COMPUTERS IN
BUSINESS

K201

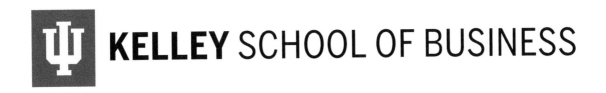

KELLEY SCHOOL OF BUSINESS

COMPUTERS IN BUSINESS

K201

Kelley School of Business Faculty

INDIANA UNIVERSITY PRESS

Bloomington and Indianapolis

This book is a publication of

Indiana University Press
Office of Scholarly Publishing
Herman B Wells Library 350
1320 East 10th Street
Bloomington, Indiana 47405 USA

iupress.indiana.edu

The paper used in this publication meets the minimum requirements of the American National Standard for Information Sciences—Permanence of Paper for Printed Library Materials, ANSI Z39.48-1992.

Manufactured in the United States of America

ISBN 978-0-253-02653-8 (pbk.)
ISBN 978-0-253-02663-7 (e-bk.)

1 2 3 4 5 21 20 19 18 17 16

TABLE OF CONTENTS

Appendix

Welcome! This is the official textbook for K201—*Computers in Business*. This course has been designed to offer a rigorous introduction to the contemporary world of business computing and is the first of two required technology courses in the Kelley School of Business.

Each chapter is divided into three sections: Research & Exploration, In-Depth Case Application, and Review Problems.

RESEARCH & EXPLORATION

This section is designed to introduce you to concepts and methods that are integral to being prepared for each class.

Research

Necessary key terms and concepts to be researched are provided and should be well understood before continuing onto the Exploration section.

Exploration

Complex concepts are explained in detail and hands-on exercises walk students through the application of these concepts and others introduced in the Research section. These exercises should be completed before the start of each class.

IN-DEPTH CASE APPLICATION

This section builds on the concepts and methods covered in the Research & Exploration section. It consists of hands-on exercises led by the instructor and is centered on Premiere Foods, a locally sourced and organic grocery store.

If a student misses class, he or she must work through this section before returning to class. Instructors provide important explanations, concepts, methods, and other important discussions in class, however, so simply working through this text should not be regularly substituted for attending class.

REVIEW PROBLEMS

This section provides you with hands-on exercises to complete on your own in order to practice the concepts and methods covered in the previous two sections. Completing the review problems after each class is essential to mastering the materials and doing well in the course.

Knowledge Checks

At the end of many chapters will be Knowledge Check problem(s) in the Review Problems section. These problems are designed to assess your understanding of the various topics covered in lab. Once you have completed the steps, go to the course website to answer Koin-earning questions.

Throughout this book, you will notice this icon in the margin of some of the hands-on exercises:

This indicates that there is a video available of the steps in the exercise being completed. You may find these videos helpful if you run into issues while trying to complete the steps on your own. These videos are avaialble under Modules in your K201 section of Canvas.

The key to mastering the lab material is practice! We provide you with the necessary materials and help—the rest is up to you.

COMPUTERS IN
BUSINESS
K201

K201 Introduction

Chapter 1

Outline

- Research & Exploration: Course Structure, Navigating Course Resources

- In-Depth Case Application: Course Logistics, Course Files

- Review Problems: Understanding Course Structure and Policies

Objectives

- Understand the goals of this class and how the class will be structured.

- Use Canvas to access important class resources.

- Access your K201 files in Box.

- Understand the importance of maintaining backup files.

- Identify a strategy for keeping copies of course files and assignments.

RESEARCH & EXPLORATION

Research

For K201 lab, the only required book is this K201 e-book. However, you will at times find it necessary and extremely beneficial to use additional online resources such as the <u>IU Knowledge Base</u>, <u>Microsoft Office Support</u>, and video tutorials on <u>YouTube</u>, among others.

Each chapter in this e-book comprises three distinct sections:

Research & Exploration

This section contains information on various concepts and methods as well as hands-on exercises that will help you prepare for each class. Students who do not prepare for each class will have extreme difficulty keeping up during class.

In-Depth Case Application

This section builds on the concepts and methods covered in the Research & Exploration section. It consists of hands-on exercises led by the instructor and is centered on Premiere Foods, a locally sourced and organic grocery store.

Students who miss class must work through this section before returning to class. However, because instructors provide explanations, concepts, methods, and other important discussions in class, simply working through this text is not intended to be a substitute for regularly attending class.

Review Problems

This section provides you with hands-on exercises to complete on your own so that you can practice the concepts and methods covered in the two sections preceding it. Completing the review problems after each class is essential to mastering the materials and doing well in the course.

Exploration

Course Resources and Syllabus

K201 is a challenging course for many. The first step to doing well is to become familiar with the course structure and policies by reading the syllabus. You will also want to familiarize yourself with all of the resources available, such as where to find important announcements, get free K201 help, earn extra credit, locate graded assignments files, and more.

1. Log into Canvas, then locate your K201 Lab section.

2. Explore the Canvas site until you find the link to the course syllabus.

3. Read the syllabus, then further explore the site.

Activating your Box at IU Account

Throughout the semester, you will be responsible for many different files associated with this course. We will place all the files you need to get started in your IU Box account during the first week of classes. All IU students and faculty and staff members get unlimited free storage space on Box at IU to store anything they wish. This storage space isn't just for K201—you can use it to store, share, and access photos, music, videos, and so forth from anywhere.

1. To activate your Box at IU account, simply log on using your IU username and passphrase.

Your Box at IU account will be automatically created the first time you log into Box at IU. Here you can upload, download, and share files. For more information on how to use IU Box, read this IU Knowledge Base article.

IN-DEPTH CASE APPLICATION

Who Is In Your Lab Classroom?
Instructor

Responsible for the class, office hours, and grades.

Teaching Assistant (TA)

Typically runs the computer, answers questions, and manages the peer tutors. TAs are paid undergraduate students who have served as a peer tutor in the past.

Peer Tutors

Students who did exceptionally well in K201 and are invited to come back as volunteers in the classroom. Peer tutors help answer student questions and also help students who fall behind during class. Some sections have as many as six peer tutors. Peer tutors begin offering tutoring during week 2.

Software Requirements

The lab component of K201 teaches Microsoft Access and Microsoft Excel. Microsoft Office 2016 for Windows is required and is the only acceptable software for this course. This software is installed on all PCs in (Student Technology Center (STC) computer labs and can also be downloaded to a personal PC from IUware using the Office 365 link.

If you are going to use your personal computer, it is your responsibility to make sure you have the necessary software installed. Check the K201 syllabus for more detailed information.

What About Using a Mac?

None of the Macintosh operating systems or Microsoft Office versions for Mac is acceptable. You may install Windows on a Macintosh either as the only operating system or as a dual-boot option. Using Boot Camp Assistant, you can partition your hard drive and install Windows and MS Office on your Macintosh computer so that you can complete K201 assignments.

If you wish to use your Mac for K201 but do not want to partition the hard drive, you can use IUanyWare. IUanyWare is a client virtualization service available to IU students, faculty, and staff. With IUanyWare, you can use a web browser or mobile app to run certain IU-licensed software applications without having to install them on your computer or mobile device. All you need is a high-speed Internet connection.

For more information on how to set up and use IUanyWare, read this IU Knowledge Base article.

Authorize Cloud Storage Services

Cloud Storage is easy to set up and to use. Simply authorize your storage accounts, after which they'll show up just like a hard drive within any virtual app though IUanyWare or on any lab computer.

1. Go the IU Cloud Storage Configurator at https://cloudstorage.iu.edu.

2. Click **Login**; if prompted, type your IU username and passphrase.

3. Click **Login** again, or press **Enter**.

4. Click the **arrow** to the right of the Box cloud storage option, then click **Authorize**.

5. In the page that opens, click **Grant access to Box** to authorize access to all files stored in your Box at IU account.

6. Repeat steps 4 and 5 for any other preferred cloud storage options.

Once this has been done, you will be able to access your K201 files on a Mac or on other devices using IUanyWare. Additionally, when you log into any PC in an STC computer lab, you will be able to access all your Box files under This PC.

Accessing Your K201 Files in Box

If you are officially enrolled in the course and have activated your Box at IU account as instructed in the Research & Exploration section, then you will find that many of the K201 files you will need have already been uploaded to your Box at IU account.

1. Log onto https://box.iu.edu using your IU username and passphrase.

   Alternatively, if you have authorized your IU account to access your Box at IU files and are in an STC computer lab, you can double-click **This PC** and then double-click the **Box** drive located under Network Locations.

2. Locate and open the **My Courses** folder.

3. Locate and open the **current semester** folder, then open the **K201 Files** folder.

4. Browse the folder structure to locate the PowerPoint slides summarizing the course.

5. Locate files needed for the next class.

6. Locate the Knowledge Check files.

You must take good care of your files. You must not allow another student to have access to your files. If you allow another student access to your files, academic misconduct charges will be sought.

If you have taken K201 before, you cannot turn in old files. Please make sure to keep old and new files separate.

Backing Up Your Files

Box at IU has a version management feature that automatically creates backups of your files each time you upload a new version. This can be very useful in the event of a file's becoming damaged, a computer's becoming lost or damaged, or a file's being accidentally deleted. This feature also allows you to revert to an earlier version of a file if needed.

1. To access the version history of a file, click the version number, located in the small red box underneath the filename.

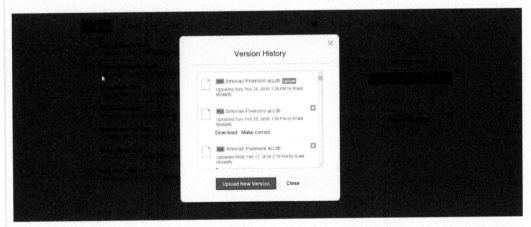

2. The Version History box can be used to download previous versions of a file or override the current version with an earlier version.

It is your responsibility to manage all your course files. Although you are not required to use Box at IU, you may find this and other features useful.

Additional IT Help

The IU Wells Main Library at 10th and Jordan has a University Information Technology Services (UITS) Computing Support Help Desk that gives all IU students free computer help. It's located on the first floor behind the coffee stand. You can even bring your laptop or other computing device in to the IU experts (bring your IU ID card, too). They can help answer your questions about IU Cloud Storage, IUanyWare, installing Windows on a Mac, getting the correct version of MS Office installed, and so forth.

You can also contact UITS tech support by phone 24/7 at (812) 855-6789, chat with tech support live at http://ithelplive.iu.edu, or e-mail tech support at ithelp@iu.edu.

REVIEW PROBLEMS

Review Problem 1

It is extremely important that you be fully aware of course expectations and policies. After locating and reading the syllabus, exploring the K201 Canvas site, reviewing the Research & Exploration and In-Depth Application sections of this book, and reviewing the PowerPoint slides presented on the first day of class, you should be able to answer the following questions:

1. What are the dates for all four K201 exams?

2. What free resources are available to help you with K201?

3. What are graded projects, lab checks, and knowledge checks?

4. Which version of Microsoft Office is required?

5. If you plan on using your Mac for the course, what are your only two options?

6. What is the policy on sharing course files?

Access Introduction

Chapter 2

Outline

- Research & Exploration: Understand the Purpose of Relational Databases
- In-Depth Case Application: Organize Graded Projects, Understand Database Basics
- Review Problems: Sort on One Field, Sort on Multiple Fields, Solve a Business Problem, Knowledge Check 1

Objectives

- Research terms using the define: operator.
- Understand relational database objects and concepts.
- Understand the structure of the database used in lab.
- Understand how to access and manage graded project files.

RESEARCH & EXPLORATION

Research

Databases play an integral role in the world—at work, in school, and in our personal lives. However, most people know very little about what databases are and how they work. Database design theory and development can get complicated, so let's begin by obtaining a basic definition of a database.

Go to your preferred search engine and type the following:

define: database

Using *define:* before your search term will narrow search results to those found among online glossaries and encyclopedias. This can be a good way of exploring what the consensus is on a term's meaning. Run the search. Look over the first page or two of results.

Now that you have a basic understanding of what a database is, the next step is to understand why you would want to use one. Read this Knowledge Base article that explains the benefits of using a relational database.

By now you should know the basic definition of a database and have some notion of why databases are useful. However, you may discover that in many organizations around the world, people use Excel to manage their data when they should be using Access. Read Using Access or Excel to manage your data to understand when each software application is appropriate.

Last, much of the terminology associated with databases may be confusing. So that you can speak about databases, read the Overview section of the following article: Learn the structure of an Access database.

Exploration

In K201, we will use one company's database as our teaching file to illustrate database concepts. To fully understand the examples used in class, it is important that you have some background information on the company and the structure of its database.

Premiere Foods started as a small monthly newsletter written and distributed as a hobby by a few organic food aficionados. Their informal product reviews soon grew popular with friends and then with friends of friends, and they eventually began a small organic local and healthy foods grocery store.

Eventually they took their nonperishable foods online. Word of mouth (along with attention to quality) made the website popular.

In addition to an online business, Premiere Foods now has stores in Indiana and Illinois. Its customers are environmentally conscious and very loyal, and sales are strong.

You will be working to understand and improve upon a database that contains data related to 2015 sales to customers who registered to be Premiere "members" and receive special product discounts. (Note: this database does not contain all Premiere's sales, nor even all sales for 2015, and it does not attempt to represent all business functions.)

Premiere Database Precautions

For many of you, this is your first time working with a database. Be aware that there are a few precautions you must take to ensure you do not lose any work that you complete throughout the first half of the course:

- Always be sure that your database is saved to your computer before working on it. If you are using https://box.iu.edu or another cloud storage service, be sure to download the file to the computer and then open the downloaded copy.

  Databases require access to your computer's resources and will not operate properly if opened directly from any cloud storage service, including Box at IU, Google Drive, or OneDrive.

- Once you have finished working on the database file and before you log off the computer, be sure to upload the updated version of the database file back to your cloud storage service, USB flash drive, or so forth. This will ensure that you always have access to the most up-to-date version of your database.

Browse the Database

Spend a few minutes opening the database tables and examining the data in them.

1. Log onto Box at IU, then navigate to the K201Files folder, located in the My Courses folder.

2. Download the **Premiere.accdb** file, located in the Access folder, to your computer.

3. Open the downloaded database file.

First of all, recognize that this database tracks sales revenue (not employee hours worked, accounts payable, or any number of other things for which a business might use a database).

The *tblProduct* table contains the items carried in the store or in the online catalog. The *tblMember* table contains personal information about customers who have enrolled in the Member Club. The *tblTransaction* table is a record of sales receipts printed, with each transaction representing one receipt. Notice that there is also a table called *tblTransactionDetails*. Open and examine the contents of each of these tables, reflecting on the articles you read in the Research section, and then consider the answers to the following questions:

- Why does MemberID appear in the *tblTransaction* table when this table is intended to store information only about the transactions?

- What are some of the unique identifiers you discovered in the tables?

- Why do you think the database designer chose to use two tables to store transaction information?

- What is the name for the database object that stores the data?

- How could you find out what a customer owed for each transaction?

In-Depth Case Application

Managing Course Files

You are responsible for maintaining all your files for this class. Let your lab instructor or TA know if you have any questions after completing this exercise.

Creating a Folder to Organize Graded Projects

1. Log into Box at IU.

2. Navigate to and open the **K201Files** folder located inside the My Courses/Current Semester folder.

3. Open the **Graded Projects** folder. There should already be folders inside for all the graded projects except GP1.

4. Click **+New**, then select **Folder** to create a new folder inside Graded Projects.

5. Name the folder **GP1**, then click **Okay**.

Creating a Subfolder to Back Up Graded Projects

1. Open the **GP1** folder you just created.

2. Inside the GP1 folder, create another folder and name it **done(backup)**.

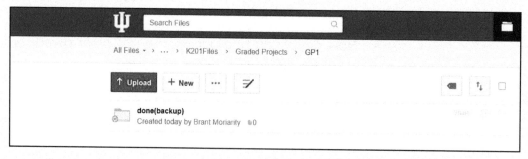

Each of the 9 GP folders now has a done(backup) folder inside. As you complete and submit each graded project, place a copy of your project file in this folder, making sure not to open or modify it after the deadline. This will ensure that you have a completed backup copy of your work in case your submitted file is lost or corrupted.

Downloading the Graded Project Files

1. Using the Edge browser, log onto Canvas, then go to your K201 lab section. Click **Files** in the left navigation, then click **Graded Projects**.

2. Locate and click the **K201 GP 1** link.

3. Click the **Download** link, then click **Run**.

4. In the self-extracting archive dialog box, click the [...] button.

5. Navigate to the **Desktop**. Click **OK**, then click **Extract**.

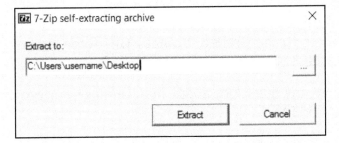

Renaming and Opening the Grading Project File

Once the GP1 files have finished extracting, you will find several files on your Desktop. As of now, everyone's GP1 file is named exactly the same. However, since you logged into Canvas to download the file, it is already associated with your IU account. Accordingly, it is important that you rename the file so there is no question about which file belongs to you.

1. Locate and right-click the file named **K201_GP1... .accdb**.

2. Select **Rename** from the right-click menu.

3. Add your IU username, followed by a hyphen, without spaces, to the beginning of the filename. The name of this file should now be **yourusername-K201_GP1... .accdb**.

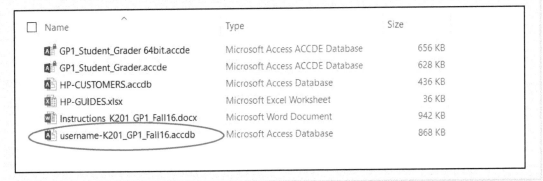

The file you renamed is your Graded Project 1 file. Over the next few chapters, you will learn about how to import data into a database, select appropriate data types, and improve the overall design of the tables. You will then apply these concepts to GP1.

4. Open the **Instructions_K201_GP1... .docx** file, then browse through the document to get an idea of how the graded projects are structured. Pay particular attention to Section A, on how to open the graded project file and how to use the student grader.

Uploading GP1 Files to Box

Now that you have extracted all your Graded Project 1 files, you should upload them to the Graded Projects/GP1 folder in Box so that you will be able to access them later.

If you have any questions about maintaining your project files, talk to your instructor or TA.

Exploring the Premiere Database

1. Navigate to your **K201Files/InClass Files/Access** folder in Box.

2. Locate the **Premiere.accdb** database file, then click the pencil icon, next to the filename, to edit the name.

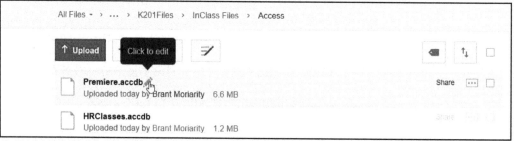

3. Much as with the Graded Project 1 file, add your IU username and a hyphen to the beginning of the filename, then click **Save**.

4. Download your **username-Premiere.accdb** database file to your computer, then open the local copy of the file.

   Note: It is extremely important that you save the database file to your computer and then open the copy residing on your computer. If you click Open File directly in Box, all changes will be lost.

All the various database objects that make up the Premiere Foods database are located in the Navigation Pane on the left. These objects are organized by type: Tables, Queries, and Forms.

5. Explore the various tools available on the Ribbon. You will become more familiar with these as you progress through the course.

6. Double-click **tblEmployee** to open the table.

7. Notice the small arrows to the right of each field name. These can be used to sort data in ascending or descending order and to filter the records in the table.

8. Click the **arrow** next to the JobTitle column heading. Click the **Select All** check box to deselect it.

9. Click the **Customer Service Associate** check box, then click **OK** to view only the employees who have that job title.

Being able to sort and filter data in tables can make it easier to locate a particular record or group of records.

10. Click the same **arrow** again, then click **Clear filter from JobTitle** so that all records are visible.

11. Close **tblEmployee** without saving the changes.

Uploading Your Revised Database

You may have chosen to store your K201 files on a USB drive, Box at IU, or another cloud storage service. Regardless of your method, it is crucial that when you are done working with your files you save them back to the source so that you always have access to the most up-to-date version.

1. Close your Premiere database.

   Note: You must close the database file before uploading saved changes back to Box or to your USB drive.

2. Navigate to your **K201Files/InClass Files/Access** folder.

3. Click **Upload**, then click **Files**. Navigate to your **username-Premiere.accdb** file, then upload your revised file. The version number increases by 1, indicating that a new version has been uploaded.

REVIEW PROBLEMS

Review Problem 1

To quickly locate data in a table, sort the data on one or more fields.

Sort on One Field

1. In your copy of the Premiere database, open **tblProduct**.

2. Click the **arrow** next to the CatalogPrice column heading, then click **Sort Smallest to Largest**. Sorting the data in this manner makes it easy to locate the lowest-priced items at Premiere Foods.

Sort on Multiple Fields

When you want to sort on multiple fields, the fields to be sorted must be contiguous, and the primary sort field must be the leftmost field. For example, if you want to easily locate the lowest-priced items within each category, you will need to sort first by Category and then by CatalogPrice.

1. Click the **CatalogPrice** column heading to select it, then click and drag the column to the left so that it is positioned just to the right of the Category field.

2. Click the **Category** column heading and then, without releasing the mouse button, drag to the right to select both the Category and the CatalogPrice fields.

3. If necessary, click the **Home** tab on the Ribbon; then, in the Sort & Filter group, click **Ascending**.

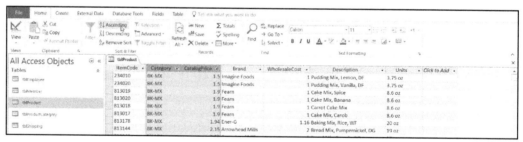

Review Problem 2

Solve a Business Problem

Now that you have a better understanding of how the Premiere database is structured, try navigating though the various tables to solve the following business problem:

Premiere Foods sells a Spectrum brand eggless mayo spread. There is a defect causing it to spoil before the expiration date. Spectrum is doing a recall, and you need to alert people who purchased this product. Find the name and phone number of one such person. Do this by opening database tables, sorting on fields as necessary, and tracking relevant information as you go.

Save and Back Up

When you are finished with your work, close the Premiere database file, then upload the revised version to Box. We strongly suggest that if you are using a flash drive you also place a copy of your work on cloud storage.

Knowledge Check 1

File Management

Files Needed

- All files in the Knowledge Checks/PF folder

The PF folder contains image files, spreadsheets, and other files for Premiere Foods. The prior intern did not implement any file management structure. You, the current intern, know that it is dangerous not to manage your files in folders. Accordingly, in this Knowledge Check, you will set up a folder system to manage these files.

Your task is outlined hereafter. As you do this, pay special attention to whether these instructions ask you to move or create a copy of the various files.

1. Locate the PF folder, then download it to your Desktop.

Before working with the files inside the PF folder, you will need to extract the files.

2. Locate and click the **PF** folder, using the File Explorer to select it.

3. Once selected, click the **Extract** contextual tab that appears at the tip of the File Explorer window.

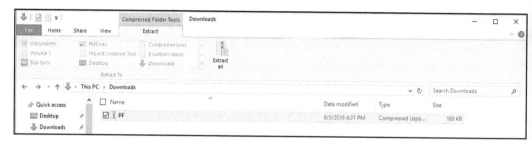

4. Click **Extract All** and then, in the dialog box that appears, click **Extract**.

There is now a PF folder with another PF folder inside that contains all the files you need.

5. In the innermost PF folder, create three new folders: **Revenue Backup**, **Farmer Markets**, and **Web Site Pictures**.

6. Move all of the files having .jpg extensions to the Web Site Pictures folder.

7. Rename the Revenue Qtr1.xlsx file to **Quarter 1-2015.xlsx**. In a similar fashion, rename the other three revenue spreadsheets appropriately.

8. Copy the revenue files into the Revenue Backup folder.

9. Within the Web Site Pictures folder, create a subfolder named **Food**. Move the rice, veggies, eggs, and peppers files from the Web Site Pictures folder into the Food subfolder.

10. Move the three files related to farmer markets from the PF folder into the Farmer Markets folder.

After completing these steps, go to the course website to answer Koinearning questions.

Importing Data, Keys, and Relationships

Chapter 3

Outline

- Research & Exploration: Research Various Types of Keys and Relationships in Relational Databases, Import Data into a Database, Create a Composite Key, Create a Relationship between Two Tables

- In-Depth Case Application: Import Data from Various Sources into Access, Define Keys, Create Relationships

- Review Problems: Finish Creating Relationships, Knowledge Check 2

Objectives

- Use Access to import data from various types of files.

- Understand and create composite primary keys.

- Create relationships between tables.

- Understand referential integrity.

- Know the purpose of the Cascade Update and Cascade Delete settings.

RESEARCH & EXPLORATION

Research

The Premiere Foods database you will be using throughout the first 11 chapters of this book has already been created using various database design principles. Read Database design basics to gain an understanding of the basic design principles used in the development of the Premiere Foods database. After reading this article, you should be able to easily answer the following questions:

1. What is a primary key? Can you think of any examples?

2. What is a foreign key?

3. What is a composite key?

4. What are the three types of table relationships?

Exploration

Up to this point, Premiere has been keeping employee records and other data in separate databases and spreadsheets. Premiere plans to integrate these systems into the Premiere database and wants to start by importing the employee training data from its HR database.

Preparing to Import Data into Access

To begin, you cannot import files from a cloud storage tool such as Box at IU. Please complete the following steps in order to import data from external sources into your Premiere database.

1. Log onto Box at IU, then navigate to the Access files in the K201Files folder.

2. Check the box for the following files: your Premiere database, **HRClasses.accdb**, and **Enrollments.xlsx**.

3. With all three files selected, click the **download** ⬇ button, and then click **Okay**.

When multiple files are downloaded from Box, they are placed inside a compressed zipped folder.

4. Once the files have been downloaded, open the **Access-Selected** folder to view the contents. The files inside the zipped folder cannot be modified until they have been extracted.

5. In the File Explorer window, on the Compressed Folder Tools Extract tab, click **Extract All**.

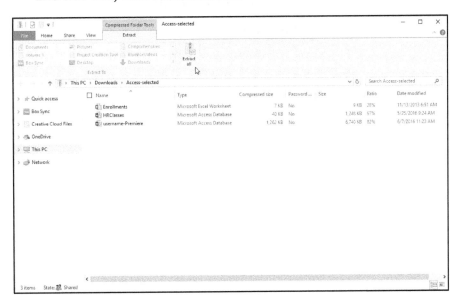

6. In the Extract Compressed (Zipped) Folders dialog box, click **Browse**. Locate and click the **Desktop** folder, then click **Select Folder**.

7. Click **Extract** to extract the downloaded files from the compressed folder onto the Desktop.

Importing Data from Another Access Database

The HRClasses database contains a list of all training classes offered to Premiere employees in a table called CLASSES. You will need to import the CLASSES table into your Premiere database.

1. Open your Premiere database.

2. Click the **External Data** tab, in the **Import & Link** group, and then click **Access**.

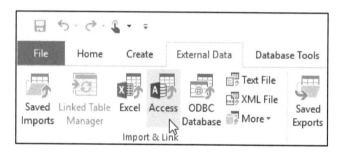

3. In the Get External Data—Access Database dialog box, click **Browse**, locate and click the **HRClasses.accdb** file on the Desktop, and then click **Open**.

   Troubleshooting
   Access will show only those files that match the file type selected before the import began. If you cannot locate the HRClasses.accdb file on the Desktop, it is possible that you did not correctly click **Access** in the Import & Link group on the External Data tab. Click **Cancel** to cancel the import, then try again.

4. Be sure the **Import tables, queries, forms, reports, macros, and modules into the current database** option is selected, and then click **OK**.

5. In the Import Objects dialog box, on the Tables tab, click **CLASSES**, and then click **OK**.

   After the Import Wizard runs, a window appears allowing you to save the import steps. If you ever have a file that needs repeated importing, this option is useful.

6. You need these data imported only once, so click **Close**.

7. In the Navigation pane, right-click the **CLASSES** table, then select **Rename**. Type **tblClass** as the table name, then press **Enter**. Now the table you imported matches the naming convention of the other objects in your Premiere database.

Importing Data from an Excel File

Enrollments.xlsx is an Excel file that the company has been using to keep track of which classes each employee has registered for. You will bring these data into the database as a new table.

1. On the External Data tab, in the Import & Link group, click **Excel**.

2. In the Get External Data—Excel Spreadsheet dialog box, click **Browse**, locate and click the **Enrollments.xlsx** file on the Desktop, and then click **Open**.

3. Be sure the **Import the source data into a new table in the current database** option is selected, and then click **OK**.

4. In the Import Spreadsheet Wizard, make sure that the box is checked to indicate that the first row contains column headings, and then click **Next**.

5. In the next step, you can indicate what type of data you are importing in each field. You can also choose to omit fields. You do not need to change anything here, so just click **Next**.

6. Next you are asked to designate a primary key. Neither of the fields in this file contains a set of unique values, so the requirements of a primary key are not met. We also do not want Access to create a primary key field, so select **No Primary Key**, then click **Next**. You will return to the idea of a key for this table later.

7. In the last step, name this table **tblEmployeeTraining**, click **Finish**, and then click **Close**.

8. Before proceeding, check your work to make sure that all the records imported correctly. You should have the following number of records in each table.

Table name	# of records
tblClass	11
tblEmployeeTraining	104

Creating a Composite Key

The tblEmployeeTraining table contains two fields: EmployeeID and ClassID. Each of these two fields is a foreign key, because each is a primary key in another table. EmployeeID is the primary key of tblEmployee, and ClassID is the primary key of tblClass. When you imported the Employee Training data, you decided not to have a primary key. Because several employees could enroll in a single class—or one employee could enroll in several classes—there are likely to be many duplicates; thus, neither the ClassID nor the EmployeeID meets the requirements of a primary key field. However, each class offered has a unique ClassID, and an employee should never need to enroll in the same class more than once. To represent this fact in the database, you will set a composite primary key using both the **EmployeeID** and **ClassID** fields.

1. Right-click **tblEmployeeTraining** in the Navigation pane, then select **Design View**.

2. Point to the field selector area to the left of the EmployeeID field. Your mouse pointer will change to a rightward-facing black arrow. Click and drag down to select both EmployeeID and ClassID.

   Troubleshooting
   If you were unable to select both fields simultaneously, click one of the rows below the ClassID field to cancel the selection, then try again.

3. Click the **Primary Key** button.

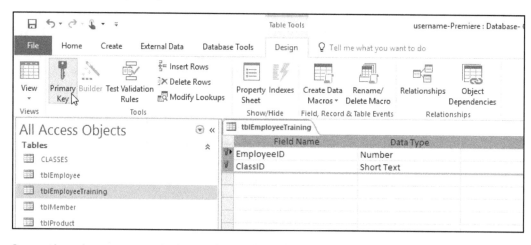

4. Save the changes, and close the table.

Creating a Relationship between Two Tables

For you to take full advantage of a relational database, relationships need to be established between tables using the primary and foreign keys created in the tables. These relationships are what allow you to retrieve data from multiple tables in order to answer questions such as "Which employees have enrolled in each of the classes offered at Premiere?"

1. Make sure all database tables are closed.

2. Click the **Database Tools** tab; in the Relationships group, click the **Relationships** button.

3. On the Relationship Tools Design tab, in the Relationships group, click **Show Table**.

4. Double-click the **tblClass** table to add it to the Relationships window. Add the **tblEmployee** and **tblEmployeeTraining** tables as well, then close the Show Table dialog box.

To create relationships between the tables, click and drag to connect the fields they have in common. In other words: connect a **primary key** to its matching **foreign key**.

5. In the tblEmployee table, click **EmployeeID**, then drag to the EmployeeID field in the tblEmployeeTraining table.

Troubleshooting
If you see an error message about tables being locked, then at least one of the tables that you are connecting is open. Close the table or tables, then try again.

6. In the Edit Relationships dialog box, click to check **Enforce Referential Integrity** and **Cascade Update Related Fields**. (The purpose of this will be explained in class.) Then click **Create**.

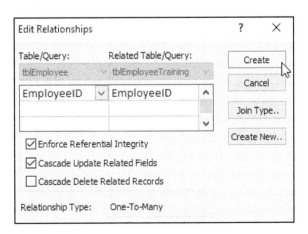

7. Do the same to connect **tblEmployeeTraining** to **tblClass** using **ClassID**.

8. Save the changes to the Relationships window, then close the database.

Save and Back Up

When you are finished with your work, close the Premiere database file, then upload the revised version to your Box account. We strongly suggest that if you are using a flash drive you also place a copy of your work on cloud storage.

IN-DEPTH CASE APPLICATION

Importing Data into the Premiere Database

*Note: To complete the exercises in this section, you will need to download the following files to your computer in addition to your Premiere database: **new_state_data.txt**, **Member_ratings.xlsx**, and **More_ratings.xlsx**.*

Sometimes the data needed for a database table already exist elsewhere. If the data are in another Access database, you may decide to (1) copy and paste the desired records into a table that you have defined or to (2) import an entire Access table, structure and all, into your database.

You can also import data from an Excel file by importing an entire worksheet or by specifying a named range to import. Other common types of external data are data in delimited text files, in which special characters known as delimiters determine the breaks between fields.

Importing Data from a Tab-Delimited Text File

The tblStateTaxAndShipping table is currently incomplete, lacking data for nine states. In addition, tax rates and shipping and handling fees for a number of states have gone up. You have been provided with a file to use to replace the current data.

1. Open the **tblStateTaxAndShipping** table.

2. Click in the top-left corner of the table to select all the records, then press **Delete**.

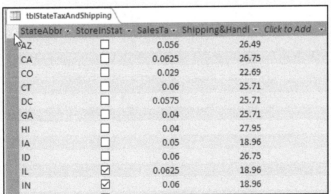

3. Access will warn you that you are about to delete 42 records and that this action cannot be undone. Click **Yes** to delete the records.

4. Close the table.

5. Click the **External Data** tab; in the Import & Link group, click **Text File**.

6. In the Get External Data—Text File dialog box, click **Browse**, locate and click the **new_state_data.txt** file, and then click **Open**.

7. Select the **Append a copy of the records to the table** radio button, and then select **tblStateTaxAndShipping** from the drop-down list of tables.

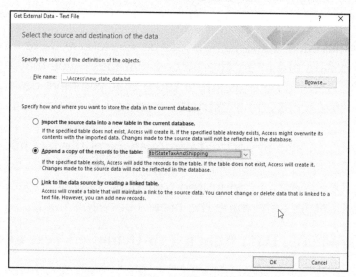

8. Click **OK** to launch the Import Text Wizard.

9. In the first step of the Import Text Wizard, Access should have determined that the data are delimited; leave the Delimited radio button selected, then click **Next**.

10. Verify that the **Tab** delimiter is selected.

11. Click the check box for **First Row Contains Field Names**. If this check box is not selected, then Access will interpret the words State, SalesTax, and so forth as data instead of as names that describe the data.

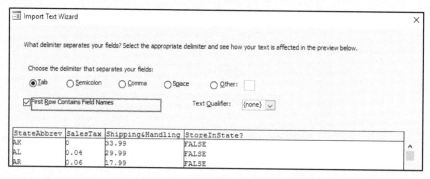

12. Click **Next**.

13. Confirm that the data will be stored in the tblSateTaxAndShipping table, click **Finish**, and then click **Close**.

14. Open the **tblStateTaxAndShipping** table, then look over the data briefly. There should now be 51 records—one for each state and one for Washington, D.C.

15. Close the tblStateTaxAndShipping table.

Importing Product Ratings from an Excel Worksheet

Premiere Foods collects ratings of the products that it sells from Premiere members and, when possible, from independent consumer ratings groups. You will add these ratings to the Premiere database as a new table.

Before you import data from Excel into Access, a basic understanding of Excel concepts such as a workbook (a file), worksheet (a page in the file), and named range (a section of one worksheet) will prove useful.

What Is a Worksheet?

A worksheet is a single spreadsheet that contains cells organized into columns and rows. There are usually several worksheets contained in a workbook.

What Is a Named Range?

A named range is a name given to a specific range of cells in a worksheet. This allows a section of data in a worksheet to be imported—as opposed to all the data. There can be many different named ranges in a single worksheet. The highlighted section of data in the following image belongs to the named range "ratings":

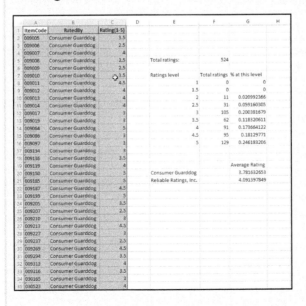

1. On the External Data tab, in the Import & Link group, click **Excel.**

2. Browse for and click the **Member_ratings.xlsx** file, then click **Open.**

3. Verify that the **Import the source data into a new table in the current database** option is selected, then click **OK.**

The first screen of the Import Spreadsheet Wizard shows that there are multiple worksheets in the workbook, along with an option to Show Named Ranges at the top—as well as a preview of the data in the selected worksheet at the bottom. The data you need to import are located on the product_ratings worksheet.

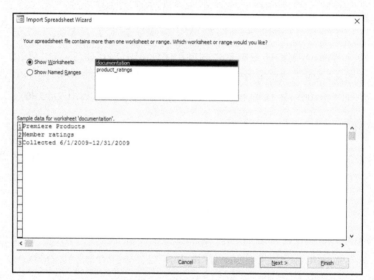

4. Click the **product_ratings** worksheet, then click **Next.**

5. Verify that the **First Row Contains Column Headings** check box is selected, then click **Next.**

6. There is no need to modify the field properties, so click **Next** again without making any changes.

7. Select **No primary key** for now, then click **Next.** You will assign an appropriate composite key later.

8. Change the table name that will be created to **tblProductRating.**

9. Click **Finish.** Do not save the import steps. Click **Close.**

Importing More Product Ratings from an Excel Named Range

Premiere Foods has also obtained product ratings from two independent ratings sources, Consumer Guarddog and Reliable Ratings, Inc. These are in an Excel file named More_ratings.xlsx, but if you open the Excel file, you'll notice that the sheet with the ratings also contains a few summary statistics. This would create a problem if you tried to import the entire sheet. To solve this, the range containing the ratings has been given the name "ratings."

1. On the External Data tab, in the Import & Link group, click **Excel**.

2. Browse for and click the **More_ratings.xlsx** file, then click **Open**.

3. Select the **Append a copy of the records to the table** radio button, then select **tblProductRating** from the drop-down list of tables.

4. Click **OK** to launch the Import Spreadsheet Wizard.

5. As you saw before, with Excel files, you can choose between importing entire worksheets or a subset of data defined as a named range.

6. Click the **Show Named Ranges** button, then select the **ratings** range.

7. Click **Next**. The box for First Row Contains Column Headings should already be checked.

8. Click **Next**.

9. Verify that Access will store these data in the tblProductRating table. Click **Finish**. Do not save the import steps. Click **Close**.

10. Open the **tblProductRating** table. You should have 1,452 product ratings from either Premiere members, represented by their MemberID, or independent consumer ratings groups—Consumer Guarddog and Reliable Ratings, Inc.

Defining a Composite Key and Creating a Relationship

Composite keys are a type of primary key comprising 2 or more fields. Together, these fields create a unique combination that identifies each record in a table. In addition to providing a way to ensure there are no duplicate records in a table, a composite key can also help to enforce company policy.

Premiere Foods encourages members to submit ratings for their products. However, it does not want the same member to rate the same product more than once. Creating a composite key with the RatedBy and ItemCode fields will ensure that the same combination of values cannot occur more than once in the table.

Also, in order to use the ratings data effectively, we need to create a relationship between tblProductRating and tblProduct. This relationship will allow us to answer questions like "Which product categories have the highest average rating?" and "Which brand has the lowest average rating?"

Defining Fields in a Table

Before a relationship can be created between tblProductRating and tblProduct, the field they have in common, ItemCode, needs to be the same data type and have the same field size in both tables. In short, they must be made compatible before a relationship can be created.

1. With tblProductRating still opened, on the Home tab, in the Views group, click **Design View**.

2. In the Navigation pane, right-click **tblProduct**, then select **Design View**.

3. Click the **ItemCode** field of tblProduct, making note of the Data Type and Field Size. Close **tblProduct**.

4. In Design View of tblProductRating, verify that the Data Type of ItemCode matches that in tblProduct.

5. In the Field Properties pane of the ItemCode field, change the Field Size property to match the value in tblProduct.

6. Click the RatedBy field, then change the field size to **30** for more efficient use of space.

7. Save the changes, noticing the warning message displayed:

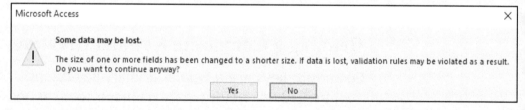

8. You will see this message any time you decrease a field size (even if you decrease a field size from 255 to 254). Click **Yes** to continue.

Creating a Composite Key

1. Select both the **ItemCode** and **RatedBy** fields of tblProductRating.

2. On the Design tab, click **Primary Key** to define these two fields as a composite key.

3. Save and close **tblProductRating**.

Creating a Relationship between Tables

1. Click the **Database Tools** tab; in the Relationships group, click **Relationships.**

2. Drag **tblProduct** from the Navigation pane into the Relationships window.

3. Drag **tblProductRating** from the Navigation pane into the Relationships window.

4. Create a one-to-many relationship between **tblProduct** and **tblProductRating** by clicking and dragging the **ItemCode** field from one table to the **ItemCode** field in the other.

5. In the Edit Relationships dialog box that appears, click the check boxes to **Enforce Referential Integrity** and **Cascade Update Related Fields.**

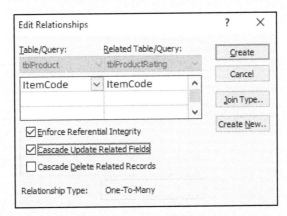

6. Click **Create** to create the relationship.

Understanding Relationship Options

- **Enforce Referential Integrity:** This option is used most often in relationships and ensures that when adding a record to the table on the "many" side of the relationship there is a matching record in the table on the "one" side of the relationship. For example, by selecting this, you stipulate that a review cannot be assigned to an ItemCode that does not exist in tblProduct. This also means that you cannot delete a product from tblProduct if that product has a record in tblProductRating.

- **Cascade Update Related Fields:** This means that if you change a product's ItemCode in tblProduct, Access will automatically update each instance of that ItemCode in tblProductRating. This ensures that data remain consistent and reliable.

- **Cascade Delete Related Records:** If you select this option, deleting a product from tblProduct would result in the deletion of all ratings assigned to that product. This setting is rarely used, and when it is, it is only used temporarily for a specific task. It is never used for this class.

Save and Back Up

When you are finished with your work, close the Premiere database file, then upload the revised version to your Box account. We strongly suggest that if you are using a flash drive you also place a copy of your work on cloud storage.

REVIEW PROBLEMS

Review Problem 1

Creating relationships between tables that share a common field is essential to being able to retrieve valuable information from any database. Create or edit relationships until your Relationships window looks like the following figure. Add and resize tables as necessary so that all fields are visible.

- Select **Enforce Referential Integrity** and **Cascade Update Related Fields** for all relationships.

- When you have finished, save your changes and close the Relationships window.

Troubleshooting Relationships

Having issues with your relationships saving? You may have created relationships involving a copy of a table instead of the original.

1. On the Relationship Tools Design tab, in the Relationships group, click **All Relationships**.

2. If you see any additional relationships appear, look for any table names with a number appended—tblProduct_1.

3. For each of these, delete the relationship line of which it is a part, and then delete the table from the Relationships window.

Save and Back Up

When you are finished with your work, close the Premiere database file, then upload the revised version to your Box account. We strongly suggest that if you are using a flash drive you also place a copy of your work on cloud storage.

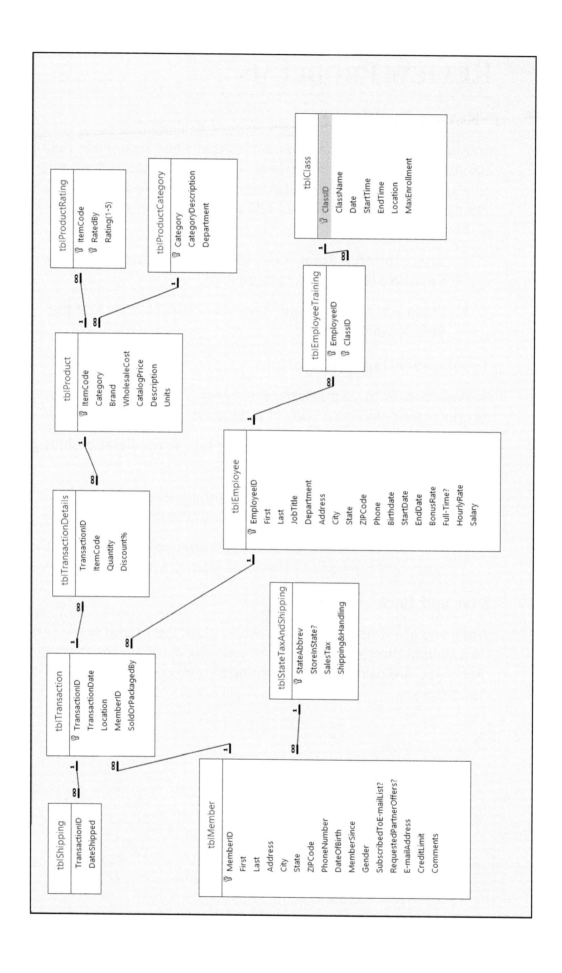

Knowledge Check 2

Importing Data into Access

Locate the file named **TheArtfulYard.accdb** in your Knowledge Checks folder. You will be using this database for every Access Knowledge Check, so be sure that you always have an up-to-date copy of the file.

1. Download and open **TheArtfulYard.accdb**.

2. Also, download the following files to import: **landscapers_1.xlsx**, **landscapers_2.xlsx**, **landscapers_3.txt**, and **landscapers_4.csv**.

Make a Backup Copy of the LANDSCAPERS Table

1. In the Navigation pane, right-click **LANDSCAPERS**, and then select **Copy**.

2. In the Navigation pane, right-click **LANDSCAPERS** again, and then select **Paste**.

3. In the Paste Table As dialog box, choose to paste the **Structure and Data**, and then name the copy **LANDSCAPERS_KC2_BACKUP**.

As you are completing this Knowledge Check, if anything should happen to the data in the LANDSCAPERS table, you can delete the LANDSCAPERS table and then make a copy of the LANDSCAPERS_KC2_BACKUP table (structure and data), naming it LANDSCAPERS. Then start over with the new LANDSCAPERS table.

Import Data into the LANDSCAPERS Table

Import new landscaper information from each of the following four files. Each time you do this, make sure that you choose to append a copy of the records to the LANDSCAPERS table—do not create a new table each time.

1. **landscapers_1.xlsx**. The data that we want are on the **new_info** worksheet. There should now be 19 records in the LANDSCAPERS table.

2. **landscapers_2.xlsx**. The data that we want are in the range named **landscapers**. There should now be 30 records in the LANDSCAPERS table.

3. **landscapers_3.txt.** The data are in tab-delimited format. There should now be 43 records in the LANDSCAPERS table.

4. **landscapers_4.csv.** This is a type of comma-delimited text file. There should now be 56 records in the LANDSCAPERS table.

When you are finished, be sure to save your database in a place where you will be able to find it again; you will need it for future Knowledge Check exercises.

After completing these steps, go to the course website to answer Koin-earning questions.

Data Types and Basic Field Settings
Chapter 4

Outline

- Research & Exploration: Research Key Terms, Enter Data
- Case Application: Understand Data Types and Basic Properties
- Review Problems: Data Types and Field Sizes, Format and Input Mask Properties, Validation Rule Property, Knowledge Check 3

Objectives

- Use the Microsoft Office website to locate helpful articles.
- Understand the importance of data types and field sizes.
- Choose the appropriate data type based on the potential use of the data.
- Understand the usefulness of field properties.
- Define and change the appropriate general field properties based on the anticipated use of data.
- Understand the use of the Date() function.
- Explain null versus zero-length string (i.e., NULL or "").

RESEARCH & EXPLORATION

Research

Remember that a field is used to store data that represents a certain attribute of an entity (table). Accordingly, a database field is like a compartment that will accept only a specified type of data, like a number, a text string, a date, or a binary value such as 1 or 0. Specifying the appropriate data type for a field is one way to ensure the accuracy, consistency, and efficiency of database contents.

Along with data types, the contents to be accepted by a field can be further stipulated by specifying several properties. Field properties are used to specify things like the maximum number of characters, the format of the displayed data, and the range of values that will be accepted, as well as whether those values are required. Some field properties can help speed the process of manual data entry and avoid common human errors. The number of properties that can be adjusted for a given field will be determined by its data type. For example, a field with a data type of Short Text will have a Field Size property, while a field of data type Date/Time will not.

Research Key Terms:

- Data type

- Field property

- Data validation

- Data entry and human error prevention

- Metadata

- MS Access Date() function

Although you can probably find plenty of information about these concepts by searching online, you might want to consider first going directly to the source. The Microsoft Office website, **http://support.office.com**, is a valuable resource for all the Office products: Word, Excel, Access, PowerPoint, and so forth. Follow these steps to search for articles specific to Access 2016:

1. At http://support.office.com, type **Data types in Access 2016** in the search field.

2. Read the article "Data types for Access desktop databases."

3. Try to find additional information about the other key terms mentioned above and read the following articles:

   - "Create a field to store dates and times"

   - "Restrict data input by using a validation rule"

   - "Guide data entry by using input masks"

You will use the information found in these articles to work on subsequent exercises.

Exploration

Explore a Table

Copy the most recent version of your Premiere database to the Desktop or to another known location on your computer's hard drive. Open the database, then follow these steps:

1. Open the **tblEmployee table**.

2. The **View** button (in the **Home** tab, **Views** group) is used to toggle between Datasheet View and Design View. Switch to the Design View of the table. Design View is where fields are created, data types are established, and field properties are specified. This is where we collect data about the data (this is called *metadata*) for all the various fields in the table. A database has "data awareness" when it has the ability to record additional data describing all its components (i.e., fields, tables, and relationships).

3. Click the **View** button to return to the datasheet.

4. Scroll to the bottom of the tblEmployee table to add a new record. Alternatively, you may click the **New** button found in the **Records** group on the **Home** tab.

5. Enter the following values in their corresponding fields. Skip over any fields for which values are not specified.

FIELD	VALUE
Employee ID:	9999

First:	John
Last:	doe
Address:	123 Elm
City:	Gosport
State:	IN
ZIP:	47433
Phone:	8125550555
Start Date:	01/01/1993
Bonus Rate:	0.1

Note: If you do this exactly as asked, you will encounter some errors; this is part of the point of the exercise. Read any error messages carefully, and modify the data being entered so that you can complete the record.

<u>Imagine This</u>!

Now try to figure out the answers to the questions that follow. Some answers may be found in the Design View of the table. Make your best guess, or conduct additional research to find the rest of the answers.

- Why are Address, City, and State separate fields?

- If you type the last name or the state in lowercase, Access capitalizes it. How?

- The State field assumes that the state will be Indiana. How?

- The Phone field provides a template featuring parentheses and a hyphen. How?

- StartDate prohibits entry of an invalid date value. How?

- You are warned if the bonus rate entered is less than 0 or greater than .09. How?

IMPORTANT: Please delete the record for John Doe before continuing. Select the record by clicking the box on the left edge of the table, then hitting the Delete key on your keyboard; alternatively, simply right-click on the box to the left of the record, then choose Delete Record from the popup menu.

Improving Table Design

Switch back to the Design View of the tblEmployee table and consider the following questions:

- Both the Last field and the State field have the symbol > in the Format property row. Take a close look at these two fields in Datasheet View. Based on your reading and what you see, what do you think this symbol does?

- The ZipCode field and the Phone field both contain numeric characters. Why do they have a Short Text data type?

- Look at the Input Mask property of the Phone field. What does this do?

- In Design View, select the BonusRate field. Look at the Validation Rule and Validation Text properties. They seem to have similar settings. What is the difference between these two properties? Why have we set both?

- Take a look at the Data Type and Format property of the HourlyRate and Salary fields. What is the difference between a Currency data type and a Currency format?

- Briefly switch to Spreadsheet view and try to change someone's HourlyRate to $10.50, then switch back to Design View and try to figure out why this not possible. Based on this finding, what change would you recommend to improve that field? Should we do the same to the Salary field?

- Which data type will automatically generate sequential numeric values that may be used for a primary key field?

Now follow these steps to improve the design of the tblEmployee table:

1. The longest value that the Department field will contain is "Human Resources", which is 15 characters long including the space. Set the field size of this field to **15** to allow entries up to 15 characters in length.

   Before continuing, save the table. You should see the following warning (it will appear whenever you have changed a field size to a smaller value):

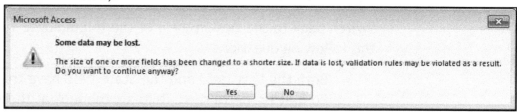

2. Click **Yes** to continue.

3. Choose an appropriate data type for the **Birthdate** and **EndDate** fields. Be careful! Dates have numeric values associated with them and must never be treated as text. If the data type of these fields is inadvertently set to Short Text or Long Text, change the data type to Number first, save, and then set to the correct data type.

4. The **Full-Time?** field indicates whether the employee is a full-time employee. Choose the appropriate data type so that this data can be displayed as a check box.

5. The **HourlyRate** and **Salary** fields both contain the rate of pay (in dollars) for each employee. Choose the appropriate data type for each of these fields.

6. Add a new field to the table. Name the new field **Notes**, and make the data type **Long Text**. (Long Text is appropriate for fields that might need to store lengthy comments.)

7. Save the changes, clicking **Yes** to continue if a prompt warns you that some data may be lost.

8. Returning to the Datasheet View, review the fields to see the result of the changes made to Data Types and Field Properties.

Save and Back Up

When you are finished with your work, close the Premiere database file, then upload the revised version to your Box account. We strongly suggest that if you are using a flash drive you also place a copy of your work on cloud storage.

Be sure to have your completed work available for the next lab meeting, either in your cloud folder or on your flash drive.

IN-DEPTH CASE APPLICATION

Primary Key

A primary key is a field or a combination of fields used to uniquely identify each record (instance) in a database table.

1. Download your Premiere database to the Desktop, then open the file.

2. Open the **tblMember** table in **Design View**, noting that MemberID is the primary key. This designation is correct. As found in your Chapter 3 research, major benefits of a primary key field include the following:

   - It guarantees that each record in the table will have a unique identifier.

   - It helps maintain the integrity of the database. If you have defined a field as a primary key, Access will require data entry in that field.

   - It guarantees that records will automatically appear in primary key sequence when viewed in Datasheet View or Form View, even if they were entered in random order.

   - It allows queries to run more quickly if the table is included in query design.

Data Types and Field Sizes

It is important to structure a database correctly in order to maintain data integrity. Setting correct data types will restrict data entry to specific types of data for the designated field. For example, when you set a Number data type, you eliminate the possibility of entering text for a field that should only contain numeric values.

Field Sizes are either assigned automatically based upon the data type designation or can be manually set by the database designer. Changing a field size restricts the number of characters that can be typed in a field and also helps to keep the database from bloating with unused spaces, thus making the database smaller and faster.

1. Change data types and field sizes according to the following table:

Field Name	Data Type	Field Size	Explanation
ZIPCode	Short Text	10	Will never need to be used in calculations; may contain characters other than numbers. Field size is 10 in case data eventually includes zip code (5) + hyphen (1) + extension (4)
PhoneNumber	Short Text	14	Same as above. Field size is 14 to allow for two parentheses, a space, and a dash.
DateOfBirth	Date/Time	Automatically set by Access to 8 bytes	While Access sees dates as numbers, specifying that this as a date field will allow it to prevent bad dates from being entered—e.g., 4/31/12 (April has 30 days).
MemberSince	Date/Time	Automatically set by Access to 8 bytes	Same as DateOfBirth.
RequestedPartnerOffers?	Yes/No	Automatically set by Access to 1 character	Use this data type for fields to indicate either Yes/No or True/False answers.
E-mailAddress	Hyperlink		When used for e-mail addresses, it will launch the default e-mail client if one is set up.
CreditLimit	Currency	Automatically set by Access—accurate to 15 digits on left side of decimal point and up to 4 digits on the right side	Used for storing and calculating monetary values. Currency data type prevents rounding off during calculations. (Note: Number data types are used for all other mathematical calculations.)
Comments	Long Text	Automatically set by Access	A Long Text field can store up to 1 GB of characters.

2. Save the **tblMember** table. You will see the warning "Some data may be lost." Access will display this warning whenever you decrease a field size.

3. Click **Yes** to continue.

Set Field Properties

Format Property

In order to give data a consistent look, you can have Access display all letters as capitals or lowercase once data is entered. This is accomplished with the Format property. (**Note:** The Input Mask property can also force capital letters. However, because a last name could be any number of characters long—from one up to the set field size—the Format property is an easier way to accomplish this.)

1. Make sure that the **Last** field is selected.

2. Type > for the **Format** property. (If you want Access to display all characters as lowercase, you would use the < symbol.)

3. Save the table, then return to the **Datasheet View** to review your results.

4. Notice now how the values in the Last field are now displayed as all uppercase. Place your cursor in the first record's Last field, noticing how the text returns to both Capital and lowercase. It's important to note that formatting does not change the underlying data—it only changes the way the data is displayed.

Input Mask Property

An input mask provides a template for data entry (e.g., spaces in which to type a Social Security number, with the hyphens already there). The Input Mask Wizard provides some predefined templates. In the Exploration section, you explored how the input mask works for phone number. During data entry, a person would have to type only 6174511970 and hyphens would be provided, resulting in (617) 451-1970. Input masks make for easier, more uniform data entry.

Create a Date Input Mask

1. Return to the **Design View** of the **tblMember** table, then select the **DateOfBirth** field.

2. Click in the **Input Mask** row in the field properties pane, then click the "build" button ⬚ that appears to the right. (Save the table if prompted.)

3. Choose **Short Date** from the list of predefined templates.

4. Click **Next**; if necessary, edit the input mask to look like **99/99/00**.

5. Click the far left side of the **Try It** box. An input mask appears for you to test. Type any date in the Try It box to make sure that you have correctly created your input mask. The input mask should allow you to enter two-digit identifiers for month, day, and year (like 082578 for August 25, 1978).

6. Click the Finish button to build the input mask.

7. Save the table, then return to the **Datasheet View** to test your input mask.

8. In **Datasheet View** click the new (blank) record button ⬚, then tab over to the DateOfBirth field. Enter **101784**, noticing how the input mask provides you with a template for entering the date correctly.

9. Once you have tested the input mask, press the **Esc** key to cancel the record.

10. Return to the **Design View**.

Format versus Input Mask Property

The **input mask** that you just created for the DateOfBirth field determines how data in that field are entered. The **format property** changes the way the dates, once entered, are displayed.

1. Change the **Format** property for **DateOfBirth** to **Medium Date**.
   Note: The DateOfBirth field should now have a Short Date input mask and a Medium Date format.

2. Save the table and return to the **Datasheet View**. Test this combination of Short Date input mask and Medium Date format in a new record. For **DateOfBirth**, enter **101784** (for 10/17/1984). The Short Date input mask allows you to enter the data this way (although you might not see slashes while you type), but the date will be formatted as 17-Oct-84 when you tab to the next field.

3. Press **Esc** to cancel the new record. Return to **Design View**.

Caption Property

A caption is used to display a descriptive, more user-friendly field name. The caption will show up as the field label in the datasheet and on forms and reports. The actual field name, however, will remain the same.

1. Return to Design View, then make sure the **Last** field is selected.

2. Type **Last Name** for the **Caption** property.

3. Save the table, returning to the Datasheet View to review your results.

Default Value Property

In order to save time with data entry, the default value property can be set to a predefined value. For example, if the majority of Premiere's members are from Ohio, then the default value for State could be set to OH. Default values can also be set for dates using the Date() function, which returns the current date. Dates are stored as numeric values, also called serial numbers. The serial number represents the number of days between 1/1/1900 and the date. For example, the date 5/1/2013 has a numeric/serial value of 41407 (that is the number of days between 1/1/1900 and 5/1/2013).

Assume that a new member's data are entered in the table the day after they become a member. Accordingly, the default value for MemberSince needs to be yesterday's date: Date()-1

1. Return to **Design View**, then make sure the **MemberSince** field is selected.

2. Type **Date()-1** for the **Default Value** property. This will not alter existing records, but when a new record is entered, the appropriate date will appear automatically. This date can then be changed if necessary.

Important Note: Access also has a Now() function. The Now() function returns the date *and* time. <u>Do not use this function unless time is needed.</u> Otherwise, if a query requests dates after 4/19/2012, the results will include anything after 4/19/2012 at 12:00 a.m. Thus, almost all of the 4/19/2012 data points (anything after midnight plus one second) will be included in the results.

3. Save the table, then return to the **Datasheet View**.

4. In **Datasheet View** click the new (blank) record button , then tab over to the MemberSince field. The default value for this field should now display yesterday's date.

5. Return to the Design View. Notice that the default values for SubscribedToEmailList? and RequestedPartnerOffers? are set to "No". This reflects Premiere Foods' official policy of not assuming that new members want to join the e-mail list or receive offers from partnering businesses.

6. Last, the majority of Premiere's members are from Indiana. Select the **State** field, setting the **Default Value** to **IN**. This will result in an error (see the image below). If you had typed **OH** for Ohio, Access would not have produced an error and would have entered **OH**. There is an operator in Access called the IN operator that allows a user to specify a list of values that Access can use to test data against. Thus, to use IN for Indiana, you must enter the value as "IN", indicating that it is a text entry and not an operator.

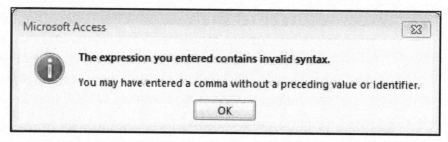

7. Save the table, then return to the Datasheet View to review your results.

Validation Rule and Validation Text Properties

If you know that only certain data will be permitted in a field, you can check data entry with the Validation Rule and Validation Text properties. These allow you to do the following:

- Define what data are permitted.

- Provide a message when an invalid value is entered.

Frequently Used Operators for Validation Rules			
Logical Operators:	And	Or	Not
Comparison Operators:	< Less than	> Greater than	= Equal to
	<= Less than or equal to	>= Greater than or equal to	<> Not equal to

Define the Validation Rule

Credit limits must not be less than 0 and not more than 3000. The **Validation Rule** property, which is an expression that defines what values are allowed in this field, can be entered in one of two ways:

- **Between 0 And 3000**

- **>=0 And <=3000**

1. In **Design View** of the **tblMember** table, define what is legal in the **CreditLimit** field using one of the two possible entries just mentioned.

Define Validation Text

1. For the **Validation Text** property, type **Value must be between 0 and 3000.** (including the period).

2. Save the table.

3. You will see the following warning:

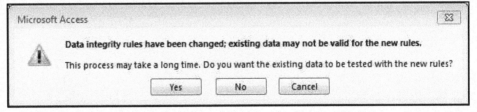

This message will appear any time a validation rule is created or altered. Access alerts you that records already in your table might not fit the definition of what is valid data.

4. Click **Yes** to indicate that you want to continue. No further warnings should appear.

5. Save the table, then return to the Datasheet View to test your Validation Rule and Validation Text.

6. In Datasheet View, click the new (blank) record button 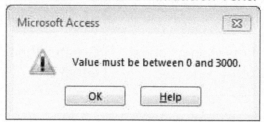, then tab over to the CreditLimit field. Enter **4000** for the **CreditLimit**. The following dialog box should appear as a result of your designated Validation Rule and Validation Text:

Microsoft Access ⌧

⚠ Value must be between 0 and 3000.

OK   Help

7. Once you have tested the input mask, press the **Esc** key to cancel the record. (You may need to press Esc twice.)

8. Return to the **Design View**.

Save and Back Up

When you are finished with your work, close the Premiere database file, then upload the revised version to your Box account. We strongly suggest that if you are using a flash drive you also place a copy of your work on cloud storage.

REVIEW PROBLEMS

Review Problem 1

Data Types and Field Sizes

Make the following changes in the **tblClass** table:

1. The **ClassName** field should not need to store more than 40 characters. Make the appropriate change to limit the length of data entered in this field.

2. You need a field to store class descriptions, which have the potential to be quite lengthy. Add a field called **ClassDescription**, then choose an appropriate data type for this field that will allow users to enter descriptions longer than a Short Text field would allow.

Review Problem 2

Format and Input Mask Properties

Make the following changes in the **tblMember** table:

1. Change the Format property for the Gender field so that the values appear as all capital letters.

2. Change the Format property for MemberSince to **Medium Date**.

3. Create a **Short Date** input mask with a 4-digit year for MemberSince field. Note that this input mask will not show up when entering a new record, because there is a default value set for the field. However, when a new date value is entered in place of the default, it must be typed in accordance to the mask—that is, the user will need to enter eight numeric characters corresponding to the desired date (e.g., 01012016).

4. Create a template so that when telephone numbers (including area code) are entered, parentheses and a dash appear automatically. In the last step of the wizard, store the data with the symbols.

5. Create a template for the **ZIPCode** field with the four-digit zip code extension. In the last step of the wizard, **do not** store the data with the symbols.

Make the following changes in the **tblEmployee** table:

The State field should have a field size of 2, allowing for a maximum of two characters in that field. However, there could still be inconsistencies with how the states are entered—for example, as IN, in, In, or iN. Placing a > (greater than) symbol in the Format property of that field would make all the state abbreviations appear as capital letters. The Input Mask property can be used to control how the state abbreviations are entered in the first place.

1. Type the following symbols in the Input Mask property for the **State** field so that each state abbreviation will require two capital letters: **>LL**

>	Forces all following characters to be uppercase
L	Requires a letter, A through Z
<	Forces all following characters to be lowercase
?	Optional letter, A through Z
0	Required number, 0-9
9	Optional number, 0-9

2. Change the **Format** property of the **Birthdate** field to **Medium Date**. Then, using the **Input Mask Wizard**, create a **Short Date** input mask.

Now a user can enter dates efficiently, in Short Date form, but view them as Medium Dates, with the month partially spelled out.

Remember this: When you add an input mask to a Date/Time data type field, the Date Picker is no longer available in Datasheet View.

Make the following changes in the **tblClass** table:

1. ClassID numbers consist of two uppercase letters followed by four numbers.

2. Set an input mask on the **ClassID** field so that data entered must fit this pattern.

Note: For a list of other Input Mask characters, you can press F1 while your cursor is in the Input Mask property or run a search on the keywords "input mask characters" within the Access Help feature.

Review Problem 3

Validation Rule Property

Make the following changes in the **tblMember** table:

1. Change the Validation Rule property for **Gender field** so that the only values allowed are **M Or F**. (Remember to put quotes around text as needed.)

2. If something else is entered, the user should see the following warning: **Please enter M or F.** (including the period).

Save and Back Up

When you are finished with your work, close the Premiere database file. If you are storing your Premiere database on the cloud, copy or upload it to your cloud folder. If you are working from a flash drive, copy or move your file to that drive, making sure to eject the drive properly before you pull it from the port. (Pulling the drive out of its port before the database is closed may damage your file.) We strongly suggest that if you are using a flash drive you also place a copy of your work on cloud storage.

Be sure to have your completed work available for the next lab meeting, either in your cloud folder or on your flash drive.

Knowledge Check 3

Tables, Fields, Data Types, and Field Sizes

Locate the file named **TheArtfulYard.accdb** in your Knowledge Checks folder.

The Artful Yard is a lawn and garden supply store located in Bloomington. In the PRODUCTS table, you can see that we carry everything from log cabin treehouse birdfeeders to brass Kokopelli wind chimes, and that we have products to fit a wide range of budgets. Looking at the **CUSTOMERS** table, you can see that, thanks to our catalog business, we sell to people from Maine to Utah, from Minnesota to Florida.

We started the LANDSCAPERS table as a customer service, for people whose yards need more prettying up than a Capiz Butterfly Sun catcher or a Gingerbread Style Birdhouse can provide. We have information for landscapers in and around Bloomington, and we offer this information to all interested customers.

In this exercise, you will be working to improve the **LANDSCAPERS** table.

Open the **LANDSCAPERS** table, then fill in the blanks on the next page with the appropriate data types and field sizes. Switch between Datasheet View and Design View to get a sense of the characteristics of the data in each field before making your decision.

Continues on next page.

LANDSCAPERS Table

Field name	Data type	Field size
LandscaperID	Leave as Number	Look at the current IDs. There are several field sizes that could handle the data. Of them, choose the most efficient option in terms of storage size.
LandscaperName	Leave as Short Text	What is the Maximum allowable for a Short Text field:
Distance(miles)		Single
Address		100
City		50
State		
ZipCode		You will eventually be storing zip codes with their 4-digit extensions; e.g., 47401-6002.
Phone		You will eventually be storing parentheses, a space, and a hyphen—as well as the digits, of course.
Consult/hr (hourly charge for landscape consulting)		

1. Copy and paste the LANDSCAPERS table (right-click, Copy; right-click, Paste).

2. Choose to paste the structure and the data, naming the copy LANDSCAPERS_KC3_BACKUP.

3. In Design View for the LANDSCAPERS table, implement the changes that you outlined above.

4. After each change, save the table, then check the data in the table.

5. If a change caused a problem with the data (e.g., deleting decimal values from the Distance (miles) field [none of the distances should be whole numbers] or digits from the end of each

phone number), delete the LANDSCAPERS table, and make a copy of the LANDSCAPERS_KC3_BACKUP table (structure and data), naming it LANDSCAPERS. Then start over with the new LANDSCAPERS table.

When you are finished, be sure to save your database in a place where you will be able to find it again; you will need it for future Knowledge Check exercises.

After completing these steps, go to the course website to answer Koin-earning questions.

Data Entry, Lookup Fields, and Field Properties

Chapter 5

Outline

- Research & Exploration: Define Terms, Create Lookup Fields, Create Simple Data Entry Forms

- In-Depth Case Application: Require Data Entry, Create Lookup Fields, Edit Relationships, Create Simple Data Entry Forms, Compact and Repair, Find Records Using Wildcards

- Review Problems: Create Lookup Fields, Edit Relationships, Knowledge Check 4

Objectives

- Create lookups using the Lookup Wizard.

- Define and change the appropriate lookup field properties based on the anticipated use of data.

- Create and use simple forms for data entry.

- Set properties in forms to protect data integrity.

- Create lookups by typing possible values.

- Create lookups using multiple fields from a table.

- Edit relationships to preserve data integrity.

- Ensure database safety by compacting and repairing.

- Choose the appropriate wildcard characters to facilitate data searches.

RESEARCH & EXPLORATION

Research

Setting up a database requires more in-depth knowledge of the data types and properties than is required for simply entering data into a database that is already created. If a database is used by multiple people and each user enters a piece of data in a slightly different way, then the data may look sloppy and unprofessional. Having every piece of data entered by typing can also become a time-waster and cause dirty data. When tables are set up, properties can be put in place to make data entry more efficient with the use of drop-down lists that allow users to simply choose the correct data.

The database designer constructs the tables with their properties and lists, but generally the data entry person is the one who actually enters the data using simple, visually appealing forms. The properties that were established in the tables carry over to the form so data can still be populated while lessening the risk of entry errors.

As the database grows, its file size can become large and cause the database to run slowly, which can be an annoyance. Compacting and repairing the database eliminates unused space in the file and can help fix damaged databases.

Use your preferred search engine or the Microsoft Office Online Support website (http://support.office.microsoft.com) to research the following key terms and concepts:

- Simple form

- Zero length

- Null

Also, locate and read the following articles:

- Create a Lookup Field (this article applies to Access 2010 but is still relevant to Access 2016)

- Guide to Table Relationships

- Compact and Repair

- Examples of Wildcard Characters

Exploration

Go to your storage device or cloud storage, download your most recent **Premiere** database to the Desktop, and then open it.

Using the Lookup Wizard

Employees at Premiere have specific bonus rates. When new employees are entered into the database, they are assigned a bonus rate. Before now, the data entry person typed these rates into the table, which caused mistakes such as an employee being assigned a 30% (.3) bonus rate instead of a 3% (.03) rate. Those mistakes have been fixed, but now your job is to create a drop-down list to make the data entry easier and more accurate for the future:

1. Open **tblEmployee.**

2. Look at the BonusRate field. Employees are given a bonus rate in the form of a decimal representing a percentage. The field can be left empty (NULL), or it can contain a zero value or one of a range of decimal numbers. Create a drop-down list that a data entry person can use to enter this data easily and accurately.

3. In Design View, select the **BonusRate** field. Note that the data type is Number, because these values will be used in calculations.

4. Note the field size is Double, which allows decimals to be used and ensures a high level of precision.

5. Click the **Data Type** arrow to show the drop-down list. At the bottom of the list, click **Lookup Wizard**. Running the wizard will not change the data type.

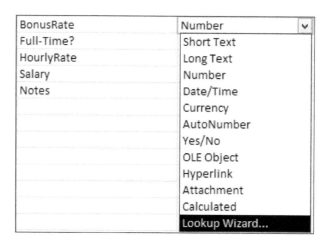

6. In the first step of the wizard, choose **I will type in the values that I want.** Click **Next.**

7. Keep the number of columns at 1, and begin typing your list in the box. *Do not hit Enter during this process; that will take you to the next screen!* Either use your Tab key to move to the next cell, or click on the next blank cell. Type the following list: **0, .01, .02, .03, .04, .05, .06, .07, .08, .09.** You can expand the width of the column to fit the entries in the list if you wish. Click **Next.**

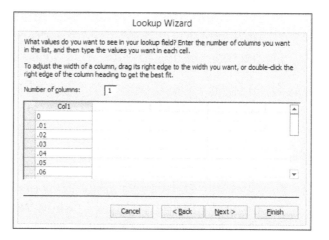

8. On the final screen of the wizard, keep the name BonusRate as the label for the lookup field, and click the **Limit To List** check box so that someone cannot enter values that are not in the list you defined, making sure that the Allow Multiple Values check box is NOT selected.

9. Click **Finish.** Save the table, then switch to **Datasheet View.**

10. Tab to the BonusRate field. The drop-down list should look like this:

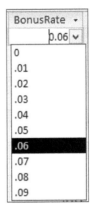

11. Save and close **tblEmployee.**

Imagine This!

Imagine you are improving data entry in a database for a locally owned gym that offers classes two or three times a week. You are setting up the table of classes, and you want to create a drop-down list for the DaysOffered field so that the abbreviations for the days of the week stay consistent. How would you set up the drop-down list to allow a class to be offered on more than one day of the week?

Using Forms for Data Entry

Users rarely enter data directly into tables. Instead, forms are used as a user-friendly interface for viewing or entering data into one or more tables. Forms can be designed so that the focus is on one record at a time, or they can be designed to allow the viewing of multiple records at once.

Create a Simple Form

1. Select, but do not open, **tblEmployee** by clicking on the table name in the Navigation pane once.

2. Click the **Create** tab on the ribbon.

3. In the Forms group, click **Form**.

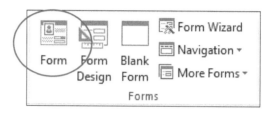

4. A form is created using all of the fields in the tblEmployee table. The form displays only one employee record at a time.

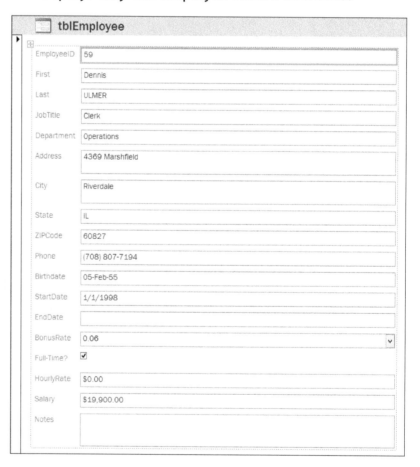

5. Save the form as **frmEmployee**, then close it.

<u>Troubleshooting</u>

The layout of the fields may be different from the image shown depending on your screen resolution. This is not a problem.

If your form looks drastically different from the image shown, you likely did not correctly follow the steps above, or you may have selected the wrong table. Simply delete the form you created and try again.

Save and Back Up

When you are finished with your work, close the Premiere database file, then upload the revised version to your Box account. We strongly suggest that if you are using a flash drive you also place a copy of your work on cloud storage.

IN-DEPTH CASE APPLICATION

Opening Your Premiere Database

Go to your storage device or cloud storage, download your most recent Premiere database to the Desktop, and then open it.

Requiring Members' Last Name Be Entered

For a Short Text, Long Text, or Hyperlink field type, you can use the field properties Required and Allow Zero Length to force users to enter text in that field for each record. For instance, for every new member record entered in the tblMember table, you might want to ensure that the user enters a last name.

1. Open **tblMember** in Design View.

2. Click the **Last** field and then, in the Field Properties pane, click inside the **Required** property.

3. Change the property value from No to **Yes**.

4. Also, click inside the **Allow Zero Length** property, then change the value from Yes to **No**. You must change the Allow Zero Length property so that Access does not allow a zero-length string as a member's last name.

Note: Allowing a zero-length string in a field that is required is a way to bypass that requirement. For example, some stores have computer systems that require the cashier to ask for an e-mail address to complete the transaction. If the customer does not wish to provide an e-mail address, the employee can enter a zero-length string ("") into the field to complete the transaction without entering an actual valid e-mail address. If the company requires an e-mail address when completing a transaction, then the field should be set to not allow zero-length strings.

5. Save your changes, clicking **Yes** in response to any warning messages.

6. Close **tblMember**.

Creating a Lookup Field to Ensure the Accuracy of Store Locations

Premiere Foods has three locations, labeled IN store, IL store, and Online. You will create a lookup field in the tblTransaction table to aid entry of the store location. You will create this Lookup Field using the three values just listed for the Location field.

1. Open **tblTransaction** in Design View.

2. On the Location field, click the **Data Type arrow** to show the drop-down list.

3. Select **Lookup Wizard**.

4. In the first screen of the wizard, choose **I will type the values that I want**. Click **Next**.

5. In the second screen of the Lookup Wizard, type **IN store, IL store, Online**, then click **Next**.

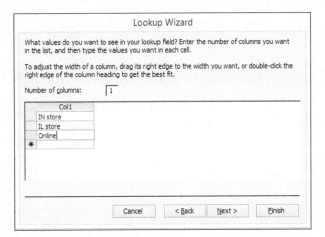

6. Keep the label **Location** for your lookup field, check the box to **Limit to List**, and click **Finish**. Do NOT change Allow Multiple Values from the default value of No. This setting cannot be undone.

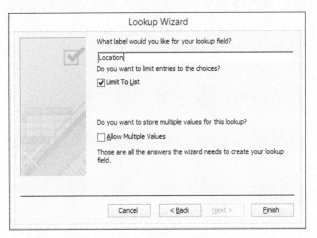

7. Save and return to **Datasheet View** to check your work.

Creating a Lookup Field to Reduce Errors in the tblTransaction Table

In the tblTransaction table, the SoldOrPackagedBy field contains the identification numbers of employees who either completed the transactions at the stores or packaged the online orders in the warehouse. It would be helpful, and would reduce errors, if the person entering this data could see not only the EmployeeIDs but also employee names in a drop-down list and simply choose the correct employee from that list. Accordingly, you will create a lookup field in the SoldOrPackagedBy field using multiple fields from the tblEmployee table. Since the SoldOrPackagedBy field is used to create the relationship to the tblEmployee table, the field cannot be modified until the relationship is deleted.

Deleting an Existing Relationship

1. If necessary, close **tblTransaction**.

2. Click the **Database Tools** tab on the Ribbon; in the Relationships group, click **Relationships**.

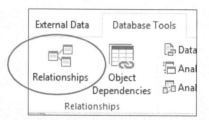

3. Click the **relationship line** that connects tblEmployee to tblTransaction, then press **Delete**.

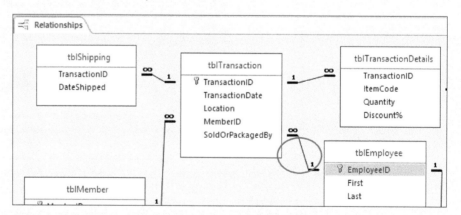

4. Click **Yes** on the message box that appears asking whether you are sure you want to permanently delete the relationship.

5. Save and close the **Relationships** window.

Creating a Multi-Field Lookup

1. Open **tblTransaction** in Design View.

2. Click the **Data Type arrow** for the SoldOrPackagedBy field, then select **Lookup Wizard**.

3. Select **I want the lookup field to get the values from another table or query**. Click **Next**.

4. Select **tblEmployee**. Click **Next**.

5. On the next screen, choose **EmployeeID**, **First**, and **Last** as the fields you want for your drop-down list. Click **Next**.

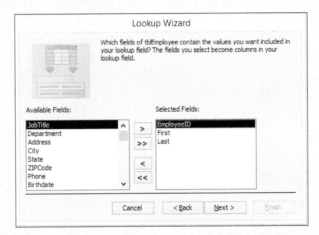

6. Sort **Ascending** by **Last** and then by **First**. Click **Next**.

7. Even though the Lookup Wizard recommends doing so, do NOT hide the key column. Click the **Hide key column** check box to clear it so that EmployeeID will be visible in the drop-down list. Click **Next**.

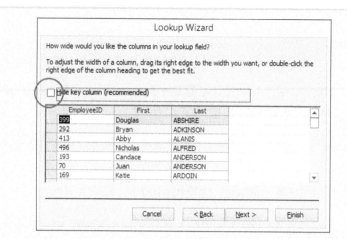

8. Choose the **EmployeeID** as the value to store, then click **Next**.

9. Do not change the label for the lookup field, but do click to **Enable Data Integrity**. Do not choose to Cascade Delete. Click **Finish**.

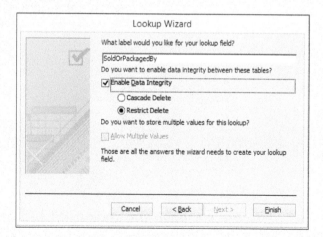

10. Save the table when prompted to allow the relationship to be created.

11. Click the **Lookup** tab in the Field Properties pane, click inside the **Column Heads** property, and change the value from No to **Yes**.

12. Switch to **Datasheet View** to view the results.

13. Close **tblTransaction**.

Edit Relationships to Ensure Data Integrity

Creating lookup fields re-creates the relationships between the tables that you deleted. However, the relationships are not complete. You must edit the relationships to Cascade Update Related Fields.

1. Click the **Database Tools** tab on the Ribbon; in the Relationships group, click **Relationships**.

2. Double-click the **relationship line** between tblTransaction and tblEmployee.

3. In the Edit Relationships dialog box, check the box next to **Cascade Update Related Fields**.

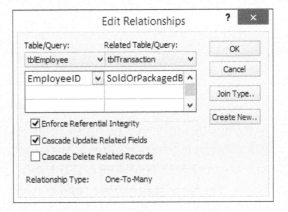

4. Click **OK**. Close the **Relationships** window.

Creating Simple Forms for Data Entry

In the business world, users usually do not enter data directly into tables. Instead, forms are created that are used to enter data into tables.

Create a simple form based on the tblClass table:

1. Select, but do not open, **tblClass**.

2. Click the **Create** tab on the Ribbon.

3. In the Forms group, click **Form**.

A simple form based on the tblClass table will appear. At the top, this form contains the class information; at the bottom, it contains the EmployeeIDs of those who have registered to take this class. The navigation buttons underneath the EmployeeIDs indicate that 11 employees have registered for the Computing Basics class. Alternatively, the navigation buttons at the bottom of the form indicate that there are 11 forms, one for each class.

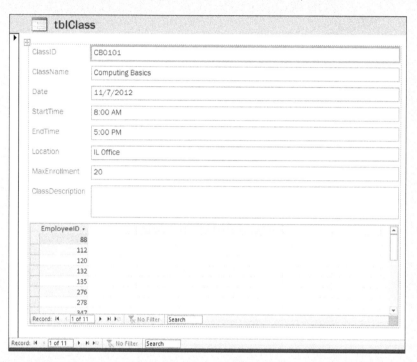

4. By default, forms open to an existing record and in Layout View. Switch to **Form View**, then enter the Class data into the form. To enter NEW data into the form, go to the bottom of the form and click the **New (blank) Record** button.

5. Enter data by typing, then press the Tab key after entering each piece of data to move the cursor to the next field. As you enter data into the form, observe that input masks, formatting, and validation rules are present in the form because it was created based on the tblClass table, in which those properties were set. Properties for data should always be set in the Design View of a table, not in a form. You can set rules for a text box in a form, but these properties only apply to the form text boxes, not the table fields.

ClassID	DA1245
ClassName	**Data Analysis for Decision Making**
Date	**01/25/15**

StartTime	**13:30**
EndTime	**15:00**
Location	**IN Office**
MaxEnrollment	**30** (after validation text is displayed, change the value to **25**)

6. Save and close the form with the name **frmClass**.

Compact and Repair the Premiere Foods Database

In chapter 3, you added data to Premiere by importing from other Access databases, Excel files, and text files. You also deleted some old data during this process so that when you imported new data, it would be accurate. In chapters 3 and 4 as well as in this chapter, you changed field types and properties to make data entry easier and ensure accuracy. While making changes to databases is necessary, Access does not automatically free up space in the database each time you delete data; it reserves that space as if there were still data in it. Also, when you are performing a task in Access, it sometimes creates hidden objects to help it complete the task. Access does not always get rid of these objects on its own, even after the tasks are completed.

As the database grows, its performance slows, and the likelihood increases that the file will become corrupted. The Compact and Repair command automatically cleans up your database, making it smaller and helping correct and prevent database file problems. It is important to do this operation on a local hard disk, not on a network drive or on removable media.

To compact and repair your Premiere file, do the following:

1. Click the **File** tab on the Ribbon.

2. Click the **Compact & Repair Database** button.

3. Wait while Access does its work. You will then be returned to the Home tab on the ribbon.

Finding Records

You have already found data by sorting on a field or fields. When you need to be more specific in your search, you can establish search criteria. Open the

tblProduct table, click inside the appropriate field, and then click the **Find** button (on the Home tab, in the Find group).

Note that you can change options in this dialog box to search in particular ways. Sometimes you know the exact terms for which you would like to search, but other times you only know part of the data, such as the first letter of a person's name or the last four digits of a credit card number. Select methods from the drop-down lists to suit your needs.

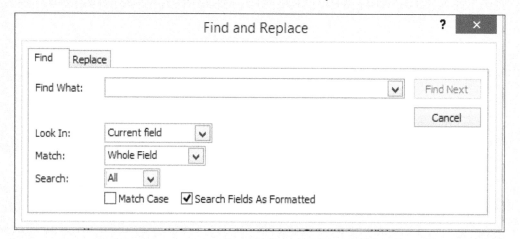

If you need to search for records that have no data entered—for example, records that are blank—you will need to use the word Null as your search criteria. You will also need to clear the Search Fields as Formatted check box. If you keep that box checked, Access will return no results even when there are blank entries.

In tblProducts

1. Enter search criteria that will allow you to find the records requested:

    - How many Cedar Lane products are there?

    - How many products are related to or made from tofu?

2. Close **tblProduct**.

In tblEmployee

1. Find out how many employees still work for Premiere. Consider which field tells you whether an employee is still working for Premiere. Search that field using the search term that indicates that the records are blank, since the employee is still employed with Premiere. If Access gives you no results, confirm that you have unselected the check box next to Search Fields as Formatted, then try again. Carefully count how many employees are still working for Premiere.

2. Close **tblEmployee**.

You can use wildcard characters to represent unpredictable or unimportant characters. Wildcards will become extremely useful when establishing criteria in queries.

Wildcards	
Character	Represents
*	Any number of characters, including none
?	Any one character
#	Any one numeral

In Various Tables

Enter search criteria that will allow you to find the records requested:

- A lady who reminds you of your grandmother always arrives with a smile on her face and a friendly greeting. You were chatting with her one day and found out that her birthday is the same as your sister's (September 17), but you cannot remember this lady's first name, and you would like to be able to welcome her using her first name the next time you see her. Search the appropriate field and find the customer who fits this description.

- Your boss wants to know how many of Premiere's employees live in the Bloomington area (which means their zip code begins with 47). Search the appropriate field, carefully counting to ensure that the data you give your boss is correct.

- A customer approaches you because he cannot remember the brand of teriyaki sauce that he bought a few months ago. He says it was the best he has ever used, and he wants to find it again to see if that brand sells any other sauces. He knows the brand was three letters, then a hyphen (-), then the letter J. Search the appropriate field to find the brand, confirm that this brand makes teriyaki sauce, and find out for the customer what other sauces this brand also makes.

Save and Back Up

When you are finished with your work, close the Premiere database file, then upload the revised version to your Box account. We strongly suggest that if you are using a flash drive you also place a copy of your work on cloud storage.

REVIEW PROBLEMS

Review Problem 1

Create Lookup Fields

In the tblMember Table

1. Create a drop-down list for the State field, using the StateAbbrev field in the tblStateTaxAndShipping table as the source for the values.

2. You will first need to delete the relationship between the tblMember table and the tblStateTaxAndShipping table.

3. Sort the values in ascending order.

4. Keep the label **State** for your lookup field, and be sure to **Enable Data Integrity.**

In the tblProduct Table

1. Create a drop-down list for the **Category** field. You will first need to delete the relationship between the two tables.

2. All categories are already listed in the tblProductCategory table; use this as the data source for the lookup field.

3. The list should use only the **Category** field, sorted alphabetically in ascending order.

4. Click the **Enable Data Integrity** check box so that any category selected must exist in the tblProductCategory table.

5. Once you have finished, return to **Datasheet View.** There now should be a drop-down list that provides possible categories from the tblProductCategory table. (If you add a new category to the tblProductCategory table, it will automatically become available in this drop-down list.)

Review Problem 2

Edit Relationships

In this lab, you had to delete several relationships before creating lookup fields based on other tables. Return to the **Relationships** window, then locate the relevant relationships:

- tblEmployee/tblTransaction

- tblProductCategory/tblProduct

- tblMember/tblStateTaxAndShipping

If you did not choose to enforce referential integrity when creating the lookup, the Lookup Wizard implements only the most basic relationship type, so you will see that the lines joining these lack the one-to-many symbols that you see on the other relationship lines.

Check each of these relationships, making sure that both **Enforce Referential Integrity** and **Cascade Update Related Fields** are selected.

Save and Back Up

When you are finished with your work, close the Premiere database file, and then upload the revised version to your Box account. We strongly suggest that if you are using a flash drive you also place a copy of your work on cloud storage.

Knowledge Check 4

Before starting Knowledge Check 4, make sure you have completed Knowledge Check 3.

Data Types

Check all data types and field sizes in the LANDSCAPERS table, making sure that they are appropriate for the data stored. (If you completed Knowledge Check 3 satisfactorily, they should be.) For some fields, you may have to look at the data to figure out what the field size should be.

Improve the Design of the LANDSCAPERS Table

1. Make the appropriate field the primary key.

2. Make Access display landscaper names in uppercase.

3. Create a drop-down list for the City field that gets its data from the AREA CITIES table. Use only the CityName field, then sort in ascending order by this field.

4. Since most of the landscapers with whom you put customers in contact will be in Indiana, eliminate the requirement for IN to be

entered in the State field; make this value appear automatically as new records are entered.

5. While IN is currently the only state for which we have landscaper information, this might change someday. To help with the possible future need to use other state abbreviations, create a drop-down list for the State field that pulls its data from the STATE INFO table. List state abbreviation and then state name, then sort ascending by state name. Be sure to choose StateAbbrev as the value to store. Your list should look like the following graphic:

6. For the Phone field, create a guide for data entry so that the parentheses, space, and dash are there already and all that needs to be typed are the ten digits. Use the # character as a placeholder, and select the option to store the data with symbols. (There is already a guide on this field; replace it with a new one that meets the description above.)

7. Minimize errors in the Consult/hr field by making values outside a certain range illegal. For the upper limit of the range, use the value 75. Set this up so that Access will return a warning (using a message of your choice) if a value outside the allowed range is entered.

8. Take some work out of data entry by having Access automatically enter the current date (whatever that may be) for DateAdded when a new record is entered.

9. For people who can never remember whether, for example, 7 means June or July, set up the DateAdded field so that it will be obvious when looking at the data what the month is by making the dates display with 3-letter month abbreviations instead of digits.

Improve the Design of the AREA CITIES Table

10. Create a drop-down list in the SizeDescr field with the following four options: **large city, medium city, small city, town.**

After completing these steps, go to the course website to answer Koin-earning questions.

When you are finished, be sure to save your database where you can find it again; you will need it for future Knowledge Check exercises.

Basic Select Query Design, Criteria, and Total Row

Chapter 6

Outline

- Research & Exploration: Research and Create Basic Select Queries
- In-Depth Case Application: Create Single- and Multitable Select Queries Using Appropriate Criteria
- Review Problems: Designing Select Queries, Knowledge Check 5

Objectives

- Understand the purpose of a select query.
- Understand which tables to include in a query and how additional tables affect the result.
- Use exact match and pattern match to limit the records selected.
- Use Comparison operators.
- Use Logical operators (AND, OR, NOT).
- Use Special operators (Between, Is Null, Is Not Null, Like).
- Use the And and Or conditions.
- Use the Total row to group duplicate records.
- Use Where to conflate records and hide criteria fields.

RESEARCH & EXPLORATION

Research

Your Premiere database now has 11 separate tables that contain the 2015 normalized data related to Premiere Foods' employees, members, products, transactions, and so forth. In order to turn these data into meaningful information for decision making, you need to be able to retrieve appropriate data from the tables in your database. Select queries allow you to do this by asking questions and retrieving data from one or more tables. After you run a select query, the results display as a dynaset (dynamic set of data) in the query's Datasheet View.

Query results are narrowed down by specifying criteria or conditions that must be met.

Go to the Microsoft Office Online Support website, http://support.office.microsoft.com, and locate the following articles:

- Introduction to queries 2016

- Query criteria access 2016

- Table of operators (this article applies to Access 2007 but is still relevant in Access 2016)

- Join data sources in a query (this article applies to Access 2013 but is still relevant in Access 2016)

Research the following key terms and concepts:

- Select query

- Text field criteria

- Number and Currency field criteria

- Yes/No field criteria

- Date/Time Criteria

- Comparison operators

- Logical operators (And, Or, and Not)

- Totals query

Exploration

Guidelines for Writing Queries

Use the following basic guidelines to help you create the following select queries in order to return the desired results. (Read "Guide to Creating Queries," located in the appendix, for more details regarding these guidelines.)

1. Read the problem thoroughly, then determine the fields that you need to display, specify criteria for, and/or use in a calculation.

2. Open the Relationship window, noting the table(s) that contain the needed fields. (If a field you need exists in more than one table, use the table in which the field is the primary key.)

3. Create your query in Design View, adding only the necessary table(s) to the top half (field list area) of the query design window. Be sure to keep the following table inclusion rules in mind:

   - Don't add unnecessary tables. Adding too many tables can lead to incorrect results.

   - Exception: All added tables must be joined by relationships. If not, you <u>must</u> add the table(s) that will complete the join(s).

4. Add fields to the bottom half of the design window (the design grid) in the order requested, then run your query.

5. Add one criterion at a time, running the query to audit your results before specifying additional criteria.

6. Create calculated fields as needed.

7. Turn on the Total row only to group data so you can eliminate duplicates or aggregate data.

8. Sort your results in Design View—not in Datasheet View. Queries sort from left to right in Design View.

9. Show only fields that you are asked to list.

   - If you're not using the Total row in your query, simply deselect the Show button to hide the field.

- If the Total row is being used in your query to aggregate data, don't just deselect the Show button. You must specify WHERE instead of GROUP BY for fields that you need to specify criteria for but don't want to display in your dynaset.

Exact Match and Sorting

Create a query that will list the **Last** and **First** name fields as well as the **Address, City, State,** and **ZIPCode** fields for Premiere Members from the city of Indianapolis. Sort in ascending order by the **Last** and then **First** name fields.

1. Open the **Relationships** window from the **Database Tools** tab, determining the table(s) you want to add to the Query Design. Remember to look for table(s) that contain the fields you need to list, specify criteria for, or use in a calculation.

2. Click the **Create** tab and click **Query Design**.

3. Double-click **tblMember** in the Show Table box to add it to the top portion of the Design View, then close the dialog box.

4. Place the fields into the query design grid in the order that they are requested by either dragging them to the design grid or merely double-clicking on the field name.

5. Run the query by clicking on the Run ⊞ button to check your results as you build the query. This action will perform the query operation and take you to the Datasheet View, where you will see the selected fields for all 2,695 Members.

   ### Troubleshooting
   Although you added the **Last** field to the design grid in Design View, the field appears as **Last Name** in the Datasheet View. This discrepancy is a result of the designated caption property when the table was created.

6. The correct fields appear in your dynaset, but you were asked to list only Members from Indianapolis. Return to the query Design View by clicking the **Design View** ⊠ icon on the Home tab.

7. Type **Indianapolis** in the criteria row of the **City** field. This type of criteria is considered an exact match and will return only records that contain the word Indianapolis. Note: After entering the criteria, it will be displayed as "Indianapolis," since the City

field is a short text field. Also, exact match criteria is not case-sensitive, but spelling MUST be exact in order to return correct results.

8. Run the query again by clicking **Run** to check your results. Your dynaset now contains only members from Indianapolis.

9. You still need to sort your results in ascending order, first by the **Last** and then by the **First** name fields. Queries must be sorted in Design View. Return to the **Design View** and select **Ascending** in the **Sort** row for both the **Last** and **First** fields. Remember: queries sort from left to right in Design View.

10. Run the query again by clicking Run to check your results.

11. Save the query as qry**RE1**.

12. Your dynaset should match the following figure:

Last Name ▾	First ▾	Address ▾	City ▾	State ▾	ZIPCode ▾
ALFRED	Pamela	7357 Oak Leaf	Indianapolis	IN	46254-
AQUINO	Thomas	1902 Christopher	Indianapolis	IN	46227-
ARVIZU	Claire	7377 Ju Dee	Indianapolis	IN	46228-
ARVIZU	Rosie	7580 Bob O Link	Indianapolis	IN	46274-
ATHERTON	Joseph	2886 Colony	Indianapolis	IN	46251-
BAKER	Jayne	3768 Martin	Indianapolis	IN	46217-
BALES	Jacob	2444 Webster	Indianapolis	IN	46202-
BALES	Mabel	4902 Pebble Place	Indianapolis	IN	46237-

Record: ◄ ◄ | 1 of 90 | ► ►► ►▸ | 🏷 No Filter | Search

Results for qryRE1 query

Is Null Operator, * Wildcard Pattern Match, and And Condition

Create a query that lists the **Last**, **First**, **Address**, **City**, **State**, and **ZIPCode** fields of **current** employees who live in Bloomington and the surrounding area. (This area is defined as those addresses with zip codes beginning with **47**.) Sort your results in ascending order, first by **Last** name and then by **First** name.

1. Open the **Relationships** window from the **Database Tools** tab, then determine the table(s) you want to add to the Query Design.

2. Click the **Create** tab, then select **Query Design**.

3. Double-click **tblEmployee** in the Show Table box, then close the dialog box.

4. Double-click on the **Last**, **First**, **Address**, **City**, **State**, and **ZIPCode** fields to add them to the design grid and run the query. The

dynaset displays all 230 employees, but you only want employees who have zip codes that start with 47.

In chapter 5, you were introduced to the use of Wildcards, which were very useful when searching for specific records while in the table's Datasheet View. These same wildcards (*, ?, and #) are extremely useful when creating select queries and are used with the Like operator to create a pattern match (e.g., Like "tofu*", Like "????", Like "??###").

5. Return to the Design View, then enter **47*** on the criteria row of the ZIPCode field. Notice that the criteria now reads **Like "47*"**.

   <u>**Imagine This!**</u>
   Imagine that you want the ZIPCode to end in 47. How would you edit the pattern match to return the correct records?

6. Run the query to check your results. You should now have 75 records listed in your dynaset, which represents all employees in the tblEmployee table whose zip code begins with 47. However, you've been asked to list only current employees (those who are still working for Premiere).

   The EndDate field in the tblEmployee table is used to designate the date when an employee ended his or her employment with Premiere. If the EndDate field is empty (contains null values or zero-length strings), then the employee is still working for Premiere. Although you don't want to list the EndDate field in your query, you will need to add it to the query design grid to specify the appropriate criterion for this field.

7. Return to the **Design View**, then add the **EndDate** field to the design grid.

8. Type **Is Null** in the criteria row for the **EndDate** field. Entering the EndDate and ZIPCode criterion on the same row results in an And condition indicating that all criteria on the same row in the design grid must be TRUE to return the correct result. Note: Entering """ (quotes with no space) can also be entered as the criterion to indicate that the field value is empty.

   <u>**Imagine This!**</u>
   What would you enter for the criterion in the EndDate field if you want your dynaset to return records for employees who are no longer working for Premiere?

9. Run the query to check your results. Your query now returns 63 records with no date listed in the EndDate field. This is correct, but you don't want this field listed in your dynaset.

10. Return to the **Design View**, then deselect the checkmark on the Show row of the design grid for the EndDate field.

11. Sort the query in ascending order, first by **Last** name and then by **First** name.

12. Run the query again by clicking Run to check your results.

13. Save the query as **qryRE2**.

14. Your dynaset should match the following figure:

Results for qryRE2 query

Imagine This!

What would you type in the Criteria row of a query to locate the following records in the Premiere database?

- Members with yahoo.com e-mail addresses

- Members born on May 13 of any year

Yes/No Criteria and the ? Wildcard Pattern Match

Create a query that lists the **First** and **Last** name, **Department**, and **Salary** for **current full-time** employees whose first names contain **five** characters and start with the letter **S**. Sort by **Salary** in descending order.

1. Create the query in Design View, adding the appropriate table.

2. Add the **First** and **Last** name, **Department**, and **Salary** fields to the query design grid, as well as the **Full-Time?** and **EndDate** fields for criteria specification.

3. Run the query to check your results. All 230 employees are listed, because appropriate criteria have not yet been specified in order to return requested employee information. It's good practice to add one criterion at a time and run the query to audit your results before specifying additional criterion.

4. Return to the Design View, then enter **S????** in the criteria row of the **First** field. The entry now appears as **Like "S????"** to indicate that the employee first name must begin with an S that is followed by any four characters.

Imagine This!
Imagine that you are asked to list first names containing 5 characters no matter what the first name starts with. In this case you might be inclined to enter just **?????** for the criterion. However, this criterion will return the following error message:

Access will only place quotes around criterion and add the Like operator if the criterion is recognized as text. In this case, you would need to type **"?????"** for the criterion.

5. Run the query to make sure that all employee first names have five characters, starting with S. You should have 8 records, but your dynaset still needs to be narrowed down to display only current full-time employees.

6. Return to the Design View and enter **Yes** in the criteria row of the **FullTime?** field. Note: In a Yes/No field, True can also be entered to designate a Yes field value. A No field values is designated with either No or False. Do not put quotes around Yes/No field criteria.

7. Run the query to check your results. You should see that one of the employees listed is no longer working for Premiere.

8. Return to the Design View, then enter the appropriate criterion for the EndDate field so that only current employees are displayed in the dynaset. Be sure to run your query to check your results.

9. Return to the Design View, then sort your results in descending order by **Salary**. Also, make sure that only the **First, Last, Department**, and **Salary** fields are shown in your dynaset.

10. Run the query to check your results.

11. Save the query as **qryRE3**.

12. Your dynaset should match the following figure:

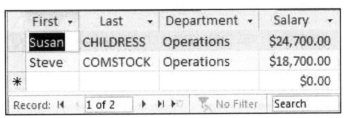

Results for qryRE3 query

Imagine This!
What would you type in the Criteria row of a query to locate ClassIDs that begin with the letters SM, followed by 4 digits?

Comparison Operators

Create a query that will list **First** and **Last** name, **Department**, and **HourlyRate** for **current part-time** employees who make at least $10 per hour. Sort your query by **HourlyRate** in descending order.

1. Add the employee **First** and **Last** name, **Department**, and **Hourly Rate** to the query design grid.

2. Add additional fields to the design grid, then enter appropriate criteria that will limit the query result to include only current part-time employees. Be sure to run the query to test your results after you enter each criterion.

3. You will need to use a comparison operator to designate that the hourly rate needs to be at least $10. Common comparison operators are shown in the following table:

Operator	Stands for	Example
=	Equal to	=10 (the = can be omitted)
>	Greater than	>10
>=	Greater than or equal to (at least)	>=10
<	Less than	<10
<=	Less than or equal to (no more than)	<=10
<>	Not equal to	<>10 (can also enter Not 10)

Type **>=10** on the criteria row for **HourlyRate**, then sort by **HourlyRate** in descending order.

4. Run the query to test your results.

5. Save the query as **qryRE4**.

6. Your dynaset should match the following figure:

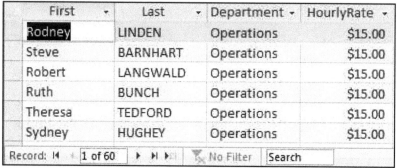

Results for qryRE4 query

Imagine This!

Imagine that you want to further refine your query to only include current part-time employees hired before 2009 who are making at least $10.00 per hour. What field would you add to your query design grid, and what criteria would you designate for this field?

Between and Or Operators

Create a query that will list the **First** and **Last** name and **Phone** number for all employees from Oklahoma and Illinois who were hired between the years 2010 and 2014. Sort the results in ascending order, first by **Last** name and then by **First** name.

1. Add the employee **First** and **Last** name and **Phone** number fields to the query design grid.

2. Add the **State** and **StartDate** fields to the design grid to specify criteria that will limit the result to only Oklahoma and Illinois for the designated time period.

3. Type **OK Or IL** on the criteria row for **State**, then run the query.

   ### Troubleshooting
   A common mistake is to type OK And IL because of the way the question is worded. This criterion would, of course, not work, since the field value for State cannot be both OK and IN.

4. Run the query to test your results.

5. The Between Operator determines whether a numeric or date value is found within a designated range (e.g., Between 50 and 100; Between #1/1/2015# And #3/31/2015#). Query results using the Between Operator will include both the beginning and ending numeric or date values in the designated range.

   Enter **Between 1/1/2010 And 12/31/2014** on the criteria row for **StartDate**.

6. Run the query to check your results.

7. The query instructions ask you to list the First field and the Last field in the query design grid, but you are told to sort first by Last name and then by First name in ascending order. Remember, all sorting needs to be done in the query Design View and Access sorts from left to right.

   Return to the **Design View**, then drag the **Last** field from into the first column of the design grid. Your design grid should now look like the following image:

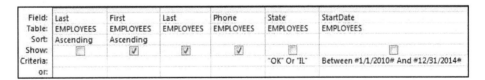

Field:	Last	First	Last	Phone	State	StartDate
Table:	EMPLOYEES	EMPLOYEES	EMPLOYEES	EMPLOYEES	EMPLOYEES	EMPLOYEES
Sort:	Ascending	Ascending				
Show:	☐	☑	☑	☑	☐	☐
Criteria:					"OK" Or "IL"	Between #1/1/2010# And #12/31/2014#
or:						

8. Sort Ascending for the first **Last** field that is listed, then deselect the show button. Sort Ascending for the **First** field.

9. Run the query to check results.

10. Make sure that your dynaset displays only the requested fields.

11. Save the query as **qryRE5**.

12. Your dynaset should match the following figure:

First	▾	Last	▾	Phone	▾
Douglas		ABSHIRE		(847) 514-9225	
Abby		ALANIS		(708) 608-7126	
Eric		ATHERTON		(847) 749-5483	
Harold		BARNETTE		(708) 554-7221	
Al		BINGAMAN		(708) 905-2900	

Record: I◄ ◄ 1 of 36 ► ►I ►⧉ 🔽 No Filter Search

Results for qryRE5 query

Imagine This!

You might be inclined to use the or row of the query design grid to return the requested records for the qryRE5 query by placing the state criteria for OK on the Criteria row and IL on the or row. This technique is acceptable; however, you must be very careful! Remember, criteria on the same row in the query design grid results in an And condition, indicating that all criteria on the same row must be TRUE in order to return the correct result. What would happen if your design grid looked like the following image?

Field:	Last	First	Last	Phone	State	StartDate
Table:	EMPLOYEES	EMPLOYEES	EMPLOYEES	EMPLOYEES	EMPLOYEES	EMPLOYEES
Sort:	Ascending	Ascending				
Show:	☐	☑	☑	☑	☐	☐
Criteria:					"OK"	Between #1/1/2010# And #12/31/2014#
or:					"IL"	

Would your dynaset have more records, or would it have fewer? What records would actually be displayed in your dynaset? What would you need to do in the query Design View to make sure that the correct records are returned?

Combined And and Or Conditions

Create a query that will list employee **State**, **First** and **Last** name, **Department**, and **Salary** for **current full-time** employees from Indiana who have salaries of at least $50,000 as well as employees from Illinois who have salaries of at least $40,000. Sort by State in ascending order and by Salary in descending order.

1. Create the query using what you've learned from designing the previous queries.

2. Save the query as **qryRE6**.

3. Your dynaset should match the following figure:

State	First	Last	Department	Salary
IL	Dave	CABUTO	Operations	$57,000.00
IL	Patsy	CRISWELL	Operations	$50,500.00
IL	Megan	JOHNSON	Operations	$44,000.00
IL	Jonathan	KEELING	Operations	$44,000.00
IL	Sharon	KETCHAM	Operations	$41,800.00
IL	Adrienne	LINDSEY	Operations	$41,400.00
IL	Gretta	LOVING	Operations	$51,600.00
IL	Dawn	MULLIS	Operations	$40,600.00
IL	Adam	PRIETO	Operations	$49,400.00
IL	Marjorie	ROSENHEIM	Operations	$55,800.00
IL	Charlene	VERDUGO	Operations	$52,400.00
IL	Eugene	WESTBROOKS	Operations	$51,300.00
IN	Benjamin	DRIVER	Human Resources	$74,400.00
IN	Velma	FRIEDRICHSEN	Accounting	$73,500.00

Record: I◄ ◄ 1 of 21 ► ►I ►☐   ☐ No Filter   Search

Results for qryRE6 query

Troubleshooting

If you are get an error message when you try to enter IN for the state criteria, place quotes around it: "IN". (This is necessary because IN is a reserved word—an operator.)

IN-DEPTH CASE APPLICATION

Creating Mailing Labels

Your supervisor in the marketing department at Premiere has asked you to provide mailing labels for Premiere Foods Club Members. She'd like the resulting labels sorted in alphabetical order by member's last name. To do this, you must first create a query that lists all the information that would be suitable for a mailing label. The resulting query will then be used as a basis for generating a Labels Report.

Table Selection and Field Inclusion

1. Download your Premiere database to your Desktop, then open the file.

2. Click **Relationships** on the **Database Tools** tab. You learned from completing this chapter's Research & Exploration sections that it is good practice to inspect the Relationships window before you begin writing a query in order to determine the table(s) that contain the fields that you need to list in your query. Think about what fields are suitable for a mailing label and about what table(s) you need to include in your query design to accomplish this. In this case, the table that is needed should be very evident. Leave the Relationships window open as a reference as you build your query.

3. Click **Query Design** on the **Create** tab, then add the **tblMember** table, since this is the table that holds the fields that you need to list for the labels (First, Last, Address, City, State, ZIPCode).

4. Since the **First, Last, Address, City, State** and **ZIPCode** fields are listed contiguously in the table field list, you can select all the fields, then drag them into the design grid at once instead of adding them one at a time.

   Click on the **First** name field, press and hold Shift, and then click the **ZIPCode** field to select the desired fields and drag the highlighted fields into the design grid.

5. Sort by **Last** name in ascending order, then run the query to examine your dynaset. Your dynaset will return all 2,695 from the **tblMember** table but will only list the fields that you included in the design grid.

> **Query Advice:** *Include table(s) in your query for fields you need to display.*

Working with Multiple Tables and Grouping Records Using the Total Row

Your supervisor now decides that she wants mailing labels only for customers who have made a purchase. Since the tblMember table does not contain this data, you need to once again examine the Relationships window and find the table that contains data related to member purchases:

1. Return to the **Design View**, then drag the **tblTransaction** table into the design area.

2. Run the query, then examine the data.

   Members who have never made a purchase will not be displayed in the dynaset, because they do not have related records in the **tblTransaction** table. However, there are some members who have made multiple purchases (e.g., Douglas Abel is listed three times because he made three separate transactions). If labels are generated based on the current query result, members will receive multiple mailings resulting in higher cost to Premiere.

3. To eliminate (conflate) the duplicate records, you must add the Total row to your design grid.

4. Return to the **Design View**, then click the ⬚ icon on the **Design** tab to show the **Total** row in the query design grid. Notice that each field now has **Group By** designated by default.

5. Run the query to check your results. The duplicate records have now been eliminated (conflated) as a result of the Group By designation in the Total row, and you should now see 2,071 records in your dynaset.

> **Query Advice:** *Make sure you only include table(s) that are necessary and/or allow you to specify necessary criteria. Also,* you MUST have a reason to use the Total row in a query. Adding the Total row to the design grid when it's not necessary may return incorrect results.

And versus Or Conditions, Exact Match, Pattern Match, Or and Not Operators, and Using Where on the Total Row

You are now told that your supervisor wants to use the mailing labels to mail coupon promotions to members who made their purchase at brick-and-mortar locations. She does not want to include any purchases that were made online. Because the two brick-and-mortar stores are located in Bloomington, Indiana, and Chicago, Illinois, she wants to mail coupons only to folks who live in those areas.

Specifically, the following conditions need to be met in the query in order to return the requested records.

- Members who live in Bloomington, Indiana.

- Members who live in the Chicago, Illinois, area. This will include those who have zip codes in Illinois starting with **60** and those who have zip codes in Indiana starting with **464** (for the Northwest Indiana region).

- Members whose purchases did NOT occur online.

It's good practice to specify criteria one at a time in the query design grid, making sure to run the query after the addition of each criterion in order to make sure that all conditions are met and correct records are returned.

Remember: Access evaluates criteria on each line as an And condition. The phrase "on the same line at the same time" might help you remember this rule. Multiple lines used in the design grid represent an Or condition.

1. Enter the criteria on the Criteria row of the design grid that will return records for purchases that were made by members from Bloomington, Indiana. (Don't forget to put quotes around IN, since IN is an operator.) Run the query to check your results. The dynaset should list 54 records.

2. Return to the Design View, then enter criteria on the or row that will return Illinois members whose zip code begins with 60. Be sure to use

the * wildcard pattern match correctly for the zip code. Run the query to check your results. The dynaset should now list 252 records.

3. Return to the Design View, then enter criteria on the next row of the design grid that will return Northwest Indiana members whose zip code begins with 464. Run the query to check your results. The dynaset should now list 260 records.

   Tip: Rather than use three rows for the criteria, you can streamline your query design by placing both zip code criteria on the or row using an Or operator. The resulting design grid would look like the following image:

Field:	First	Last	Address	City	State	ZIPCode
Table:	tblMember	tblMember	tblMember	tblMember	tblMember	tblMember
Total:	Group By	Group By	Group By	Group By	Group By	Group By
Sort:		Ascending				
Show:	☑	☑	☑	☑	☑	☑
Criteria:				"Bloomington"	"IN"	
or:						Like "60*" Or Like "464*"

4. You still need to indicate that the purchases were made only at the Brick and Mortar store locations and not online. Examine the fields in the **tblTransaction** table, opening the table if necessary to validate the field that should be added to the design grid.

5. Add the **Location** field to the query design grid.

6. Enter **Not Online** criterion for **Location** field, making sure that this condition is met for all records that are shown in the resulting dynaset. (Remember: "on the same line at the same time.")

   Note: You can use either the **<>** or the **Not** operator to specify criteria for members who did not make an online purchase. The Not operator will be displayed as <> when the query is saved and reopened. The <> cannot be used if there is a wildcard also being used in the criterion.

7. Run the query to check your results. The dynaset now contains 285 records, but notice that Howard ABEL is showing up twice again. When you examine his records, you'll see that Howard made purchases at both the Illinois store and the Indiana store. Accordingly, his records are now being grouped individually by two unique Location values.

   Since the Location field is only being used in this query to specify the needed criteria and you don't want it to show up in your dynaset, your first inclination might be to deselect the Show button. Merely deselecting the Show button will not affect the records being grouped by the Location Value, and you will still have duplicate records listed for Premiere members.

8. Return to the Design View and change Group By to **Where** on the **Total Row** of the **Location** field. Notice that the Show button is automatically deselected.

9. Run the query to check your results. You should now have 258 records in your dynaset.

> **Query Advice:** *When the Total row is in use and you have fields being used ONLY for criteria that are not to be displayed in the results, change Group By to Where in the Totals row for those fields.*

Multiple Table Joins and the Between Operator

Your boss reveals that she is thinking of carrying a brand-new, all-natural, organic brand of unscented antiperspirant, so she wants to send the promotional coupons only to people who purchased products belonging to the **personal hygiene** department in the warm months of the year, from **May** through **September** of **2015**.

1. You need to once again inspect the Relationships window in order determine the table(s) containing field values related to the personal hygiene department.

2. Drag the **tblProductCategory** table into the design area, then add the **Department** field to the design grid and run the query to check your results. You should still see 258 records listed in the dynaset, but this result is not correct.

3. Return to the Design View. Notice that there is no relationship (join) between the tblTransaction and tblProductCategory tables.

   Hint: When tables in queries are not joined, dynaset results will be incorrect and could cause your screen to freeze when you run the query. If your query is taking an extraordinarily long time to run, or if it seems frozen, check to see whether all tables are joined. If all tables are not joined, press the **CTRL+BREAK** keys simultaneously to stop the execution of the query, then add the necessary tables to the query design.

   > **Query Advice:** *All tables included in a query should be connected with relationships. If necessary, add tables to join tables together, even if you are not listing or specifying criteria for fields in the added tables.*

4. Inspect the Relationship window again, then add the table(s) that will complete the join. You don't need to use any fields in the added table(s), but they must be in the query design so that all tables are joined together.

5. Add the **Personal Hygiene** criteria to the appropriate row(s) in the query design grid, then run the query to check your results. There are now 246 records listed, which proves that incorrect result will occur if all tables are not joined in the query design.

6. Finally, you need to return records only purchased in the warm months of the year, from **May** through **September** of **2015**. Since dates are actually numbers, you can use comparison operators (>=, <=) or the reserved words Between and And to specify a particular range of dates.

   Add the needed field, then enter the following on the appropriate criteria line(s):

   Between 5/1/2015 and 9/30/2015

   Once entered, the dates with have # signs surrounding the designated dates, since these are exact dates. Be careful when entering exact dates without using the # signs (e.g., entering **Between 5/1/2015 and 9/31/2015** will actually enter the criteria **Between #5/1/2015# And #9/1/1931#/2015**, since there are only 30 days in September).

7. Run the query to check your results. Arthur ABSHIRE has three records listed.

8. Return to the **Design View**, make appropriate changes on the Total Row to eliminate the duplicate records, and run the query again.

9. Run the query to check your results.

10. Save the query as **qryCA1**.

11. Your dynaset should match the following figure:

First	Last Name	Address	City	State	ZIPCode
Arthur	ABSHIRE	1829 Viva	Rankin	IL	60960-
Albert	ALANIS	7644 Glen Ridge	Bloomington	IN	47401-
Derrick	ALBER	6128 Bagby	Dundee	IL	60118-
Brandi	ANGULO	6655 Bainbridge	Chicago	IL	60616-
Barbara	AQUINO	2364 Clarizz	Bloomington	IN	47404-
Jerome	ARCE	7658 Wisley	Fox River Grove	IL	60021-
Ada	BACKUS	129 Collinswood	Arlington Heights	IL	60006-

Record: ◄ ◄ 1 of 151 ► ►► No Filter Search

Results for qryCA1 query

REVIEW PROBLEMS

Create the indicated select queries while keeping the following in mind:

- Use the Research & Exploration and In-Depth Case Application sections of this chapter as a reference when writing the queries.

- Place only tables in the query Design View that contain tables that hold fields that you need to list, specify criteria for, or use in a calculation. If all tables are not joined, add any additional tables that will complete the join. Be sure to use the Relationships window and to inspect table data to determine which tables to use in your query.

- Add necessary fields to the design grid.

- Run the query without specifying criteria, then look at the data.

- Be sure to use appropriate criteria or operators while creating your query,

- Specify one criterion at a time, running the query after each criterion is added to see whether the results continue to make sense.

- Pay close attention to any And and Or conditions that need to be met. Remember: "on the same line at the same time."

- Eliminate duplicate records with Totals Row, using Group By and Where when necessary.

- Review the wording of the problem to determine which fields need to be displayed.

- Designate sorting in the query Design View.

Review Problem 1

E-mail Problems

Jeff Pratt, a Premiere Foods member, asked yesterday whether our e-mail list has been discontinued; it has been months since he has received e-mail from us.

Open the **tblMember** table and check into this. You should find that while Jeff is listed as wanting to receive our e-mails, we don't have his e-mail address. (One possibility: someone deleted his address when mail sent to him started bouncing back to us.)

1. Create a query listing members who are in this situation (wanting to receive e-mail from Premiere but not able to do so because there is no e-mail address for them in the database). List their **First** and **Last** names and **PhoneNumber** so that they can be contacted about this. Sort by **Last** name in ascending order.

2. Save the query as **qryReview1**. The dynaset should match the following figure:

First	Last Name	PhoneNumber
Chad	ABEL	(313) 670-2260
Dale	ADKINSON	(517) 702-4644
Kenneth	ALONSO	(812) 389-4282
Mark	ALSTON	(260) 220-9844
Walter	ARDOIN	(619) 943-1733
Victoria	ARDOIN	(217) 811-4043
Cynthia	ARRIAGA	(217) 546-6201

Record: I◄ ◄ 1 of 393 ► ►I ►✱ No Filter Search

Results for qryReview1 query

Review Problem 2

Member Day Invitations

Once a year, Premiere Foods invites members who live in cities where Premiere has stores (Bloomington, Indiana, and Chicago, Illinois) to attend Member Night for food, fun, and special buys.

1. The invitation should go out to people in those two cities who have been members since 2005 or earlier. Create a query that lists mailing information (**First**, **Last**, **Address**, **City**, **State**, and **ZIPCode**), sorted by **Last** name in ascending order.

2. Save the query as **qryReview2**. The dynaset should match the following figure:

Results for qryReview2 query

Review Problem 3

Mailing List

It's the time of year when Premiere Foods mails member appreciation coupons, good for 5% off any product. These should go out to all members who have made a purchase between October and December of 2015.

1. Create a query that lists mailing information for these members (**First**, **Last**, **Address**, **City**, **State**, and **ZIPCode**). Sort the results by **Last** name in ascending order.

2. Save the query as **qryReview3**. The dynaset should match the following figure:

Results for qryReview3 query

Review Problem 4

Partner Offer

Another business partner, Organic Juice, is launching a new kind of organic drink with apple juice in it. You have agreed to create a mailing list of members who have requested partner offers who live in Indiana and Illinois who have purchased any drink that both (1) has "Apple" in the description and (2) is organic ("OG" represents organic in the database).

Hint: Look for how organic is described, and remember that you would not want a result such as "Pecan Date Log" (which nonetheless has the letters "og" in it).

1. Create a query that lists the mailing information (**First**, **Last**, **Address**, **City**, **State**, and **ZIPCode**) to be sent only to Premiere members who meet Organic Juice's criteria. Be sure that each member is listed only once, and sort by **Last** name in ascending order.

2. Save the query as **qryReview4**. The dynaset should match the following figure:

First	Last Name	Address	City	ZIPCode
Vicki	CALVERT	5100 Hillcrest	Bloomington	47401-
Justin	CLAUSSEN	3878 Swinging	Lamar	47550-
Angela	HANES	6121 Petersburg	Fort Wayne	46855-
Benjamin	HIGHSMITH	319 Epson	Patricksburg	47455-
Albert	LENA	5371 Bob O Link	Allendale	62410-
Cindy	LINCOLN	337 Stillwell	Brownstown	47220-
Cindy	LOWE	7279 Grant	Chicago	60668-
Raymond	MAJOR	3806 Buick Cadillac	Rosedale	47874-
Beulah	MCBRIDE	3280 Will Sowders	Aurora	47001-
Florence	MCQUEEN	325 Hollyhock	Clinton	47842-
Belinda	NESTER	2824 Cottage	Hope	47246-
Albert	REA	6790 Sunny Slopes	Newport	47966-
Louis	ROSE	3105 Arbors	Indianapolis	46214-
Stacy	SMITH	6797 Morning Glory	Nashville	47448-
Miguel	STINNETT	2185 Spruce	Lawrenceburg	47025-
Nina	THOMPSON	4066 Beringer	Chicago	60690-
Dale	WALSTON	2513 Harvey	Carthage	46115-

Record: I◄ ◄ 1 of 19 ► ►I 🖼 No Filter Search

Results for qryReview4 query

Knowledge Check 5

Before starting Knowledge Check 5, make sure you have completed Knowledge Check 4.

Creating Single- and Multitable Queries

Create queries in **TheArtfulYard.accdb** database to solve the problems outlined. Make use of the Relationships windows in the Database. Name the queries as instructed, and sort as instructed in the Design View of each query.

When you are finished, be sure to save this database where you can find it again; you will need it for future Knowledge Check exercises.

Create Mailing List for Store Opening Announcement

The company will soon be opening a store in Springfield, Illinois, and would like to send announcements to customers in the surrounding area.

1. Create a query that will list complete mailing information for all customers who have a 217 phone number area code and have elected to receive mail from us. Note: You might have to put quotes around the criterion for the phone number.

2. Sort ascending by **Last Name**.

3. Save this query as **qryKC1**.

Answer Customer Request

A customer called to ask if you sell any fairly inexpensive wind chimes ($6 or less) or birdhouses ($8 or less) that she could pick up today and place in a friend's new convertible as a joke.

1. Create a query that will list the description, product category, and selling price for each such product we currently have in stock. (You might notice that one of the items listed is missing a description; you will fix this in a later exercise.)

2. Sort ascending by the category and then descending by selling price.

3. Save this query as **qryKC2**.

Perform Fourth-Quarter Product Sales Analysis

Gardeners in the Northeast and the Midwest have to deal with harsh winters, and Marketing is curious to find out what sells in these two areas at the end of the year.

1. Create a query that will list the Order ID, Product ID, Product Category, Region, and Order Date for all orders placed by these customers between October 15 and December 31, 2005.

   (Note: if you think it would be difficult to tease out patterns just by looking over this long list of records, you're right. The second step might be to copy this list to Excel, where there are a number of powerful data analysis tools that could help you make sense of the data.)

2. Sort ascending by Order ID and then by Product ID.

3. Save this query as **qryKC3**.

Find Problematic Data

An astute employee has noticed a problem with some of the product data: some products lack a description, and some have apparently not yet been assigned to a warehouse.

1. Create a query to locate all problematic records, listing Product Category, Product ID, Description, and Warehouse, so that the person responsible for each category can address these problems.

2. Sort ascending by Product Category, then by Product ID.

3. Save this query as **qryKC4**.

Mailing Promotion for Bird Lovers

The Artful Yard has discovered that it has a large number of customers who are bird lovers. Several new items have been added to this product line, the company would like to send promotional coupons to those of their customers who have purchased bird-related items.

1. Create a query that will list mailing information for customers who purchased bird-related items in the fourth quarter of 2005. List only customers who are on the mailing list.

   These items should be actual items for birds (e.g., birdhouses), not items that just happen to have bird features (e.g., hummingbird chimes).

2. Sort ascending by Last Name.

3. Save this query as **qryKC5**.

After completing all 5 queries, go to the course website to answer Koin-earning questions.

When you are finished, be sure to save your database where you can find it again; you will need it for future Knowledge Check exercises.

Concatenation, Calculated Fields, and Aggregate Functions

Chapter 7

Outline

- Research & Exploration: Research and Create Concatenated, Calculated, and Aggregated Fields in Queries

- In-Depth Case Application: Use Mathematical Formulas and Aggregate Functions in Queries to Calculate and Summarize Data

- Review Problems: Practice Creating Calculated Fields and Aggregating Data in Queries, Knowledge Check 6

Objectives

- Create a concatenated field.

- Create queries with calculated fields.

- Create queries using aggregate functions: AVG, MIN, MAX, SUM, COUNT.

- Review and understand the difference between the Group By and Where operators.

RESEARCH & EXPLORATION

Research

Queries can do more than just return unique field values from a table. Queries can perform calculations, combine field values, and summarize data.

Go to the Microsoft Office Online Support website, http://support.office.microsoft.com, and locate the following articles:

- Introduction to queries 2016

- Build an expression 2016

- Sum data by using a query

- Count data by using a query

The built-in help feature in Access is also an excellent resource. After opening Access, press the F1 Key to launch Access Help with access to many of the aforementioned articles.

Research the following key terms and concepts:

- Concatenation operators

- Arithmetic operators

- Calculated field

- Concatenated field

- Totals query

- Aggregate functions

- Expression

Exploration

Create Calculated Fields and Concatenated Fields

To perform a calculation and create a calculated field in a query, you must define an expression (formula) in the query Design View that contains a combination of field names, constant values, functions, and mathematical operators. Calculated fields result in multiple rows of data (records) in the dynaset, with the calculation being performed on each row.

Concatenated fields allow you to combine two or more text fields and characters into a single field using the **&** (ampersand) operator. These fields are also created by defining appropriate expressions in the query Design View.

Keep the following tips in mind when creating calculated fields and concatenated fields:

- Make sure that you place the table(s) in the field list area of the query design that contain the fields you want to use in your expression.

- Place the expression on the Field row in a blank column of the query design grid.

- An easy way to write the expression is to first right-click in the field row of the blank column where you are going to write the expression, then click **Zoom**. This provides you with a large window for writing your expression.

- Expressions should begin with a self-selected field name (followed by a colon) that you want Access to give the calculated or concatenated field result in the dynaset.

- When writing expressions, be sure to put square brackets [] around all field names and to type the field name *exactly* as spelled in the table. Note: Field name designations are not case-sensitive and can be entered with or without capital letters.

- Text and other characters should be enclosed in quotes in a concatenated field.

- Do not place quotes around values or functions in a calculated field.

- Be sure to use the standard order of operation in calculated field expressions.

- In Design View, change field properties such as format, decimal places, and so forth by right-clicking the expression/field and selecting Properties.

- Examples of calculated and concatenated expressions follow:

  - Age: (Date() - [DateOfBirth])\365

- EmployeeName: [FirstName] **&** " " **&** [LastName]

Calculate Employee Bonuses

Create a query that lists all current full-time employee names in a field named EmployeeName and calculates each employee's bonus in a field named **BonusAmt**. The EmployeeName field should combine the First and Last name separated by a space. The bonus should be 5% of the employee's salary and should calculate the bonus amount only, not the wage with bonus. Format the BonusAmt as currency, and sort by **BonusAmt** in descending order.

1. Open the Relationships window from the Database Tools tab to determine the table(s) you want use in the query. Remember to only include table(s) in your query that contain fields that you need to list, specify criteria for, or use in a calculation.

2. Click the **Create** tab, then click **Query Design**.

3. Add the **tblEmployee** table to the Design View, since this table contains all needed fields for the query.

4. Right-click in the **Field** row of the first blank column, then select **Zoom**. You can change the Font size to make your entry more readable.

5. Type **MemberName: [First] & " " & [Last]**, click **OK** to close the Zoom dialog box, and then run the query to check your results.

   <u>Imagine This!</u>
   What expression would you enter for the new MemberName field if you want to instead display the employee's last name and first name, separated by a comma (e.g., Kinser, Amy)?

6. Return to the Design View, then type **BonusAmt: [Salary]*.05** in the next blank field row of the design grid.

7. Right click on the newly created **BonusAmt** field in the design grid, and select **Properties**. In the Property Sheet that appears, set the Format property to **Currency**, then run the query to check your results.

8. Return to the Design View, then complete the query design to list only the MemberName and BonusAmt for current full-time employees; be sure to sort the query as requested.

9. Run the query to check your results.

10. Save the query as **qryRE7.**

11. Your dynaset should match the following figure:

MemberName	BonusAmt
Benjamin DRIVER	$3,720.00
Velma FRIEDRICHSEN	$3,675.00
Sydney WINCHESTER	$3,450.00
Dale ZELLER	$3,225.00
Nicholas WILMOTH	$2,850.00

Record: I◄ ◄ 1 of 101 ► ►I ►⊞ 🔾 No Filter

Results for qryRE7 query

Calculate Employee Ages

Create a query of current employees that lists the **EmployeeName** and a calculated field named **Age**. The EmployeeName field should display the employee's Last name and First name, separated by a comma and space (e.g., Moriarity, Brant). Sort by **Age** in ascending order.

1. Create the query using the **tblEmployee** table again.

2. Create the **EmployeeName** in the first blank column of the design grid.

3. Calculate the employee's age in the second blank column of the design grid. To calculate age, use the following formula:

   Age: (Date()-[Birthdate])\365

   The foregoing formula first calculates the number of days in between the current date represented by the Date() function and the employee's birthdate. It then divides the resulting number of days by 365 to calculate the approximate number of years. This calculation ignores leap years, which you won't worry about. Also, notice that you use "\" instead of "/" to divide; this returns the integer of the number and thus does not round up decimal places.

   ### Troubleshooting
   Did the Age calculation return an incorrect answer? If so, double-check the formula's order of operation.

   ### Imagine This!
   Access has a DateDiff function that can be used to calculate the number of time intervals between two specified dates (months, days, years, etc.). Why would it be inappropriate to use the

DateDiff function with a year ("yyyy") interval in Access to calculate someone's age? Use Access Help (F1) as a resource to answer this question.

4. Add additional field(s) specifying necessary criteria, and sort as requested. Remember to show only fields that you were asked to list in your query.

5. Run the query and check your results by noting a few employees' birth dates in the tblEmployee table and making sure that the age that your formula returns is correct.

6. Save the query as **qryRE8**.

7. Your dynaset should resemble the following figure. (Note: Age may change depending on the employee birthdate and when you run the query.)

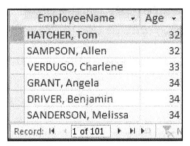

Results for qryRE8 query

Create Aggregate Functions

Aggregate functions yield summary data. While calculated fields perform the calculation for *each* record, the aggregate functions summarize a *group* of records (e.g., sales average, grand total, number of sales) that are listed in a column.

Some oft-used summary (aggregate) functions follow:

Function	Description
Sum	Total of the field values for selected records (how much)
Avg	Average of the field values for selected records
Min	Lowest field value for selected records
Max	Highest field value for selected records
Count	Number of records (how many)

Calculate Departmental Bonuses

Create a query that lists the **Department** and calculates the **BonusAmt** for each of Premiere's departments for current full-time employees from Indiana and Illinois. The bonus should, again, be 5% of the employee's salary. Format the BonusAmt as currency, and sort by **Department** in ascending order.

1. Add the required table(s) to the query design.

2. Add the **Department** field to the design grid, then create the **BonusAmt** field, formatted as currency, in the second column.

3. Add other needed fields to the design grid, specifying criteria to limit the **BonusAmt** to only current full-time employees from Indiana and Illinois. Be sure to run the query after adding each criterion in order to check your results, and sort the query in Ascending order by **Department**. Don't deselect the Show button for fields that you don't want to list in your query at this time.

4. After completing these steps and running your query, your dynaset should match the following figure. (Note: The order of the State, Full-Time?, and EndDate fields does not matter.)

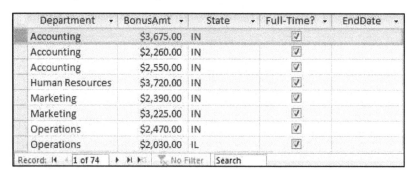

Department	BonusAmt	State	Full-Time?	EndDate
Accounting	$3,675.00	IN	☑	
Accounting	$2,260.00	IN	☑	
Accounting	$2,550.00	IN	☑	
Human Resources	$3,720.00	IN	☑	
Marketing	$2,390.00	IN	☑	
Marketing	$3,225.00	IN	☑	
Operations	$2,470.00	IN	☑	
Operations	$2,030.00	IL	☑	

Record: ◄ ◄ 1 of 74 ► ►► ☜ No Filter | Search

5. You can see that the dynaset displays only records for current full-time employees from Indiana and Illinois; however, Departments are listed multiple times. You want the dynaset to summarize (aggregate) the results for *each* Department.

6. Return to the **Design View**, then click the **Totals** [Σ Totals] button from the Design tab to show the Total row in the query design grid. (Note: You can also right-click on any field in the design grid and select Totals.)

    By default, Group By is displayed on the Total row for each field in the design grid. Click on the **down arrow** on the Total row of the BonusAmt field, then change Group By to **SUM**.

7. Run the query to check your results. Your dynaset should now match the following figure:

Department	BonusAmt	State	Full-Time?	EndDate
Accounting	$8,485.00	IN	☑	
Human Resources	$3,720.00	IN	☑	
Marketing	$5,615.00	IN	☑	
Operations	$61,475.00	IL	☑	
Operations	$48,720.00	IN	☑	

Record: I◄ ◄ 1 of 5 ► ►I ▸ 🏷 No Filter Search

Troubleshooting

The dynaset now displays 5 records instead of 74 records, and the BonusAmt has been summed for all departments—except Operations, which is displayed twice. Why is this happening? Remember, when you add the Total row to the design grid, all fields are automatically grouped by unique values in each field. Since IL and IN are unique values in the State field, Access is summing the BonusAmt for each state. How can this issue be remedied? Remember, when the Total row is in use and you have fields being used to specify criteria but you don't want the fields to be displayed in your dynaset, change Group By to Where for those fields in the Totals row. If you merely deselect the show button, the field will still be grouped by unique values.

8. Return to the Design View, then change the **State**, **Full-Time**, and **EndDate** fields to **Where**; run the query to check your results.

9. Save the query as **qryRE9**.

10. Your dynaset should match the following figure:

Department	BonusAmt
Accounting	$8,485.00
Human Resources	$3,720.00
Marketing	$5,615.00
Operations	$110,195.00

Record: I◄ ◄ 1 of 4 ► ►I ▸ 🏷 No F

Results for qryRE9 query

Troubleshooting

After saving and closing the qryRE9 query, open the query again in Design View. Notice that the SUM function has been replaced with Expression in the Total row for the calculated BonusAmt field and that the Field road now reads BonusAmt: Sum([salary]*0.05). Is this something that you should be worried about? Why is this happening? Could you have created the BonusAmt field like this initially?

Summarize Hourly Rates

Create a query that lists the highest, lowest, and average hourly rates for current part-time employees hired in the year 2015. Name the fields **HourlyMax**, **HourlyMin**, and **HourlyAverage**, respectively. The query should return only one record.

1. Begin creating the query using the correct table(s), then add the **HourlyRate** field three times to the design grid.

2. Run the query to check your results. Since you added the same field three times in the Design View, notice that the first two columns are named Expr1000 and Expr1001 and that the third column is named HourlyRate. This happens because Access will not allow you to have multiple fields with the same name listed in the dynaset.

3. Return to the Design View, then change the three field names by typing the requested field name followed by a colon in front of each of the HourlyRate field names in the design grid (e.g., HourlyMax: HourlyRate). Note: It is not necessary to place square brackets around the HourlyRate field in this case, since it is the only designated field and is not being used in a formula.

4. Run the query again and check your result. The dynaset should return 230 records, and the three field names should now be displayed as HourlyMax, HourlyMin, and HourlyAverage.

5. **Imagine This!**
   What do you think the three columns of values presently represent? How can you quickly summarize the data in each newly created field? How many records do you really want to end up with in your dynaset?

6. Return to the Design View and add the **Total** row to the design grid. For the field now named HourlyMax, change Group By to **Max**. Use the **Min** and **Avg** for the other two fields in order to correctly summarize the Hourly Rate results.

7. Run the query to check your results. Your dynaset now summarizes the values in each column, but you still need to make sure that the summary data represents only current part-time employees who were hired in 2015.

8. Return to the Design View, then add other needed fields to the design grid, specifying criteria that will limit the results for only current part-time employees hired in 2015. Be sure to run your query to check your results after adding each of the criterion.

9. Save the query as **qryRE10**.

10. Your dynaset should match the following figure:

Results for qryRE10 query

Troubleshooting
Does your dynaset display multiple records again? If so, return to the Design View, then make sure that you have made appropriate Total row designations for all fields.

Imagine This!
How can you quickly edit this query to list the HourlyMax, HourlyMin, and Hourly Average for each JobTitle?

Save and Back Up

When you are finished with your work, close the Premiere database file, then upload the revised version to your Box account. We strongly suggest that if you are using a flash drive you also place a copy of your work on cloud storage.

In-Depth Case Application

Creating Sales Revenue Line Items

Your supervisor wants to be able to generate receipts for purchases made by Premiere's members that display the **TransactionID**, **ItemCode**, **Description**, and **Subtotal**. To do this, you must first create a query that will list these fields and calculate the subtotal for each item purchased in the transaction.

Create a query that will show the following fields: **TransactionID**, **ItemCode**, **Description**, and a calculated field called **Subtotal**. Sort in ascending order, first by **TransactionID**, then by **ItemCode**.

1. Open the Relationships window to determine the table(s) that you need to use in your query in order to list the requested fields and calculate the subtotal.

   In the Premiere database, the subtotal calculation must take into account the quantity purchased, the catalog price, and the discount percentage (which reflects any promotions or coupons applied). Note: In other databases, there may not be a discount field, or the discount might be in terms of dollars rather than a percentage. You will need to carefully evaluate the specifics of each database you work with before creating calculated fields.

2. Create your query in Design View, adding the tables(s) that contain the fields that you need to list, specify criteria for, and use in your subtotal calculation. Note: If you are listing fields that are shown as the primary keys in one table and the foreign key in a second table, it's good practice to add the table that contains the primary key and to add that field to your query design grid.

3. It is not necessary to add the fields to the design grid that you need to use in the calculation; however, add the Quantity, CatalogPrice, and Discount% fields at this time in order to check the calculation results of the Subtotal field when you run the query.

4. Type the following expression in the first blank column of the design grid:

   Subtotal: [Quantity]*[CatalogPrice]*(1-[Discount%])

5. Format **Subtotal** as currency by right-clicking its column, selecting **Properties**, and setting the Format property to **Currency**.

6. Sort the query as requested, then run the query to check your results.

7. Since you listed the Quantity, CatalogPrice, and Discount% fields in the query design, you can quickly check the subtotal calculations to make sure they are correct.

8. Return to the **Design View** and delete the **Quantity**, **CatalogPrice**, and **Discount%** fields.

9. Run the query to check your results.

10. Save the query as **qryCA2**.

11. Your dynaset should match the following figure:

TransactionID ▾	ItemCode ▾	Description ▾	Subtotal ▾
1	045516	Figs, Black Mission, OG	$12.60
1	050573	Sunflower Seeds, OG	$1.90
1	213042	Coffee, Grd, House Bld, Decf, OG	$10.60
1	370828	Pumkies, Original	$18.25
1	402704	Kelp Powder, OG	$5.88
1	832414	Vinegar, Apple, raw, unfil, OG	$9.14
1	848046	Jarlsberg Cheese	$8.50
1	867315	Brown Rice Vinegar, Kyushu, OG	$4.90

Record: I◄ ◄ 1 of 60299 ► ►I ►❑ ❚❚ No Filter | Search

Results for qryCA2 query

Calculating Total Sales Revenue

In addition to listing the subtotals for the products purchased in each sale for the sales receipt, your supervisor wants to know the grand total for all transactions in the database.

Create a query that will list one field, named **GrandTotal**, that calculates the total revenue for all transactions.

1. Begin creating your query by adding the tables that contain the fields needed to calculate the total sales revenue. Your expression for revenue will be the same but will be named GrandTotal.

   GrandTotal: [Quantity]*[CatalogPrice]*(1-[Discount%])

2. Format the field as currency, then run the query to check your results.

3. The dynaset now contains 60,299 records, which is actually the Subtotal for each item purchased. You want to add these values together to return the grand total for all items.

4. Return to the Design View, add the **Totals** row to the design grid, and then change Group By to **SUM**.

5. Run the query again to check your results.

6. Save the query as **qryCA3**.

7. Your dynaset should match the following figure:

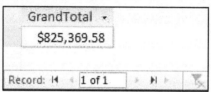

Result for qryCA3 query

Calculating Shipping Delays

The shipping manager wants to know how long it takes Premiere's Oklahoma warehouse to ship orders. Also, what is the longest and shortest time it has ever taken an order to ship? Note: On occasion, customers will place a special order in one of the stores and have it shipped to their home. Thus not all orders are online orders.

Create a query that will list these three values in fields named **AverageDelay**, **MaxDelay**, and **MinDelay**. Also create a field called **TotalShipments** that lists the total number of shipments made.

1. To calculate the time that it takes to ship an order, you must find the difference between the date when the purchase was made and the date when it was shipped. Open the Relationships window to determine which table(s) contain the fields that you need to use for this calculation.

2. Add the appropriate table(s) to your query, then write the expression in three columns of the design grid to create three calculated fields. One will become the average, one the max, and one the min.

3. Rename the three fields by replacing Expr1:, Expr2:, and Expr3: with **AverageDelay:**, **MaxDelay:**, and **MinDelay:**, respectively, then run the query to check your results.

4. The resulting dynaset returns 996 records, each representing the shipping delay for each purchase. The three columns have correct field names, but you need to summarize results in each column to return the average, longest, and shortest shipping delay for all purchases. You also want to list a fourth column that counts the total number of shipments that were made.

5. Return to the **Design View**, then click the **Totals** button to add the Total row to the query design grid. For the field now called **AverageDelay**, choose the **Avg** function. Use the **Max** and **Min** functions for the other two fields, respectively.

6. Format the **AverageDelay** field as **Standard**, with **1** decimal place. Note: You may have to run the query once before being able to select number of decimal places for a calculated field.

7. For the **TotalShipments** field, use the **TransactionID** from the Transactions table, then choose the **Count** function in the **Total** row. Don't forget to name this field.

   Note: When both a foreign key and primary key field are available for use in the query, always use the primary key. Using a primary key will cause queries on large data sets to run more efficiently.

8. Save the query as **qryCA4**.

9. Your dynaset should match the following figure:

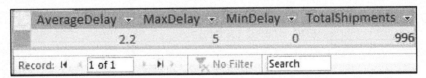

Result for qryCA4 query

Donations Earned for the Hunger Project

Nature's Way ran a special promotion in 2015, lasting from April to June. For every dollar spent during those months to purchase products made by Nature's Way, the company donated 5% to the Hunger Project (http://www.thp.org/).

Premiere Foods advertised this heavily, even going so far as to hold a competition among locations, promising to give employees from the winning location a prize.

Create a query that displays **Location** and a field named **DonationsEarned** that determines how much revenue each sales location (IN store, IL store, and Online) raised. Sort by **DonationsEarned** in descending order.

1. Considering that you need to list **Location** and the calculation already described, refer to the **Relationships** window to determine which table(s) your query must use.

2. List the **Location** field, then calculate the **DonationsEarned**, which is 5% of total sales revenue:

   DonationsEarned: .05*([Quantity]*[CatalogPrice]*(1-[Discount%]))

3. Be sure to specify the appropriate criterion for the dates of the promotion, and make sure to specify only **Nature's Way** brand products.

4. Click the **Totals** button to display the Total row. For the field now named **DonationsEarned**, choose the **Sum** function. Format this field as **Currency**.

5. Sort by **DonationsEarned** in descending order.

6. Run the query to check your results. This calculates the donations earned for each location but lists them on a day-by-day basis (by when the sale was made)—because the results are being grouped by each unique TransactionDate.

7. Return to **Design View** and examine the fields with Group By selected in the Total row. Change Group By to **Where** for the **TransactionDate** and **Brand** fields.

   Translating the query design into a normal language statement might help the use of Where on the Total row make more sense. Once you choose Where for TransactionDate, you are instructing Access to do the following: "calculate DonationsEarned, organized by (Group By) Location, Where the brand is Nature's Way and Where the TransactionDate is between April 1 and June 30, 2015."

8. Run the query again to check your results. You should now see the DonationsEarned listed for each location.

9. Save the query as **qryCA5**.

10. Your dynaset should match the following figure:

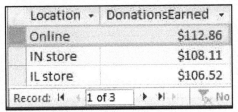

Location	DonationsEarned
Online	$112.86
IN store	$108.11
IL store	$106.52

Record: ◄ ◄ 1 of 3 ► ►► ▼ No

Result for qryCA5 query

REVIEW PROBLEMS

Review Problem 1

Product Markups

Management wants to know, for each department, how many items Premiere Foods carries and what the average price markup is. The markup must take into account the catalog price and the wholesale cost. (If you sell an item for 150% of its wholesale cost, that's a markup of 50%.)

List **Department** along with fields named **#ItemsCarried** and **AvgMarkup%**. Format the **AvgMarkup%** field as percent, then sort by **Department** in ascending order.

1. Determine what table(s) your query must use.

2. Use an appropriate field and function from the Total row to calculate the number of items carried. Don't forget to name the field as directed.

3. The expression that you write for the AvgMarkup% field should be either of the following:

   - **([CatalogPrice]-[WholesaleCost])/[WholesaleCost]**

   - **([CatalogPrice]/[WholesaleCost])-1**

   Note: Premiere has four brochure products that are $0.00. Make sure you exclude these using criteria, or Access will give a divide-by-zero error.

   Don't forget to name the field as directed or to have Access calculate the average.

4. Save the query as **qryReview5**.

5. Your dynaset should match the following figure:

Department	ItemsCarrie	AvgMarkup%
Drinks	78	52.78%
Frozen Foods	29	42.80%
Non-perishable Foods	1975	48.66%
Other	186	44.27%
Perishable Foods	561	49.42%
Personal Hygiene	1657	44.54%

Record: 1 of 6 — No Filter — Search

Results for qryReview5 query

Review Problem 2

Sales Revenue by State

You calculated Premiere's 2015 total sales revenue in the CA3 query created in the In-Depth Case Application. Now consider sales revenue from another angle. Create a query that tells you how much members in each **State** spent in 2015. List the member's **State**, then calculate the revenue in a field called **StateTotal**. Sort by **StateTotal** in descending order, then format this field as currency.

1. Considering that you need to list State and the calculation already described, determine what tables your query must use.

2. Write the expression for **StateTotal** based **on the** quantity sold, the catalog price, and the discount%.

3. Save the query as **qryReview6**.

4. Your dynaset should match the following figure:

State	StateTotal
IN	$284,222.01
IL	$183,381.33
OH	$121,305.48
KY	$70,556.19
CO	$29,628.19
NM	$19,907.58
CA	$19,815.52

Record: 1 of 28

Results for qryReview6 query

Review Problem 3

Summer Revenue and Sales Volume

Premiere Food's busy season is June 1 through August 31. For future summer season planning, it would be helpful to know how different departments performed during this period in 2015 in terms of both sales revenue and sales volume. (**Note:** Volume means quantity sold.)

1. Create a query that lists three fields—**Department**, **SummerRevenue**, and **SummerVolume**—for combined transactions from June to August 2015.

2. Sort by **SummerRevenue** in descending order.

3. Format **SummerRevenue** as currency.

4. Save the query as **qryReview7**.

5. Your dynaset should match the following figure:

Department	SummerRevenue	SummerVolume
Personal Hygiene	$111,386.91	12908
Non-perishable Foods	$94,267.98	15084
Perishable Foods	$22,703.15	2914
Other	$10,877.99	1476
Drinks	$3,765.14	630
Frozen Foods	$1,011.66	174

Record: ◄ ◄ 1 of 6 ► ►► ▼ No Filter | Search

Results for qryReview7 query

Save and Back Up

When you are finished with your work, close the Premiere database file, then upload the revised version to your Box account. We strongly suggest that if you are using a flash drive you also place a copy of your work on cloud storage.

Knowledge Check 6

Calculated Fields and Aggregate Functions

For this Knowledge Check, create queries to solve the problems outlined. Make use of the Relationships windows in the Database. Name the queries and sort as instructed in the Design View of each query.

Restocking Inventory

Management wants to know which products need to be ordered and how much it will cost to order each product.

1. Begin creating a query that will list the Product ID and Product Category.

2. In a new field named Number to Order, calculate the quantity of each product to order on the basis of the number of each product currently in stock and the number that should be present when fully stocked (the latter is given in the Max Units field).

3. In another new field called Order Cost, calculate the amount that an order for each product will cost (we pay wholesale price for each product ordered).

4. Do not list products that don't need to be ordered.

5. Sort ascending by Product Category and descending by Number to Order.

6. Save this query as **qryKC6**.

Sales Rep Customer Overcharges

In theory, the price quoted by a rep should not exceed our regular selling price for the product as given in the PRODUCTS table. It has been discovered, though, that a number of customers were accidentally overcharged by reps.

1. Create a query that will identify each of these customers, listing their First Name, Last Name, and Phone Number and calculating the amount of the overcharge in a field named Overcharge. (This should take into account the number purchased—if a customer

was overcharged $0.50 for an item and bought 30 of those items, that amounts to a $15 overcharge.)

2. List the Rep ID and first and last name of the rep responsible for each overcharge.

3. Format the Overcharge field as currency.

4. Sort ascending by Rep ID, then by customer last name.

5. Save this query as **qryKC7**.

Regional Sales Revenue and Sales Volume

Management would like to know the Sales Revenue and Sales Volume broken down by Region.

1. Create a query that lists, for each region, total sales volume, total sales revenue, and total dollar amount of discounts given.

2. Name the three new fields Sales Volume, Sales Revenue, and Discounts Given. (For revenue, use the price that the customer was quoted, and don't worry about the fact that some customers were overcharged.)

3. Format Sales Revenue and Discounts Given as currency, and sort ascending by Region (each region should be listed only once).

4. Save this query as **qryKC8**.

Management would also like to see the same information in the previous query, but only for the period between March 1 and September 15, 2005.

1. Create a query identical to the KC8 query, but limit the results to sales made between March 1 and September 15, 2005 (the most important time for The Artful Yard's business).

   Each region should still be listed only once.

2. Save this query as **qryKC9**.

Sales Volume of Bird-Related Items by Region

Management would like to know the total sales volume of bird-related items for each region during a particular period.

1. Create a query that lists the region and a field representing the sales volume for bird-related items sold between March 1 and September 15, 2005.

   These should be items for birds (e.g., birdfeeders), not items that just happen to depict birds (e.g., not metal hummingbird wind chimes).

2. Name the new field Bird Items Sold.

3. Save the query as **qryKC10**.

After completing all 5 queries, go to the course website to answer Koin-earning questions.

When you are finished, be sure to save your database where you can find it again; you will need it for future Knowledge Check exercises.

Parameter Query and
Query on Queries

Chapter 8

Outline

- Research & Exploration: Research and Create Parameter Queries and Queries Based on Other Queries

- In-Depth Case Application: Write Queries Based on Other Queries

- Review Problems: Practice Using Multiple Queries to Solve Problems, Knowledge Check 7

Objectives

- Create a parameter query.

- Understand why some queries must be based on other queries.

- Solve business problems using queries based on multiple queries.

RESEARCH & EXPLORATION

Research

Up to this point you've been creating queries based on tables in the Premiere database. There are, however, times when you will find that you need to use the results of one or more queries as the basis for your query.

Also, there are times when queries need to be more interactive, prompting users for one or more criteria that meet their specific needs each time the query is run.

Go to the Microsoft Office Online Support website, http://support.office.microsoft.com, and locate the following article:

- Use parameters to ask for input when running a query

Research the following key concept:

- Parameter query

Exploration

A parameter query prompts you for criteria each time you execute the query. The difference between a parameter query and an ordinary select query is the way in which the criteria are specified. A select query contains the actual criteria in the query design grid for specific fields in order to filter the data. A parameter query, however, prompts the user to enter the criteria when the query is executed.

Parameter Query

Create a parameter query that Premiere sales employees can use to retrieve customer shipping information on demand. The query should ask for a member's ID number and then return the selected **MemberID** along with the member's first and last name in a single field (named **Name**), **TransactionDate**, and **DateShipped**. Sort by **DateShipped** in descending order.

1. Add the required table(s) to the query design.

2. Add the fields that you want to list in the query design grid.

3. To cause this query to request a member's ID number, type the following on the Criteria row under **MemberID**, including the square brackets:

   [Enter Member ID:]

   This causes a parameter value prompt to appear when the query is run:

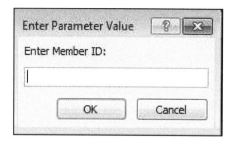

4. Any desired value for MemberID can be entered in the **Enter Parameter Value** box, and then the query will finish running using whatever value was entered as the criterion. Try typing **7** and then clicking **OK**.

5. Save your query as **qryRE11**.

6. Your dynaset should match the following figure:

MemberID	Name	TransactionDate	DateShipped
7	Theodore Ingraham	12/9/2015	12/12/2015
7	Theodore Ingraham	9/12/2015	9/13/2015
7	Theodore Ingraham	7/15/2015	7/16/2015
7	Theodore Ingraham	4/29/2015	5/1/2015

Record: I◄ 1 of 4 ► ►I 🝔 No Filter | Search

Results for qryRE11 query

Troubleshooting

Your dynaset displays more than four records when you type 7 for the MemberID. Why is this happening? What do you need to do to eliminate duplicate records?

Using Multiple Queries to Solve Problems

In chapter 7, you learned how to create queries that calculate and aggregate data. Calculated and aggregate field values generated by these queries are often needed as the basis for future calculations (e.g., finding the % of total revenue generated by each department).

Create a query that will calculate the percent of current Premiere employees from each state. The query should list the **State** field and a field named **%OfEmployees**. Format the **%OfEmployees** field as Percent, then sort the query descending by this field.

To find the percent of current employees from each state, you will need to create three queries:

- The first query will return the number of employees per state.

- The second query will calculate the total overall number of current employees.

- The third query will then divide the number of employees per state by the total number of employees.

1. Create the first query to calculate the number of current employees from each state. List the **State** field, then calculate the number of employees in a field named **#OfEmployees**.

2. Save the query as **qryRE12Numerator**, then run the query.

3. Your dynaset should match the following figure:

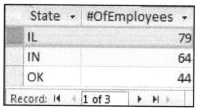

Results for qryRE12Numerator query

4. Close the query.

5. Create the second query to calculate the total number of current employees. The query must contain the same tables as the first query even if you don't use fields from all of the tables. Name the calculated field **TotalEmployees**.

6. Save the query as **qryRE12Denominator**, then run the query.

7. Your dynaset should match the following figure:

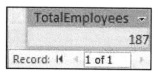

Result for qryRE12Denominator query

8. Make sure that the qryRE12Numerator and qryRE12Denominator queries are saved and closed before moving to the next step.

9. Create the third and final query to calculate the percent of current Premiere employees from each state using the results from the two preliminary queries. Begin creating the query in the Design View as you normally do, but instead of adding tables, click the **Queries** tab and add the **qryRE12Numerator** and **qryRE12Denominator** queries to your query design.

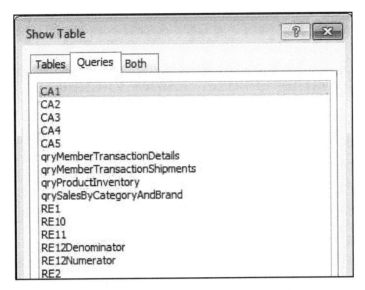

10. List the **State** field in the design grid, then create a calculated field that divides the #OfEmployees by the TotalEmployees. Name the calculated field **%OfEmployees**, formatting as Percent.

11. Save the query as **qryRE12**, then run the query.

12. Your dynaset should match the following figure:

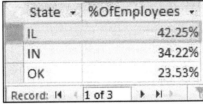

Result for qryRE12 Query

Imagine This!
How would you edit the RE12 query to have it prompt the user to enter the State field value when the query is run, thus returning only the designated state's %OfEmployees?

IN-DEPTH CASE APPLICATION

Calculating Quarter 3 Sales Volume

Assume that Premiere's fiscal year is the calendar year. Quarter 3 is a crucial time for Premiere's business. Quarter 3 performance in one year informs decisions going into Quarter 3 of the next year. For example, decisions about what product departments to expand in the summer season and what to cut back on are made partly on the basis of previous sales volume data.

Illustratively, Premiere wants to know what percentage of sales volume in Quarter 3 came from each department. This calculation would use Quarter 3 volume per department divided by total Quarter 3 volume.

Generally, to calculate a percentage, first calculate the values for the numerator and denominator separately (in two separate queries), then use the fields that generate those values in a third query in a formula that calculates the percentage. Remember: both the numerator and denominator should have the same number of tables added to the query design even if fields aren't being used from some of the tables.

1. Create one query that lists the **Department** and a field that calculates the Quarter 3 sales volume. (Be careful—you are interested in the number of products sold here, not revenue!) Name the calculated field in this query **DepartmentVolume**, and name the query **qryCA6Numerator**.

2. Create a second query with one field to calculate the total Quarter 3 sales volume. Name the field **TotalVolume**, and name the query **qryCA6Denominator**.

3. Create a third query that does not use tables but that instead uses the foregoing two queries. In this third query, display **Department** from the **qryCA6Numerator** query. Also create a field that divides **DepartmentVolume** by **TotalVolume**. Name this calculated field **%OfQ3Volume**.

4. Format the calculated field as Percent (you may have to run the query before this is an option), then sort in descending order on this field.

5. Name the final query **qryCA6**.

6. Your dynaset should match the following figure:

Department	%OfQ3Volume
Non-perishable Foods	45.37%
Personal Hygiene	38.90%
Perishable Foods	8.97%
Other	4.27%
Drinks	1.97%
Frozen Foods	0.52%

Record: I◄ ◄ 1 of 6 ► ►I ▷ | 🗋 No Filter | Search

Results for qryCA6 query

REVIEW PROBLEMS

Review Problem 1

Percentage of Shipping Delays

In a previous query, you discovered that in 2015, as many as five days passed from the time an order was placed to the time it left the Oklahoma warehouse. Your supervisor would now like to know what percentage of orders took more than three days to ship. Remember: Occasionally customers place a special order in one of the stores and have it shipped to their home. Thus not all shipped orders are online orders.

1. Create the first query with a field that counts all orders that took more than three days to ship. You will need to use two fields—count one and specify the criterion on the other. Name the field with the count **TotalDelayed**. Name the query **qryReview8Numerator**.

2. Create a second query with a field that counts all orders that have been shipped. Name the calculated field in this query **TotalShipped**. Name the query **qryReview8Denominator**.

3. Create a third query that does not use tables but instead the foregoing two queries. In this third query, divide **TotalDelayed** by **TotalShipped**. Name this calculated field **%Delayed**. Format the field as percent (you may have to run the query before this is an option).

4. Save the final query as **qryReview8**.

5. Your dynaset should match the following figure:

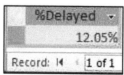

Result for qryReview8 query

> ## Review Problem 2

Advertising Spending

You have been asked to help figure out how to distribute advertising dollars to attract new members. Learning more about your current member base (e.g., what percentage of member purchases each state accounts for) would be a good place to start.

1. Create a query that lists the **State** field from the **tblMember** table and a field named **%OfSales.**

2. Name your first two queries (and the fields in them) anything you want.

3. Format the calculated field in the third query as Percent with 2 decimal places, then sort in descending order on this field.

4. Save your final query as **qryReview9.**

5. Your dynaset should match the following figure:

State	%OfSales
IN	34.44%
IL	22.22%
OH	14.70%
KY	8.55%
CO	3.59%
NM	2.41%

Record: ◄ ◄ 1 of 28 ► ►

Results for qryReview9 query

> ## Review Problem 3

Q3 Bonus Checks

In our two stores, at the end of Quarter 3, every employee with at least $5,000 in sales revenue for that quarter receives a bonus equal to 2% of his or her sales revenue for that quarter. Determine who should receive bonuses for Quarter 3 of 2015, how much they sold, and how much their bonus checks should be. **Note:** Assume that the fiscal year is the calendar year, so that Quarter 3 is July-August-September.

Hint: You do not have to use a query based on a query to solve this problem.

1. Display the store **Location**, the employee's **EmployeeID** number, the employee's first and last name separated by a space in a single field called **Name**, a field named **Q3SalesRevenue**, and one named **Q3Bonus**.

2. For the bonus, do not multiply by the employee's BonusRate; this is a flat 2% bonus.

3. You only want your result to display records for brick and mortar store sales, not for online sales.

4. Format the two calculated fields as Currency.

5. Sort by store **Location** in ascending order, then by **Q3SalesRevenue** in descending order.

6. Save the query as **qryReview10**.

7. Your dynaset should match the following figure:

Location	EmployeeID	Name	Q3SalesRevenue	Q3Bonus
IL store	151	Tiffany NOLAN	$18,692.67	$373.85
IL store	88	John JARDINE	$15,307.63	$306.15
IL store	283	Steve BARNHART	$15,225.51	$304.51
IN store	337	Hannah GOLDSBERRY	$28,171.79	$563.44
IN store	143	Billy MCMILLIAN	$23,376.21	$467.52
IN store	223	Olivia WYRICK	$13,294.65	$265.89
IN store	104	Steve PARKMAN	$8,019.74	$160.39
IN store	67	Phillip FLEMING	$7,466.88	$149.34

Record: 1 of 8 — No Filter — Search

Results for qryReview10 query

Knowledge Check 7

Using Multiple Queries to Solve Problems

For this Knowledge Check, you will create queries that require other queries to solve the problems outlined. Name the queries as instructed, then sort as instructed in the Design View of each query.

Calculating Sales Rep Revenue

Determine what percentage of sales revenue each sales rep is responsible for.

When calculating revenue, since reps can choose to quote a lower price than the selling price listed in the PRODUCTS table, use the price that the customer was quoted.

1. You will need to create three queries to accomplish your goal. Name the first two queries whatever you want. Take care to give the calculated fields in the first two queries different names.

2. The final query should be named **qryKC11** and should list three fields: **Rep ID**, rep Name (in the form last name, first name) in a single field named **Rep Name**, and a field named **Rep Revenue %**.

3. Format the Rep Revenue % field as Percent with two decimal places, then sort descending by this field.

Calculating Product Category Sales Revenue

Determine what percentage of **off-season** sales revenue each product category accounts for. (See earlier note on calculating revenue.)

Note that this database has 2005 sales only. Within a calendar year, January 1–March 1 and October 15–December 31 constitute the off season.

1. You will need to create your final query based on two other queries. Again, you can name the first two queries whatever you want.

2. The final query should be named **qryKC12** and should list two fields: **Product Category** and a field named **% of Off-Season Revenue**. You should have only one record per category.

3. Format the percentage field as Percent with two decimal places, then sort descending by this field.

After completing these steps, go to the course website to answer Koin-earning questions.

Query Wizard and Action Queries

Chapter 9

Outline

- Research & Exploration: Research and Use the Query Wizard, Build Action Queries

- In-Depth Case Application: Find Records That Have No Related Records in Another Table, Build Action Queries

- Review Problems: Practice Building Action Queries, Knowledge Check 8

Objectives

- Use the query wizard to create queries that find unmatched records.

- Use the query wizard to create queries that find duplicates.

- Use the query wizard to create a crosstab query.

- Understand the difference between a select query and an action query.

- Choose the appropriate query type depending on the required results.

- Create and run action queries.

RESEARCH & EXPLORATION

Research

In addition to writing Select queries in Design View that allow you to retrieve and display existing data in a dynaset, you can also write Action queries that allow you to build new tables, add records to existing tables, alter data in tables, and delete records from tables. Queries can also be written using the Query Wizard in order to find duplicate records in one or more tables, find records with no related records in a second table, or display results in a spreadsheet-like format.

Go to the Microsoft Office Online Support website, http://support.office.microsoft.com, and locate the following articles:

- Create a make table query

- Create and run an update query

- Create and run a delete query

- Use an append query to add records to a table

- Make summary data easier to read by using a crosstab query

- Search two tables for unmatched records

- Find duplicate records with a query

Exploration

When you first open the Premiere database, you should see a warning below the ribbon telling you that content is being blocked. Click **Enable Content** next to that warning to ensure that the Action queries created in this section will run correctly.

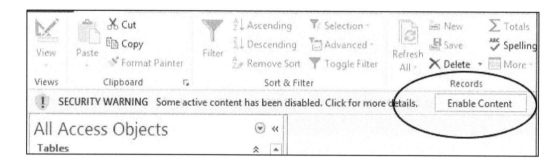

Finding Employee Classes Offered Multiple Times Using the Find Duplicates Query Wizard

You've been asked on more than one occasion to create a list of classes that are offered by Premiere. To complete this task, you need to look for records in the tblCass table that contain the same ClassName.

1. Click the **Create** tab and click **Query Wizard**.

2. In the New Query dialog box, click **Find Duplicates Query Wizard**, and then click **OK**.

3. Select **tblClass** as the table in which you want to search for duplicate fields, then click **Next**.

4. Select **ClassName** as the field that contains the duplicate field values, then click **Next**.

5. Select all the remaining available fields from the tblClass table, then click **Next**.

6. Name the query **qryRE13**, then click **Finish**. Your results are automatically displayed in ascending order by ClassName.

7. Go to the query Design View and sort in ascending order by ClassID, then run the query again.

8. Your dynaset should match the following figure:

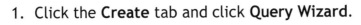

ClassName	ClassID	Date	StartTime	EndTime	Location	MaxEnrollment
Advanced Sales Management	SM0201	10/8/2012	9:00 AM	12:30 PM IN Office		15
Advanced Sales Management	SM0202	10/10/2012	9:00 AM	12:30 PM IL Office		20
Introductory Sales Management	SM0101	10/1/2012	8:30 AM	4:00 PM IN Office		15
Introductory Sales Management	SM0102	10/3/2012	8:30 AM	4:00 PM IL Office		20
Premiere Products Orientation	PP0101	10/3/2012	1:00 PM	4:00 PM IN Office		15
Premiere Products Orientation	PP0102	10/31/2012	8:30 AM	11:30 AM IN Office		15

Record: ◄ 1 of 6 ► ►I ►▢ No Filter Search

Results for qryRE13 query

Making Employee Summary Data Easier to Read and Understand Using the Crosstab Query Wizard

Your supervisor wants a summary of how many employees hold each job title in each department and would like it to be presented in a more readable spreadsheet-like format:

1. Click the **Create** tab and click **Query Wizard.**

2. In the New Query dialog box, click **Crosstab Query Wizard**, then click **OK.**

3. Select **tblEmployee** as the table that contains the fields needed for the crosstab query results, then click **Next.**

4. Since you want to summarize the requested Employee information by job title and department, first select **JobTitle** as the field to be used for the row heading, then click **Next.**

5. Now select **Department** as the field to be used for the column headings, then click **Next.**

6. To find out how many employees hold each job title in each department, select the **EmployeeID** field and the **Count** function.

7. On the same page, make sure that the **Yes, include row sums check box** is selected in order to include the Department row sum and click **Next.**

8. Name the query **qryRE14**, then click **Finish.**

9. Your crosstab query results are automatically displayed in Datasheet View, and your dynaset should match the following figure:

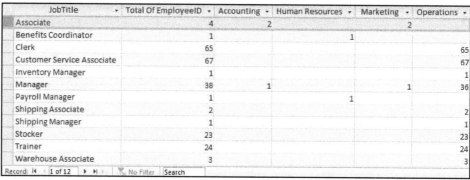

JobTitle	Total Of EmployeeID	Accounting	Human Resources	Marketing	Operations
Associate	4	2		2	
Benefits Coordinator	1		1		
Clerk	65				65
Customer Service Associate	67				67
Inventory Manager	1				1
Manager	38	1		1	36
Payroll Manager	1		1		
Shipping Associate	2				2
Shipping Manager	1				1
Stocker	23				23
Trainer	24				24
Warehouse Associate	3				3

Record: 1 of 12 ▶ ▶I No Filter Search

Results for qryRE14 query

Backing Up Employee Data Using a Make Table Action Query

A 5% salary increase was just approved for all current full-time clerks. You've been asked to update the salary field for these employees to reflect this salary increase.

Before actually updating these employee salaries, it is highly recommended that you first create a backup table of the records that you will be changing—just in case you encounter problems.

1. Begin creating your backup table by first creating a Select query in Design View that will list the **EmployeeID** and **Salary** for all current full-time clerks.

2. Rename the Salary field **SalaryBackup**, then run the query first as a Select query to be sure that it selects the correct records.

3. Your dynaset should match the following figure:

EmployeeID	Salary
59	$19,900.00
63	$18,700.00
64	$23,700.00
67	$18,700.00
70	$18,100.00
72	$18,900.00

Record: 1 of 41 ▶ ▶I

Troubleshooting
Does your dynaset have more than 41 records? If so, make sure your list only includes full-time clerks who are still working for Premiere.

4. Return to the Design View, then click **Make Table** in the **Query Type** group.

5. In the Make Table dialog box that appears, type **tblClerkSalaryBackup** as the table name to be created.

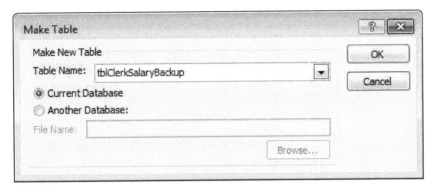

6. Click **OK**. You have now completed the setup for the Make Table query but have not yet performed the action to create the tblClerkSalaryBackup table.

7. Click the **Run** button to perform the Make Table action. You will be notified that you are about to paste 41 row(s) into the table. These are the 41 records that you saw displayed earlier in the Select query dynaset.

8. Click **Yes** to confirm that you want to create the new table.

9. Verify that the tblClerkSalaryBackup table exists by checking the Tables group in the Navigation Pane. Open the table to make sure that it lists the 41 requested records.

10. Save the query as **qryRE15MakeTable**.

Troubleshooting

You realize that you misspelled the table name when you were setting up the Make Table query. What should you do? Your first instinct is probably to just rename the actual table that was created after running the Make Table query. The problem with this approach is that when you run the Make Table query again, the resulting table name will still be misspelled. You must instead edit the Make Table query in Design View. To edit a Make Table query or any Action query, don't just double-click the query in the Navigation Pane to try to get to the query's Design View. Double-clicking will actually run the query and perform the action. Instead, right-click the query, then click Design View from the drop-down list.

Complete the following steps to fix a misspelled table name in a Make Table Query:

1. Delete the misspelled table in the Navigation Pane.

2. Right-click the Make Table query in the Navigation Pane, then click Design View.

3. Click Select in the Query Type group, then click Make Table. The Make Table dialog box will appear.

4. Correct any misspelled table names in the Make Table dialog box, then click OK.

5. Run the query again, verifying that the resulting table is spelled correctly.

6. Close the edited Make Table query, making sure to save your changes.

Updating Employee Data Using an Update Action Query

Now that you've successfully created a backup table that contains the records for the current full-time clerks, you can update the salary field for these employees to reflect the requested 5% salary increase.

1. Begin creating your Update query by once again creating a Select query in Design View that lists the **EmployeeID** and **Salary** for all current **full-time clerks**.

2. Run the query as a Select query to check your results. You should once again see 41 records listed as shown in the following dynaset.

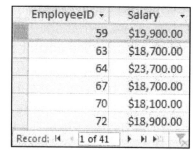

EmployeeID ▾	Salary ▾
59	$19,900.00
63	$18,700.00
64	$23,700.00
67	$18,700.00
70	$18,100.00
72	$18,900.00

Record: ◄ 1 of 41 ► ►I ►▪

3. Return to the Design View and in the Query Type group, click **Update**. An Update To: row should now appear in the design grid.

4. Under the Salary field on the Update to: line, type **[Salary]*1.05**

5. Run this query—but only once! (Running the query additional times will increase the salaries even more.) You should see a warning box telling you that you are about to update 41 rows.

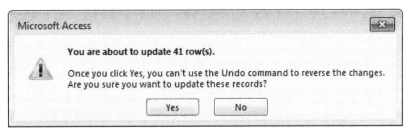

6. Click **Yes** to run the query.

7. To check your update results, open the **tblEmployee** table, then compare it to the **tblClerkSalaryBackup** table. If you've updated the records correctly, employee 64 (Richard Rivero) should now have a salary of $24,885.00.

8. Save the query as **qryRE16Update**.

Troubleshooting

Did you make a mistake updating the current full-time clerk salaries? If so, follow these steps to restore the original salary values, and then try again.

1. Create a query that uses the **tblEmployee** table and the **tblClerkSalaryBackup** table.

2. Join the tables, if necessary, on the primary key field (the same way you would in the Relationships window—by clicking and dragging).

3. Change the query type to an **Update** query.

4. Add the **Salary** field from the **tblEmployee** table to the query design grid.

5. On the **Update To** row, type the following:

   [tblClerkSalaryBackup].[Salary]

6. Run the query to restore the original Salary field values.

7. Check the tblEmployee table to make sure that the Salary field matches the Salary field in the tblClerkSalaryBackup table.

IN-DEPTH CASE APPLICATION

Finding Members Who Have Never Made a Purchase

Premiere Foods does not require people to purchase items in order to be a member and receive newsletters, partner offers, and the like. Management is aware that there are some members who have never purchased anything but does not know how many or who they are.

Create a query that will display the **First**, **Last**, **Address**, **City**, **State**, **ZipCode**, and **Member Since** fields for all members who have never made a purchase from Premiere Foods. Sort the results in **ascending** order by **Last** name and then by **First**.

Use the **Query Wizard** to create a **Find Unmatched Query**. The Find Unmatched Query is appropriate because it will allow you to retrieve a list of all Members from the **tblMember** table with no matching (unmatched) **MemberID**s in the **tblTransaction** table.

1. Click the **Create** tab, then click **Query Wizard**.

2. In the New Query dialog box, click **Find Unmatched Query Wizard**, and then click **Next**.

3. Select **tblMember** as the table that contains records you want to list in your query result, then click **Next**.

4. Select **tblTransaction** as the table that contains the related records, then click **Next**.

5. Make sure that the MemberID field is selected as the matching field in each table, then click **Next**.

6. Select the **First**, **Last**, **Address**, **City**, **State**, **ZipCode**, and **MemberSince** fields as the fields you want to see in the query result, then click **Next**.

7. Name the query **qryCA7**, then click **Finish**.

8. After creating the query with the wizard, go to Design View and sort by **Last** and then by **First** in **ascending** order.

9. Your dynaset should match the following figure:

First ▾	Last Name ▾	Address ▾	City ▾	State ▾	ZIPCode ▾	MemberSince ▾
Nicholas	ABEL	1304 Auto Mall	Adrian	IL	62310-	23-Dec-08
Vicki	ABRAMSON	3598 Redbird	Latty	OH	45855-	28-Jul-06
Jeannette	ALANIS	5602 Donington	Velpen	IN	47590-	11-Dec-06
Alan	ALEXANDER	2373 Springdale	Dana	IN	47847-	22-Jun-08
Dora	ALEXANDER	1641 Clay	Cincinnati	OH	45263-	25-Nov-07
Gerald	ALFRED	575 Signature	Manchester	NH	3111-	25-Oct-07
Verna	ALFRED	2134 Valley View	Morrisonville	IL	62546-	30-Apr-06
Jean	ALONSO	2340 Oak Knoll	Le Roy	IL	61752-	31-Jan-08
Steve	ANDERSON	2926 Commerce	Los Angeles	CA	90088-	26-Nov-06
Johnny	ANDRADE	745 Bloomingdale	Ann Arbor	MI	48109-	10-Feb-06
Richard	ANDREWS	1616 Overton	Clayton	IN	46118-	13-Jan-07
Hilda	ANGULO	1180 Vine	Fisher	IL	61843-	06-Nov-06

Record: I◄ ◄ 1 of 624 ► ►I ►▻ 🏷 No Filter | Search

Results for qryCA7 query

Correcting Four-Digit Zip Codes

Member information was collected some time ago, before you knew to make ZIPCode a short text field. With this field initially defined as number, zip codes with leading zeroes (such as zip code 01139, for Springfield, MA) lost their initial zeroes. Correct this problem for all affected zip codes.

Creating a Backup Table of Premiere Members

Before updating the incorrect zip codes, it's important to use a Make Table query to back up the tblMembers table.

1. Create a Select query that lists all fields from the tblMembers table. Do not add any criteria—this table will allow us to recover the original zip codes for all customers, if necessary.

2. Run the query. Your dynaset should contain all fields for the 2,695 member records.

3. Return to the Design View and in the Query Type group, click **Make Table**.

4. Name the new table **tblMemberBackup**, then click **OK**.

5. Run the query, then click **Yes** to create the table.

6. Before continuing, verify that the tblMemberBackup table exists and that it lists all fields for all members in the database.

7. Save the query as **qryCA8MakeTable**.

Updating Incomplete Zip Codes

Use an Update Query to locate the four-digit zip codes in the tblMember table and to add a 0 to the front of each four-digit zip code.

1. Create a Select Query that lists only the member's ZipCode.

2. Type "????" for the ZIPCode criterion to locate zip codes with only 4 digits and run the query to check your results. Your dynaset should contain 68 records with four-digit zip codes.

3. Return to the Design View, and then, in the Query Type group, click **Update.**

4. Using concatenation, type **0&[ZIPCode]** on the Update To: row in the design grid to add 0 to the beginning of each four-digit ZIPCode field.

   Notice that Access automatically put quotes around the zero ("0"), because the ZIPCode field is now a short text field and quotes are always placed around text, not numbers.

5. Click the **Run** button to update the selected records. A warning dialog box will appear indicating that you are about to update 68 row(s).

6. Click **Yes** to complete the zip code update.

7. After running the update query, check the tblMember table. In Datasheet View, sort in ascending order by ZIPCode—you should see the fixed zip codes listed at the top, with their initial zeroes. Since the ZipCode field is now set to a short text data type, you will not have to worry about this kind of error happening again.

8. Save the query as **qryCA9Update.**

   Important note: If you made a mistake updating the zip codes, you can restore the original ZIPCode values by using the tblMember and tblMemberBackup tables in an Update Query.

Retaining Backups of Only the Four-Digit Zip Codes

Now that the zip code problem is fixed, you might be tempted to delete the backup table that you created. However, it might be useful to keep a record of the problematic four-digit zip codes until you are sure that the problem has been fixed throughout the company (as opposed to being fixed in just this database); this will provide a record of whose zip codes were changed.

1. Create a Select query based on the **tblMemberBackup** table.

2. List the **ZIPCode** field, specifying the criterion that will return only the nonproblematic zip codes—the ones with five digits.

3. Run the query as a Select query to verify that you have the correct records being returned. You should see 2,627 five-digit zip codes listed in your dynaset.

4. Return to the Design View, changing the query type from Select to **Delete**.

5. Click the **Run** button to delete the selected records. A warning dialog box will appear indicating that you are about to delete 2,627 row(s) from the specified table.

6. Click **Yes** to delete the records.

7. Open the **tblMemberBackup** table to verify that it now only contains the 68 records containing four-digit zip codes.

8. Close tblMemberBackup.

9. Save this query as **qryCA10Delete**.

REVIEW PROBLEMS

Review Problem 1

Creating a Table of Members Who Purchased Defective Products

Your supervisor reminds you that Spectrum is doing a recall of its eggless mayo spread because of a defect that is causing the mayonnaise to spoil before the expiration date. She has decided to personally contact each Premiere member affected by this recall and wants you to create a temporary table to which she can refer and that she can modify as she completes her calls.

1. Create a Make Table query that will generate a new table named **tblSpectrumRecall** that lists the **MemberName** and **PhoneNumber** fields for each member affected by the recall. The MemberName field should display the employee's First name and Last name, separated by a space (e.g., Amy Kinser). Sort by Last name and then by First in ascending order. (Hint: You will need to add and then hide a duplicate field in order to sort correctly.) Your supervisor is aware that the new table may not have phone numbers formatted, so don't concern yourself with this as you create the query.

2. Save the query as **qryReview11MakeTable**.

3. The tblSpectrumRecall table should contain the following records:

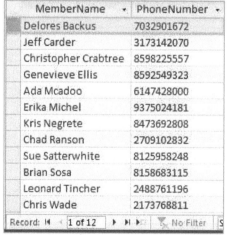

Results for tblSpectrumRecall table

Review Problem 2

Finding Underperforming Marketing Sales Reps

The Marketing Manager wants to know which of his current sales reps have never made a sale.

1. Create a query that will list the **EmployeeID**, **EmployeeName**, and **JobTitle** for employees from the Marketing department who have not yet made a sale. The EmployeeName field should display the employee Last name and then First name, separated by a comma and space (e.g., Miller, Barb). Sort the results in ascending order by employee Last name.

2. Save the query as **qryReview12**.

3. Your Dynaset should match the following figure:

Results for qryReview12 query

Review Problem 3

Summarizing Sales by Location and Quarter

Premiere's CEO wants a summary of quarterly sales for 2015 for each location, and he would like to have the sales summary displayed in a spreadsheet-like format.

1. Create a preliminary query that will list the **Location** and **TransactionDate** fields and a field named **Sales** that will calculate the sale amount for each item that was sold in 2015. Save this query as **qryReview13**. Your dynaset should match the following figure:

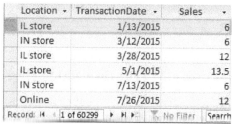

Location	TransactionDate	Sales
IL store	1/13/2015	6
IN store	3/12/2015	6
IL store	3/28/2015	12
IL store	5/1/2015	13.5
IN store	7/13/2015	6
Online	7/26/2015	12

Record: ◄ ◄ 1 of 60299 ► ►I ► No Filter Search

Results for qryReview13 query

2. Using the Query Wizard, create a second query that will display the quarterly sales summary, listing the location as the row heading and the quarter as the column heading. Base this query on the **qryReview13** query, formatting all sales values as Currency. Save this query as **qryReview14**. Your result should match the following figure:

Location	Total Of Sales	Qtr 1	Qtr 2	Qtr 3	Qtr 4
IL store	$341,968.38	$54,714.52	$50,383.00	$93,344.40	$143,526.46
IN store	$302,556.54	$38,319.68	$41,897.69	$108,203.31	$114,135.87
Online	$180,844.66	$25,994.70	$33,613.48	$40,463.77	$80,772.70

Record: ◄ ◄ 1 of 3 ► ►I ► No Filter Search

Results for qryReview14 query

Knowledge Check 8

Updating Products with Missing Descriptions

Some items in the PRODUCTS table lack descriptions. This is not currently a problem; however, when the catalog is printed, those items will have blanks where descriptions should be.

For this Knowledge Check, you will create Action Queries to address the blank description problem.

1. Create an action query that for all products without a description will update the description to read "New item! Call for more information!"

   By the time the next catalog is printed, we will have entered descriptions for all products, and only new additions to our product line will have this problem.

Now, whenever it is time to print a new catalog, this query can be run first, and every item will have either a description or a note to call for more information.

2. Run the query, then save the query as **qryKC13**.

Note that this will affect the results of your qryKC4 query from Knowledge Check 5. If you haven't answered the questions for Knowledge Check 5 yet, return to the qryKC4 query and edit it so that products whose descriptions contain the words "new item" are listed as well.

Generating Customer Purchase Data for Market Research

You occasionally sell data to market research companies without providing identifying information about your customers.

For the next three queries, you will first create a new table; the two queries that follow that will use that table so that if you make a mistake, you can simply run the first query again to re-create the table as it should be.

Make a Table Containing Customer Purchase Data

1. Create and run a Make Table query that generates a table listing customer Zip, Mailing List, Credit Limit, Order Date, product Description, Product Category, Quantity, Price Quoted, Our Selling Price, and Notes.

2. The name of the table created should be PURCHASE DATA.

3. Sort ascending first by Zip Code, then by Order Date.

4. Run this query to create the PURCHASE DATA table, on which you will base the remaining queries in this exercise.

5. Save this query as **qryKC14**.

Update the PURCHASE DATA Table

1. Using the PURCHASE DATA table, create an Update query that will add a note to the Notes field for all customers that do not have a line of credit with us.

2. The note should read: **Offer credit when taking next order.**
   Since some customers might already have notes, use the

concatenation symbol, &, to place this note after whatever note(s) the field already contains.

Note: If you make a mistake here, simply rerun the qryKC14 query to generate a new table to start over on.

3. Name this query **qryKC15**.

Delete Unwanted Records from the PURCHASE DATA Table

Finally, you need to delete some records from the PURCHASE DATA table. In its final form, the table should contain only information about fourth-quarter (October-December) 2005 orders by customers that are on the mailing list and that were given a discount (i.e., for which the price quoted was less than our usual selling price).

1. Again using the PURCHASE DATA table only, create and run a delete query to purge the PURCHASE DATA table of all records that do not meet this description.

   Hint 1: Keep in mind that your query must select the records to be deleted—and that any one of these criteria by itself is enough to cause a record to be deleted.

   Hint 2: Even if the Mailing List field in your PURCHASE DATA table has -1 and 0 instead of Yes and No, you can still use Yes or No in the criteria row.

2. Save this query as **qryKC16**.

After completing these steps, go to the course website to answer Koin-earning questions.

The IIF Function and Intro to Forms

Chapter 10

Outline

- Research & Exploration: Research the IIF Function, Create a Form
- In-Depth Case Application: Use the IIF Function, Create a Form
- Review Problems: Practice Using the IIF Function

Objectives

- Understand and use the IIF function to generate values based on a condition.
- Create a simple form.

RESEARCH & EXPLORATION

Research

Go to the Microsoft Office Online Support website, http://support.office.microsoft.com, and locate the following articles:

- IIF Function

- Create a form in Access

Research the following key terms and concepts:

- Text Box control

- Label control

- Line control

To find these controls, open the **frmClass** form that you created in chapter 5. Go to **Design View**, click the **Design** tab, and then look in the **Controls** group. Hover your mouse over each control to see its name.

Be able to identify and define the Text Box, Label, and Line controls on the following image:

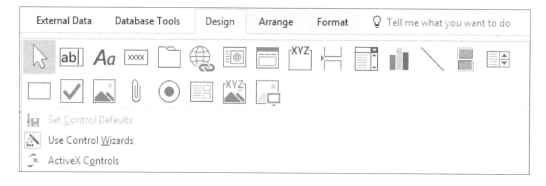

Exploration

Use an IIF Function to Determine Retirement Plan Eligibility

Any current employee who has been with Premiere Foods for at least twelve years is eligible to participate in a retirement plan.

1. Create a query in your Premiere database that lists **First** name, **Last** name, **JobTitle**, and **Department**, as well as a calculated field named **Retirement?** that should display a designation of **Eligible** or **Not Eligible** for each current employee. Sort by employee **Last** name in ascending order.

   To determine whether an employee is eligible, you will use the IIF (Immediate If) function. This is a logical function that allows you to evaluate an expression and perform one action if the expression is true but a different action if the expression is false.

   The syntax of the IIF function is as follows:

   IIF («expr», «truepart», «falsepart»)

2. Create the Retirement? field in the first blank column of the query design grid by typing the following:

   Retirement?: IIF(DATE()-[StartDate]>=365.25*12, "Eligible", "Not Eligible")

   Let's break this down:

   - *IIF* is the function name.

   - *DATE()-[StartDate]* calculates the number of days between today's date and the employee's start date.

   - *365.25 * 12* calculates the number of days in 12 years.

     Thus this expression is checking to see whether it has been at least 12 years since the employee's start date.

   - *Commas* indicate the start of the next argument.

   - If the expression is true for an employee, it will display the word "Eligible."

- If the expression is false for an employee, it will display the words "Not Eligible."

3. Run the query, saving it as **qryRE17**. Close the query.

4. Your dynaset should match the following figure. (*Remember: because you used the Date() function, your results may differ from the figure as the current date changes.*)

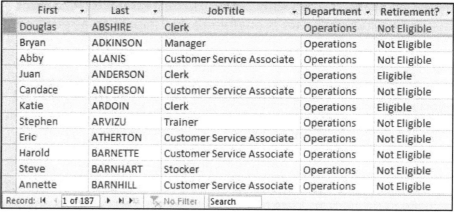

First	Last	JobTitle	Department	Retirement?
Douglas	ABSHIRE	Clerk	Operations	Not Eligible
Bryan	ADKINSON	Manager	Operations	Not Eligible
Abby	ALANIS	Customer Service Associate	Operations	Not Eligible
Juan	ANDERSON	Clerk	Operations	Eligible
Candace	ANDERSON	Customer Service Associate	Operations	Not Eligible
Katie	ARDOIN	Clerk	Operations	Eligible
Stephen	ARVIZU	Trainer	Operations	Not Eligible
Eric	ATHERTON	Customer Service Associate	Operations	Not Eligible
Harold	BARNETTE	Customer Service Associate	Operations	Not Eligible
Steve	BARNHART	Stocker	Operations	Not Eligible
Annette	BARNHILL	Customer Service Associate	Operations	Not Eligible

Record: I◄ ◄ 1 of 187 ► ►I ►⊠ 🔍 No Filter | Search

Results for qryRE17 query

Imagine This!

What would the following conditions mean in plain English when used as the first argument (expression) in an Access IIF function?

[CatalogPrice]>=150
[EndDate] is not Null
[MemberSince]<=Date()-365
[NumberInStock]<=[MinimumInventoryLevel]-2

Create the Main Form of a Multipage Form

Forms provide end users with a "window to the data," allowing them to more easily enter, view, and edit database records. The form named **frmCategoryInfoAnswer** that has already been created is a multipage form. This form helps management keep track of which brands and products Premiere Foods stocks in each product category, monitoring how sales are doing for different brands in each category. Open the form, noting its features. You will create the top section of this form (the main form) in this chapter and complete the multipage form in chapter 11.

1. Click the **Create** tab in the Forms group, then click **Form Wizard**. The form that you're creating should display items according to their category.

2. In the first step of the wizard, choose **tblProductCategory** as the table.

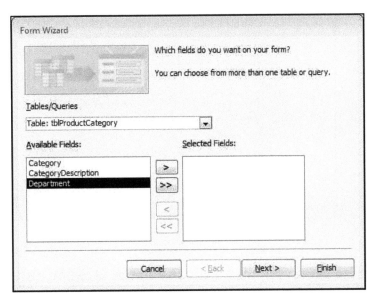

3. Add **Category**, **CategoryDescription**, and **Department** fields to the Selected Fields by clicking on the **Double Arrow**. Click **Next**.

4. Choose **Columnar** as the layout, then click **Next**.

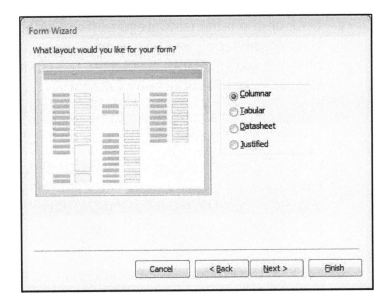

5. Name the form **frmCategoryInfo**, then click **Finish.** The form opens in Form View.

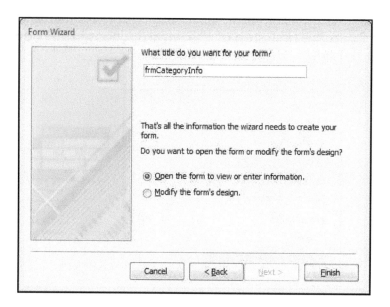

Resize the Form and Edit the Form Header and Footer

1. Switch the form to **Design View.** Click and drag the edge of the design grid, resizing it so that the form is about **8 inches wide** and the **Detail** section is about **4.5 inches tall.**

2. Edit the Form Header by completing the following steps:

   a. Click on the label **frmCategoryInfo** to select it. Click a second time on the label, and your cursor will appear in the label, allowing you to change it. Change the label in the Form Header to read **Products by Category.**

   b. Using the Format tab, make the type size **16, bold** and **blue,** and resize the label to fit the title on one line.

   c. Click on the Form Header section bar, then change the fill color to white.

   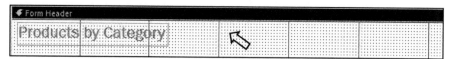

   d. Click on the Product by Category label to select it. Move your cursor to the lower right-hand corner until your cursor turns into a double-headed arrow, the resizing cursor. Click and drag upward to shorten the label to less than a half-inch tall. Move your arrow to above the Detail section bar until it turns into a line with a double-headed arrow, the resize section cursor. Click and drag up to shorten the **Form Header** design area to about **a half-inch tall**.

e. If there is a design area for the **Form Footer**, remove it by clicking its **bottom edge** and dragging it up until it is hidden/collapsed.

3. Save the form.

Format and Resize Objects

1. In Design View, use the cursor to draw a box that touches the **labels** for the **Category**, **CategoryDescription** and **Department** fields. The labels are the items on the left, not the white text boxes, as shown in the following image.

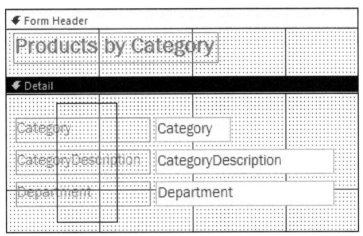

Selecting only labels

2. On the Format tab in the Font group, click the **Align-Right** icon to right-justify the text in the labels.

3. On the Design tab, change to the **Layout View** by clicking the command on the View menu. The Layout View is helpful when you want to fine-tune your form.

4. Resize the CategoryDescription label so that the text is completely displayed.

5. Change to the **Form View**. This is the default view to which you are taken when you open a form and that allows you to view, edit, and create records in the database.

6. Click on the navigation bar at the bottom of the form to move from one record to the next.

7. Return to the Design View, resetting the form width to 8 inches if necessary.

8. Save and close the frmCategoryInfo form.

IN-DEPTH CASE APPLICATION

Calculate Sales Tax for Online Orders

Premiere Foods collects sales tax on online purchases only if it has a store in the customer's state. The sales manager wants you to generate a list of online orders that includes the Location, State, and TransactionID along with a field named TaxesAssessed that calculates the tax on the order.

You will solve the problem of assessing sales tax for online transactions in two stages using the IIF (Immediate If) function.

Determine Whether Premiere Collects Sales Tax on the Order

To get an idea of how the IIF function will help determine the assessed taxes, you will first write a query that returns the text "Collect tax" if the online order was made from a state in which Premiere has a store but that returns a blank value ("") otherwise.

1. Open the Relationships window to determine the tables that need to be used in the query. Remember: you want to list the **Location**, **State**, and **TransactionID** for online purchases that were made by customers living in a state that has a brick-and-mortar store.

2. Create a query using the following tables: **tblStateTaxAndShipping**, **tblMember, tblTransaction, tblTransactionDetails**, and **tblProduct**.

3. Add the **Location**, **State**, and **TransactionID** fields to the query design grid.

4. Add a criterion for Location so that only **online** orders are displayed, then sort in **ascending** order by TransactionID.

5. Run the query, inspecting your results. At this point, the dynaset displays duplicate TransactionIDs for the online orders.

6. Return to the Design View, then edit the query so that the Location field will no longer be displayed and so that you eliminate duplicate TransactionIDs.

7. Create a new field named **Action** that will test to see whether the value in the **StoreInState?** field is Yes. If the value is Yes, then you want Access to return the words "Collect tax" as the field value; otherwise, you want the field value to be blank (""). Enter the following expression in the first blank column of the design grid to

perform the logical test: **Action: IIF([StoreInState?]=Yes,"Collect tax","")**

8. Run the query to check your results. You should now have the words "Collect tax" listed for Indiana, Illinois, and Oklahoma. (Note: Oklahoma is listed since Premiere has a warehouse in that state.)

Calculate the Sales Tax Amount

Ultimately, you need to calculate the sales taxes for each online order:

1. Switch back to Design View, then rename the Action field to **TaxesAssessed**.

2. Modify the IIF function to calculate the amount of taxes owed. Type the following:

   [Quantity] * [CatalogPrice] * (1-[Discount%]) * IIF([StoreInState?]=Yes,[SalesTax],0)

   This expression will calculate the revenue and then multiply it either by the value in the SalesTax field or by 0, depending on the outcome of the IIF function.

3. Format the **TaxesAssessed** field as Currency, then run the query to check your results. You once again see duplicate records listed for the TransactionIDs. Instead of calculating taxes for each item that was purchased in the transaction, you want to add these values together for each transaction.

4. Return to the Design View, then change the Total row for Taxes Assessed from Group By to **Sum**.

5. Run the query to check your results.

6. Save the query as **qryCA11**.

7. Your dynaset should match the following figure:

TransactionID ▾	State ▾	TaxesAssessed ▾
4	IN	$1.23
6	OH	$0.00
9	MI	$0.00
10	IN	$7.83
15	KY	$0.00
18	AZ	$0.00
24	OH	$0.00
26	KY	$0.00

Record: I◀ ◀ 1 of 993 ▶ ▶I ▷ 🏹 No Filter Search

Results for qryCA11 query

Modify the frmMemberTransactions Form

There is a basic form already created for you that contains fields from the tblMember table. You will begin modifying this form according to the following specifications:

1. Open the **frmMemberTransactions** form.

2. Switch to **Design View**, then adjust the height of the **Detail** section of the form to be 8 inches. This adjustment will make room for additional subforms that will be added in the next chapter.

3. Change the Label control in the Form Header to **Member Information**.

4. Delete the **First** and **Last** controls—both the labels and the text boxes—from the form.

5. Instead of having the First and Last name field values displayed in separate controls, you want to display the member's **First** and **Last** name separated by a space in one control (e.g., Cindy Stone). You must use a Text Box control to accomplish this. Text Box controls are used when you want to create new fields such as this or perform calculations.

6. Locate and click the Text Box [ab] control in the Controls group on the Design tab. Draw the text box control beneath the MemberID text box on your form. Notice that the right side of the new control (the text box) reads **Unbound** and that the associated label is given a generic caption: [Text20] [Unbound].

7. The text box is shown as Unbound because it is not bound to any field values. Enter the following expression in the Unbound text box to

return the **First** and **Last** name separated by a space as requested. Important: Unlike queries, all expressions in a form or report must begin with an = sign.

=[First] & " " & [Last]

8. Change the caption property of the label to read **Name**. (Label captions can also be edited by simply selecting and editing the text inside the label control.)

9. Right-align the four labels (not the text within the labels). Select all four labels, right-click any one of the selected labels, click **Align**, and then click **Right**.

10. Click the **text box** for **MemberID** to select it. In the Property Sheet, click on the **Data** tab. Change the **Locked** property to **Yes**. This will prevent a user from inadvertently changing a primary key field.

11. On the Design tab, in the Tools group, click **Add Existing Fields**. Drag **MemberSince** from the Field List pane to the form, then place it just to the right of MemberID.

12. Move the MemberSince control's text box closer to the MemberSince label by clicking the upper-left move handle and dragging it to the left.

13. Add the **State** and **ZIPCode** fields to the form, placing them to the right of City. Position the text box for these two controls closer to the associated label using the text box move handle.

14. Right-align all label controls' text, making the text **bold** using the buttons on the **Home** or **Format** tab on the Ribbon.

15. Right-click the MemberSince text box control, then choose **Conditional Formatting**. Set two new rules for the control:

    a. Customers who became members **on or before 1/1/2000** should appear with a date in **bold orange** type.

    b. Customers who became members **on or before 1/1/2007** should appear with a date in **bold blue** type.

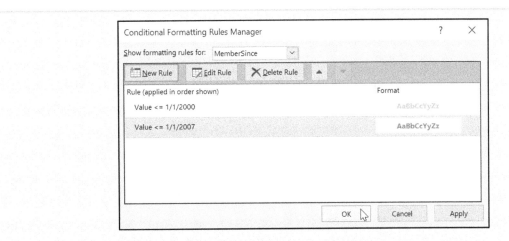

16. Save the form changes, then switch to the Form View. Use the navigation buttons to move from one record to the next, noting how the conditional formatting affects the text in the MemberSince field.

17. Switch to the Layout View and resize labels and text boxes so that all text and field values are visible. (Note: You can also resize controls in the Design View, but the Layout View provides a much nicer user interface for doing this.)

Micro-Align Controls

If fields are misaligned, the form may come across as unprofessional. Access includes tools in Design View that allow you to easily align controls to each other.

1. Return to the Design View.

2. Select all controls on the bottom of the form:

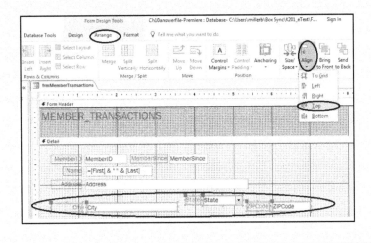

3. With the appropriate controls selected, click the **Arrange** tab on the Ribbon.

4. In the Sizing & Ordering group, click **Align**, then **Top**.

   All selected controls will adjust so that all are aligned with the topmost control in the selection.

Add a Calculated Control to Determine Shipping Method

In this part of the exercise, you will create a new calculated field that will determine the shipping method for which each member qualifies. Premiere customers who became members on or before 1/1/2000 qualify for 2-day shipping; otherwise, they qualify for 3- to 5-day shipping.

1. The Form Control necessary to create a new calculated field is Text Box. On the Design tab, in the Controls group, locate and click the **Text Box** ab| control.

2. Draw the Text Box control beneath the **City** text box on your form.

3. Change the **Label** of this new text box to read **Shipping Status**. Adjust the size and position of the text box and label so that all text is visible. Format the label to match the others, using bolding and right-alignment.

4. Enter a calculation in the text box control. Again, note that expressions must begin with an = sign. Type the following:

   =IIf([MemberSince]<=#1/1/2000#,"2 Day Shipping","3-5 Day Shipping")

5. Save the form, then switch to Form View.

6. Record 2 of the completed form should look similar to the following image:

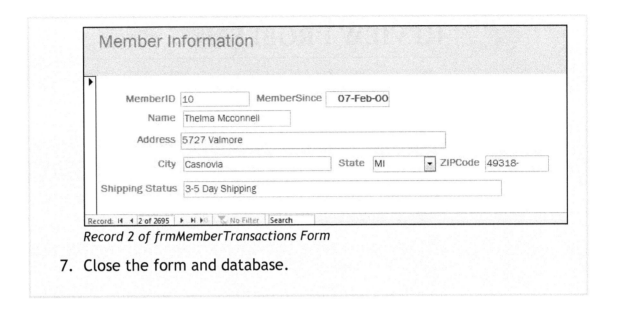

Record 2 of frmMemberTransactions Form

7. Close the form and database.

REVIEW PROBLEMS

Review Problem 1

Calculate Free Holiday Shipping

Premiere Foods has decided to offer free shipping for all transactions purchased between 11/25/2015 and 12/25/2015 whose total revenue (after discounts) is greater than $300.

1. Create a query for all transactions totaling more than $300 that have been shipped.

2. Include **TransactionID** and two new fields, named **Revenue** and **Holiday Shipping**. The Holiday Shipping field should return the text **Free Shipping** if the TransactionDate occurs within the date range listed above but should be blank if not.

3. Format Revenue as Currency, then sort by Revenue in Descending order.

4. Name the query **qryReview15**.

5. Your dynaset should match the following figure:

TransactionID ▾	Revenue ▾	Holiday Shipping ▾
4148	$565.00	Free Shipping
2126	$555.92	
1578	$555.92	
1690	$539.73	
3277	$532.97	
155	$511.44	
4498	$510.27	Free Shipping
4364	$503.65	Free Shipping
3098	$503.41	
2720	$472.23	

Record: ◄ ◄ 1 of 107 ► ►► ▾ No Filter Search

Results for qryReview15 query

Review Problem 2

Modify the frmEmployee Form

In an earlier chapter, you created a form named frmEmployee. You have been asked to modify this form to make it easier to read and edit.

1. Open the frmEmployee form in Design View.

2. Increase the width of the Detail section of the form to 8 inches.

3. Delete the form icon 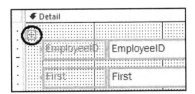 from the Form Header, then change the Form Header label to read **Employee Information**.

4. To size and move each control individually, you must first remove the layout of the controls in the Detail section:

    a. Click the EmployeeID text box in the Detail section of the form.

    b. Select the plus sign in the top left corner of the Detail section to select all controls (or press Ctrl + A to select all).

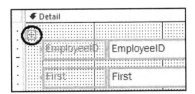

    c. On the Arrange tab in the Table group, click **Remove Layout**.

5. Right-align the text within each label, making it bold.

6. Change the property of the FullTime? text box to **Yes/No**.

7. Delete the First and Last controls, then create a new field that displays the employee Last and First name separated by a comma and space (e.g., Abbott, Megan). Change the label to read **Name**.

8. Move and resize the controls to match the following image:

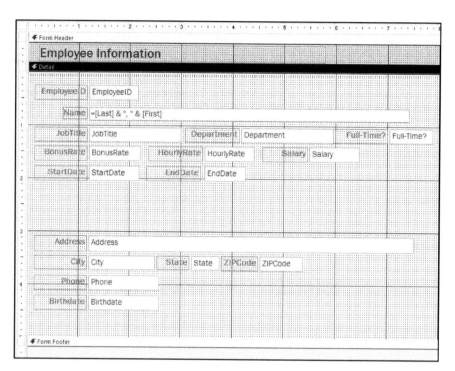

9. Add a new calculated field to the right of the EmployeeID control. The new field should test the value of the EndDate field and return the text **Current Employee** if the employee is still employed at Premiere. Otherwise, the calculation should return the text **No longer with Premiere**. Change the label of the new field to read **Status**.

10. Conditionally format the new calculated field so that the text **No longer with Premiere** appears in **bold red** type.

11. Click the Line object ⬚ in the Controls group of the Design tab, then place the line below the StartDate control. With the line still selected, click the Shift key and size the line to the width of the form.

12. Add a Text Box below the Line control and change the caption to read **Personal Info**. Change the text to use bold 14-point type.

13. Make sure all text and field values are viewable in the Form View.

14. Your completed form should resemble the following image for record 14 in Form View:

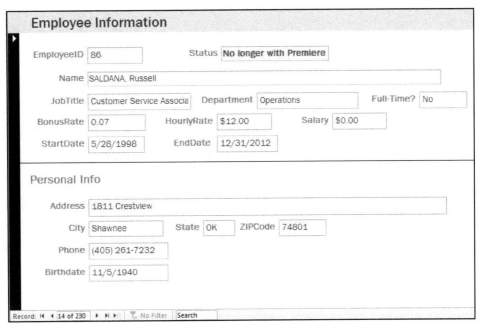

Record 14 of frmEmployee form

Multiple Page and Navigation Forms

Chapter 11

Outline

- Research & Exploration: Research Key Terms Related to Adding Pages to Forms, Identify Controls, Read a Form That Has Multiple Pages, Practice Adding Pages and Subforms to Forms

- In-Depth Case Application: Add Pages to a Form Using a Tab Control, Add Subforms to Each Page, Change Properties to Make the Form and Subforms Look Professional, Create and Format a Navigation Form

- Review Problems: Practice Adding Pages and Subforms to Forms, Adjust Form Properties, Knowledge Check 9

Objectives

- Add pages to forms.

- Add subforms/subreports to the pages.

- Create a user-friendly navigation form.

- Use calculations in a form.

- Change form properties to produce desired results.

RESEARCH & EXPLORATION

Research

As you learned in chapter 10, forms are used to provide a user-friendly interface to enter, edit, or display records in a database. Forms can display records from a single table or query in the database, but forms can also be designed to display data from multiple tables or queries. For example, a form could be created that displays customer contact information and customer purchase details on the same form. Another example is a form that contains product information as well as transactions that included the purchase of that product. Putting all the data into one form is done through the use of controls and subforms.

Use your preferred search engine or the Microsoft Office Online Support website, http://support.office.microsoft.com, to research the following key terms and concepts:

- Access subforms

- Access navigation forms

- Tab control

- Subform/subreport control

To find the controls, open a form, such as **frmEmployee** or **frmClass**, which were created in chapter 5. Go to **Design View**, click the **Design** tab, and look in the **Controls** group. Hover your mouse over each control to see its name.

Be able to identify and define the controls from the preceding list on this graphic of the ribbon:

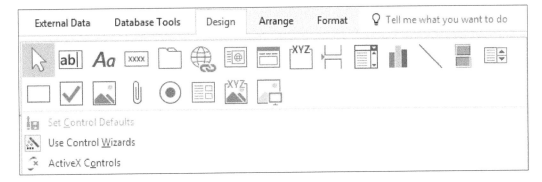

Exploration

Refer to the following form, keeping in mind the structure of the Premiere database, as you consider the questions that follow the image. Being able to answer these questions demonstrates that you can interpret the data displayed in this multipage form.

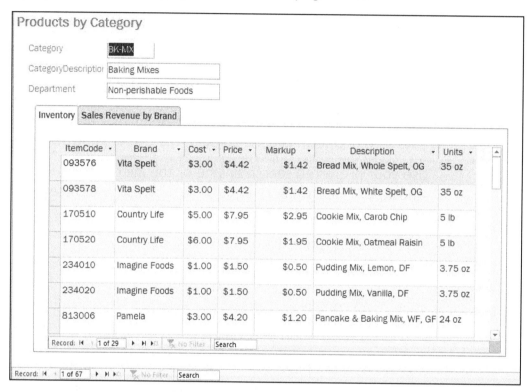

How many different product categories are there? You can confirm your answer by using the tblProductCategory table.

Where in the image can you find how many items are in the baking mixes category? How can you verify this using a table or a query?

Which of the fields displayed in the image is a calculated field? How do you know? If this were a query, what would the calculation be for that field?

Adding Data to a Form by Using the Tab Control to Create Pages

In chapter 10, you began the frmCategoryInfo form, which has a record for each product category and shows that category, its description, and department. Having the inventory and sales data for each category on the same form would be useful for store managers when they decide which products to stock in their stores. Adding data to the form can be done with the use of the Tab control, which creates pages for each set of data that you wish to display.

1. Open **frmCategoryInfo** form in **Design View.**

2. On the **Design** tab, in the **Controls** group, click the **Tab control** button ▢ once. The tab button will remain selected as you move the cursor away.

3. Add a Tab control to the form just below the **Department** field by clicking and dragging your mouse down and across the design area. When you release your mouse, the Tab control will appear, and your form should look like the following picture. The pages on your Tab control might not be called Page8 and Page9, and if so, that's fine—do not rename them!

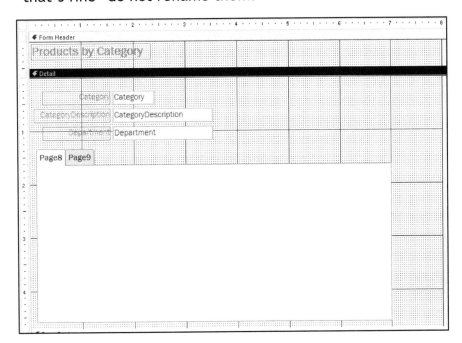

4. Widen the Tab control to about the 7-inch mark on the ruler using the sizing handles on the highlighted Tab control.

Changing the Names of Page Tabs by Using the Caption Property

1. Select the **tab** for the first page, right-click, and choose **Properties.**

2. Locate the **Caption** property (it is a Format property), then enter **Inventory** as the caption.

3. Do the same for the second page, giving it a caption of **Sales Revenue by Brand**, then close the **Property Sheet window.**

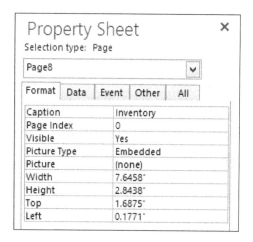

Creating an Inventory Subform

Note: In the **Controls** group, make sure that the **Use Control Wizards** option is selected. Without this, the wizard will not appear.

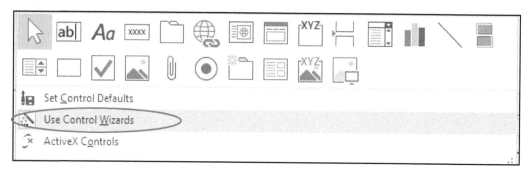

1. Click on the **Inventory** tab.

2. Locate the **Subform/Subreport** button in the **Controls** group, then click it once. The button will remain selected as you move the cursor away.

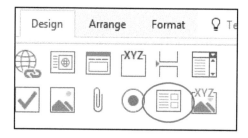

3. Move your cursor to the middle of the Tab control, then click once. Your Tab control area will turn black as you do this. After the click, your screen will look like the following image. Do not worry if the Unbound control has a different Child number.

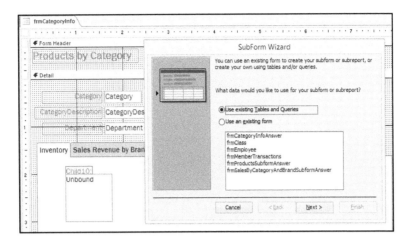

4. Make sure the radio button for **Use existing Tables and Queries** is selected, then click **Next**.

5. In the second step, choose **tblProduct** from the drop-down list. Then select all the fields in tblProduct by clicking the **double arrow** to move the fields from Available Fields to Selected Fields. Click **Next**.

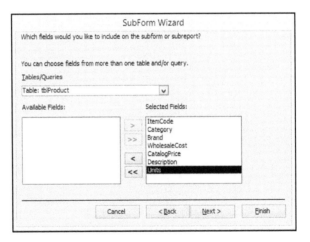

6. To be completely sure that Access correctly relates the main form, which is based on tblProductCategory, to the subform, which is based on tblProduct, choose **Define my own**, then select **Category** as the common field. Click **Next**.

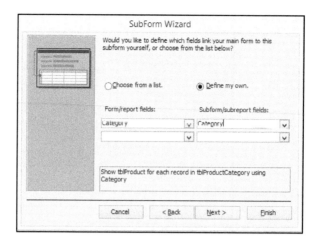

7. Accept the default name for the subform, then click **Finish**.

   In Design View, the first page of your Tab control should now look like the following figure:

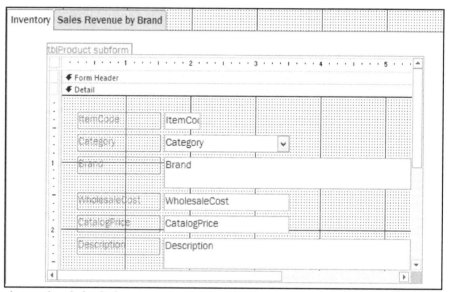

8. Delete the **label** that reads tblProduct subform.

9. Switch to **Form View**, noticing the difference between how the fields look in Design View and how they look in Form View. Since each Category has its own form, and the Category name is in the main form, it does not need to also be displayed in the subform. While in Form View, hide the **Category** field by right-clicking its column header and choosing **Hide Fields**. Another way to hide a field is to grab the column border and minimize it by dragging to the left until it is no longer visible.

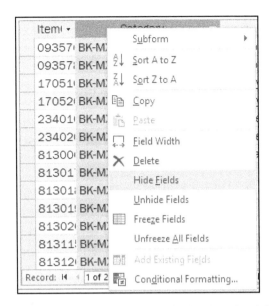

10. While in Form View, adjust **column widths** by double-clicking between column headers. You may need to return to Design View to increase the width of the subform or the Tab control, then come back to Form View to continue adjusting column widths until all column headers are visible. Move the Tab control in Design View if it seems to crowd the main form fields above it.

Adding Sales Revenue by Brand Data

1. Switch to **Design View.**

2. Select the second page of the Tab control, **Sales Revenue by Brand.**

3. Select the **Subform/Subreport** control, then place a subform on the page using all three fields from **qrySalesByCategoryAndBrand.**

4. Make sure that you choose **Category** as the field that relates the main form to this subform.

5. Accept the name that the wizard gives the subform in the last step. Click **Finish.**

6. Delete the **qrySalesByCategoryAndBrand subform** label.

7. Increase the height of the subform using the sizing handles when the subform is highlighted.

8. Format the SalesRevenue field as **Currency** by right-clicking the **SalesRevenue text box** and choosing **Properties**. Look for the **Format** property.

9. Switch to **Form View**, then hide the **Category** field.

Resizing in Layout View and Changing Datasheet Captions

1. Switch to **Layout View**.

2. On the **Inventory subform**, use the **Datasheet Caption** property to rename the **WholesaleCost** field **Cost** and the **CatalogPrice** field **Price**.

3. While still in Layout View, resize the subforms and Tab controls as needed to show all fields. Resize the columns as needed so that you use space efficiently and so that all columns' data can be read without using the horizontal scroll. Ideally, the horizontal scroll should disappear from your subform.

Hiding the Form's Record Selector

Recall that in a table under the last record is a blank row with an asterisk ⊞ to the left of the first field. This asterisk turns into a pencil 🖉 when a new record is being added to the table. If a current record in the table is being edited, the pencil will appear to the left of the row that is being edited. The place where the asterisk and pencil are located is called the Record Selector.

The Record Selector also appears in forms as a thin column that begins with an arrow near the upper left corner of the form. You can see it only in Form View or Layout View, and it looks like this: ▶. If a record were to be added or edited, the arrow would become a pencil. When the Record Selector is showing, a user could accidentally select one or more records and delete them without realizing his or her mistake. Hiding the Record Selectors can help prevent this error. The Record Selectors is a property of the form.

1. Make sure that you are in **Design View**.

2. Show the **Property Sheet** for the form.

3. Make sure you are viewing the list of properties specific to the Form. There are two ways to ensure you are viewing the correct properties:

   - Choose **Form** from the drop-down list of objects in the Property Sheet.

OR

- Select the **small square** in the upper left corner of the form where the horizontal and vertical rulers intersect.

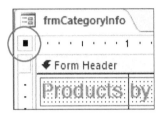

4. Set the Record Selectors property to **No**.

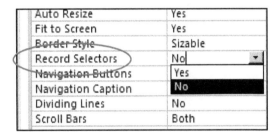

5. Return to **Form View.** Your form should look like the images on the next page.

Save and Back Up

When you are finished with your work, close the Premiere database file, then upload the revised version to your Box account. We strongly suggest that if you are using a flash drive you also place a copy of your work on cloud storage.

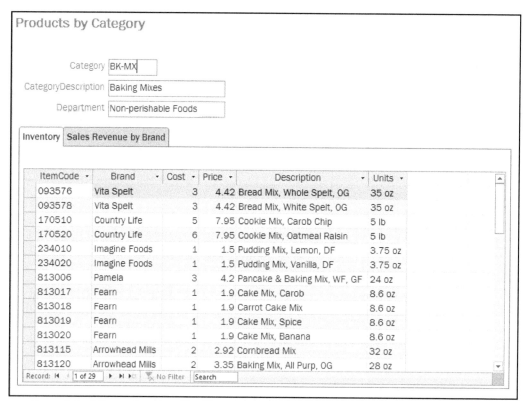

Completed form showing the first page of the Tab control

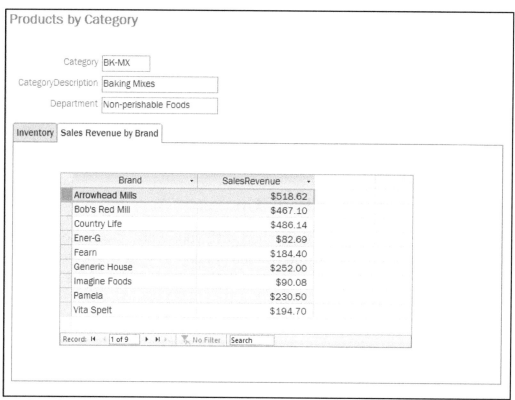

Completed form showing the second page of the Tab control

IN-DEPTH CASE APPLICATION

Adding Data to a Form by Using the Tab Control to Create Pages

In chapter 10, you began creating the frmMemberTransactions form, which right now displays basic information about each member as well as whether that member qualifies for 2-day shipping or 3- to 5-day shipping. For this form, we want to be able to add two subforms that contain data related to each member, such as additional personal details and what products they have purchased. When adding multiple subforms, a Tab control can help organize the subforms into pages.

1. Open the **frmMemberTransactions** form in Design View.

2. On the Design tab, in the Controls group, select the **Tab control.**

3. Add a Tab control onto your form beneath Shipping Status. Stretch it out to be about **7 inches wide** and **3 inches tall.** You may need to adjust more as you complete your form.

4. On the Property Sheet, select the **Format** tab, then change the Caption properties for the pages to **Member Details** and **Transaction Information**, respectively:

Shipping Status	=IIf([MemberSince]<=#1/1/200				
Member Details	Transaction Information				

Adding Data to Each Page of the Tab Control

Data can be added to the Tab control from a table, a query, or another form. To add data from a table, you select which fields you need from the Field List. To add data from a query or form, you use a subform/subreport control.

Adding Data on the Member Details Page from a Table

1. Click the **Member Details** tab to activate that page.

2. On the Design tab, in the Tools group, click **Add Existing Fields** to open the Field List to see what other data you can add to the form.

3. Hold down the **Ctrl** key and click **DateofBirth**, **Gender**, **SubscribedToEmailList?**, **RequestedPartnerOffers?**, **EmailAddress**, **CreditLimit**, and **Comments**. Release the **Ctrl** key, then drag the **selected fields** over to the Member Details page.

4. Move the **labels** for **SubscribedToEmailList?** and **RequestedPartnerOffers?** to the left of their check boxes.

5. Align and format the controls to match the following figure:

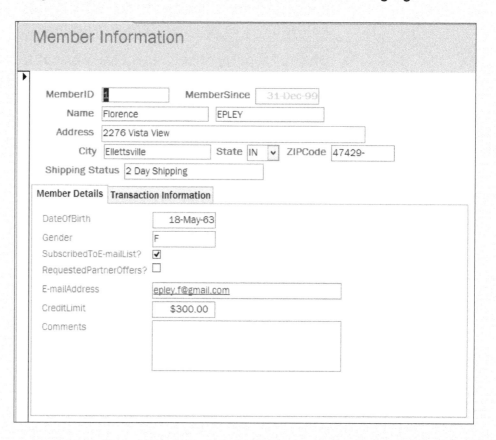

Adding Data on the Transaction Information Page from a Query

1. Switch to **Design View**, then select the **Transaction Information** tab to activate that page.

2. On the Design tab, in the Controls group, click the **Subform/Subreport** control.

3. Click inside the **Transaction Information page**. A wizard will launch.

4. Make sure the radio button for **Use existing Tables and Queries is** selected, then click **Next**.

5. Choose the query that has been made for you, **qryMemberTransactionDetails**. Add all the fields from the query by clicking the **double arrows** to move the fields from Available Fields to Selected Fields. Click **Next**.

6. Choose **Define my own**, then select **MemberID** as the field that connects this subform to the main form. Click **Next**.

7. Accept the name that Access offers for the subform, then click **Finish**.

8. Delete the default subform label from the subform.

Adjusting the Subforms

On the Transaction Information Page

1. In Form View, hide the **MemberID** field. Switch to **Layout View**.

2. Make sure the **Property Sheet** is showing, then change the following:

   a. Select the **TransactionDate** field. On the **All** tab, change the Datasheet Caption to read **Date**.

   b. Select the **CategoryDescription** field, then change the Datasheet Caption to read **Description**.

   c. Select the **CatalogPrice** field, then change the Datasheet Caption to read **Price**.

   d. Format both the **Price** and **Subtotal** fields as **Currency**.

   e. Double-click the borders of each column to auto-adjust the width to fit all contents.

f. Increase the height of the rows so that the Description column can be narrowed and have the text wrap around. However, make sure the column heading, "Description", is still readable.

g. Adjust the width of the Tab control and subform objects as necessary so that the data in the subform is displayed without having to scroll from left to right.

h. Save the form.

Notice that the Transaction Information subform has a set of Navigation Buttons that can be used to move down the list of items that the member has purchased. These subform navigation buttons could be a distraction when trying to go to another member's records, since the user could get these navigation buttons confused with the navigation buttons at the bottom of the main form. You can hide the navigation buttons in the subform to minimize this confusion.

3. Switch to **Design View**.

4. Set the **Navigation Buttons** property of the Transaction Information subform to **No**.

5. Set the **Record Selectors** property of the main form to **No**.

6. Your form, along with the second page of the Tab control, should look like the following image:

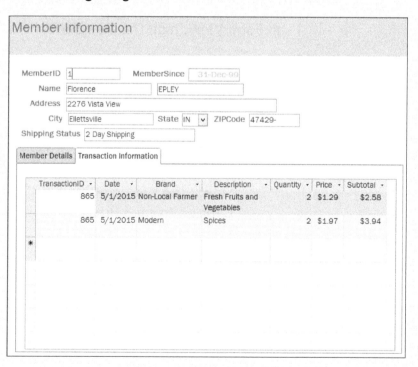

7. Save and close the **frmMemberTransactions** form.

Creating a Navigation Form

Your Premiere database now contains two main forms: frmCategoryInfo, which you created on your own at the beginning of this chapter, and frmMemberTransactions. Premiere Foods management would like a centralized location from which to easily access these two forms. A navigation form gives users an interface, much like that of a webpage, that is easy to use and that has easily understood tabs guiding the user to the data he or she wants. In this particular case, Premiere's management would like one tab to access data about the products and another tab to access data about the members.

1. Click the **Create** tab. Look in the **Forms** group, click the **Navigation** button, and then select the **Horizontal Tabs** option.

   The navigation form will open in **Layout View**.

Note: If the Field List pane shows on the right side, you may close it.

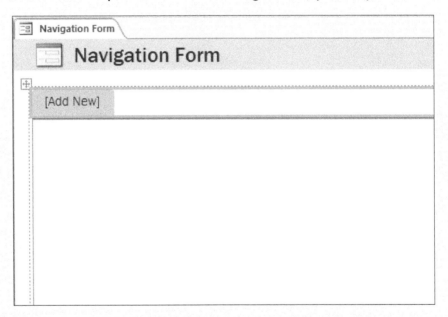

2. While in Layout View, click and drag **frmCategoryInfo** form from the objects list on the left side of your screen, then drop it on top of the **[Add New]** tab along the top of the form. Do the same with **frmMemberTransactions** form.

Format the Navigation Form

In Layout View

1. Rename the frmCategoryInfo tab by double-clicking it, deleting the text, and typing **Products** as the tab name.

2. Rename the frmMemberTransactions tab as **Members**.

3. Delete the **label** and corresponding **logo image** in the Form Header.

4. Save the form as **frmNavigation**.

5. Switch to **Form View** to view the finished navigation form, then try out each of the navigation tabs.

The Products tab of the completed Navigation Form should match the following figure:

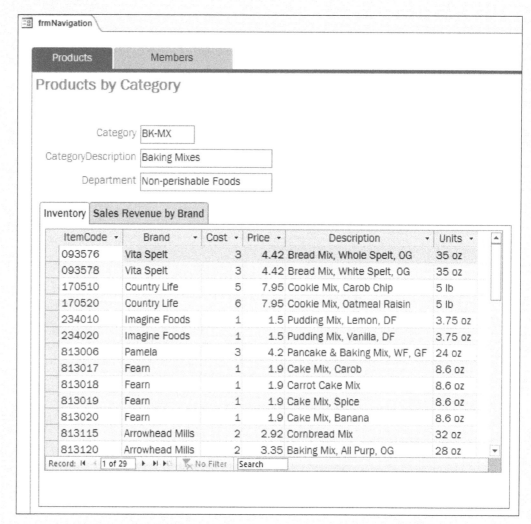

6. Close the **frmNavigation** form.

Save and Back Up

When you are finished with your work, close the Premiere database file, then upload the revised version to your Box account. We strongly suggest that if you are using a flash drive you also place a copy of your work on cloud storage.

REVIEW PROBLEMS

Review Problem 1

Add More Pages to the Tab Control

1. Open the **frmMemberTransactions** form in Design View.

2. Right-click on one of the tabs of the Tab control, then choose **Insert Page**. Now you should have three pages on your Tab control.

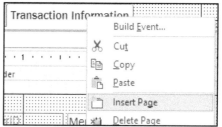

3. Change the Caption Property for the new page to **Shipping Information**.

On the Shipping Information Page

1. Add a new **Subform/Subreport** to the Shipping Information page of the Tab control. Make sure that the Shipping Information page is active before you begin.

2. Follow the wizard to add data from the existing **qryMemberTransactionShipments** query.

3. Add all **four fields**.

4. Make sure to link the subform to the main form using the key field **MemberID**.

5. In the last step of the wizard, accept the name offered for the new subform, then click **Finish**.

6. Delete the **default label** for the new subform.

7. Select both the **MemberID label** and **text box**. On the **Property Sheet**, set the **Visible** property to **No**.

8. Switch to **Form View**, then look at the subform on the **Shipping Information tab**. You may notice that you still see the MemberID field even though you set the visible property to No.

9. Switch back to Design View.

10. Select your subform on the Tab control by clicking in the box in the top left-hand corner of the subform. A black dot will appear to show you that it is selected. Your **selection type** on the Property Sheet will also say **Form**.

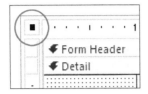 

11. Find the **Default View** property on either the Format or All tab of the Property Sheet. Change the **Default View** for the form to **Single Form**.

12. Switch to **Form View**, noticing how this changed the way the data is displayed.

13. Switch back to **Design View**.

14. Add conditional formatting to the **DateShipped** field so that dates that are at least 3 days past the TransactionDate appear in bold red type.

15. Hide the **Record Selectors** for the Shipping Information subform by setting the property to **No**.

16. Switch to **Form View**, then compare the Shipping Information page of your form to the following picture. Notice that record 1, for MemberID 1, has no shipping information, because that member has not ordered any products online. For this reason, the image shows data for record 2, MemberID 10.

17. Save and close **frmMemberTransactions**.

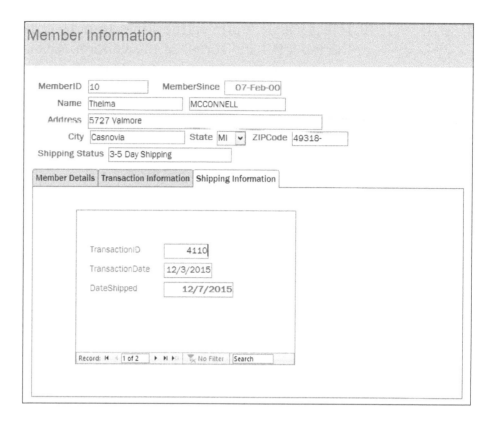

Review Problem 2

Calculating Markup on frmCategoryInfo

1. Open **frmCategoryInfo**, which was created in the Exploration section of this chapter. The inventory tab displays data from the tblProduct table and includes the Cost that Premiere pays for the products as well as the Price at which Premiere sells the products to the customer. However, there is not yet a field that calculates the Markup—that is, the amount that Premiere adds to its cost to cover expenses such as payroll and utilities.

2. In **Design View**, on the first page of the Tab control, use the **Text Box** button in the **Controls** group to draw a text box under **Units**.

3. Select the **unbound text box control**, and, to have Access calculate the dollar amount of the markup for each item, type the following:

   =[CatalogPrice]-[WholesaleCost]

4. Change the label associated with this calculated text box control to read **Markup**.

Finish Formatting frmCategoryInfo

1. Format the **WholesaleCost**, **CatalogPrice**, and **Markup** fields as currency.

2. In **Form View**, move the **Markup** column before the **Description** column. To do this, click once to select the Markup column, then click that field again and drag it to reposition it before the Description column.

3. Also in **Form View**, make the rows taller by dragging the line between two rows down. By making the rows a little taller and the Description field a little narrower, you should be able to read all the text in the Description field. Also, you should not need a horizontal scroll bar in Form View.

4. On the second page of the Tab control, use **Conditional Formatting** to format the SalesRevenue field so that if the field value is greater than 500, Access will display it in bold blue type. To do this in **Form View**, right-click the **SalesRevenue** column header, then select **Conditional Formatting**.

5. Format other labels/fields as you see fit. When you are done, your form should resemble the following figures:

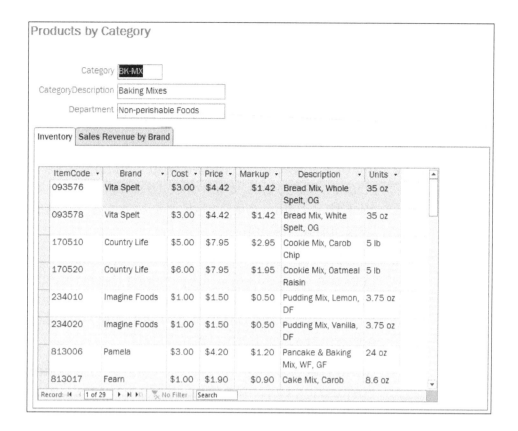

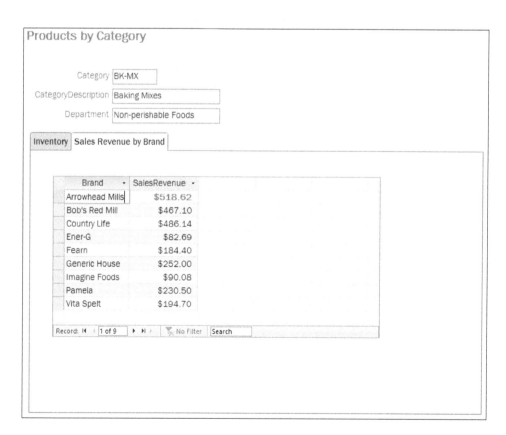

Save and Back Up

When you are finished with your work, close the Premiere database file, then upload the revised version to your Box account. We strongly suggest that if you are using a flash drive you also place a copy of your work on cloud storage.

Knowledge Check 9

Multipage Form

For this Knowledge Check, you will create a multipage form that will display information about each order placed with The Artful Yard.

Use figures 1 and 2 and the notes that accompany each figure on the following pages as a guide.

Note: Data displayed in both of the following figures is for Order ID 3. To sort the form by Order ID, in Form View, click in the Order ID field, then click the Ascending sort button in the ribbon.

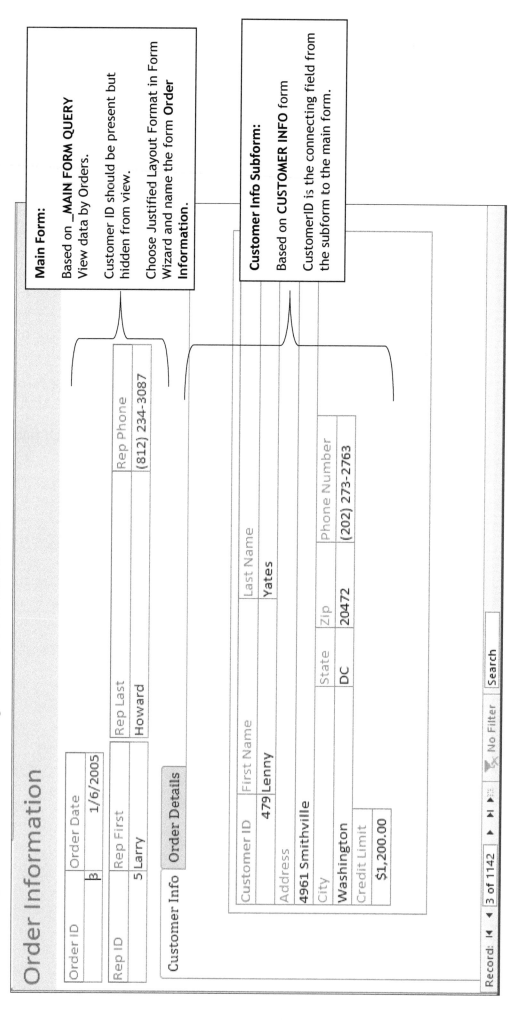

Main Form:

Based on **_MAIN FORM QUERY** View data by Orders.

Customer ID should be present but hidden from view.

Choose Justified Layout Format in Form Wizard and name the form **Order Information**.

Customer Info Subform:

Based on **CUSTOMER INFO** form

CustomerID is the connecting field from the subform to the main form.

Order Information

Order ID	Order Date
3	1/6/2005

Rep ID	Rep First	Rep Last
5	Larry	Howard

Rep Phone
(812) 234-3087

Customer Info   Order Details

Customer ID	First Name	Last Name
479	Lenny	Yates

Address
4961 Smithville

City	State	Zip	Phone Number
Washington	DC	20472	(202) 273-2763

Credit Limit
$1,200.00

Record: I◀ ◀ 3 of 1142 ▶ ▶I ▶❉   ✕ No Filter   Search

Order Information

Order ID		Order Date	
	3	1/6/2005	

Rep ID		Rep First	Rep Last		Rep Phone
	5	Larry	Howard		(812) 234-3087

Customer Info | **Order Details**

Prod ID ▾	Prod Cat ▾	Description ▾	Qty ▾	Our Selling Price ▾	Price Quoted ▾	Item Subtotal ▾	Item Savings ▾
29315	birdhouses	School House Birdhouse	2	$6.00	$6.00	$12.00	$0.00
30125	birdfeeders	Alabaster Hummingbird/Bir dhouse Feeder	3	$6.95	$6.26	$18.78	$2.07
31247	birdhouses	Wood Beach Bungalow Birdhouse	3	$7.90	$7.90	$23.70	$0.00
32194	birdhouses	Wood 3 1/2 x 5 Log Cabin Frame	4	$3.70	$3.70	$14.80	$0.00
33807	misc	Glass Hummingbirds	3	$11.60	$10.44	$31.32	$3.48

Record: I◀ ◀ 1 of 5 ▶ ▶I ▶▦ 🖫 No Filter | Search

Record: I◀ ◀ 3 of 1142 ▶ ▶I ▶▦ 🖫 No Filter | Search

Order Details Subform: Based on **_FORM PAGE 2** query; Order ID should be used but hidden from view; OrderID is the connecting field. Create two calculated fields: **Item Subtotal and Item Savings.** Change the Product ID, Product Category, and Quantity labels to **Prod ID**, **Prod Cat**, and **Qty**, respectively.

After completing these steps, go to the course website to answer Koin-earning questions.

The Power of Excel

Chapter 12

Outline

- Research & Exploration: Read, Research, and Practice in Excel
- In-Depth Case Application: Identify Various Uses of Excel, Conduct Basic Analysis
- Review Problems: Practice Basic Excel Skills

Objectives

- Understand the basics of navigating Excel.
- Interpret common errors in Excel.
- Identify order of operations.
- Identify important uses of Excel.
- Utilize the AutoFill feature.
- Solve problems with basic aggregate functions: SUM, MAX, MIN, AVERAGE, COUNT, and COUNTA.

RESEARCH & EXPLORATION

Research

Microsoft Excel is an extremely powerful application used by organizations all over the world for data analysis, data modeling, data visualization, and more. The power of Excel stems from its ability to conduct what-if analysis. When performing calculations with formulas and functions, Excel can use the values contained in other cells, referenced by their "address" (a column letter and row number), rather than requiring the user to type static numbers directly into the calculation. This allows the user to insert different values into the referenced cells to see how the new values would affect the results of the calculation without having to modify the function or formula itself. For example, when calculating revenue generated from a sale, you would multiply quantity and price. By referencing cells that contain the quantity and price values rather than typing specific numbers inside the revenue calculation, you do not need to edit the calculation itself if you want to test different quantity and price values. You can simply update the cells that hold the quantity and price data, and then the revenue calculation will recalculate. Furthermore, any other calculations that depend on quantity or price will automatically recalculate as well without your having to edit their formulas.

Use your preferred search engine to research the following key terms and Excel functions:

- What-if analysis

- Workbook

- Worksheet

- Order of operations

- Common Excel error messages

- Excel functions: AVERAGE, MAX, MIN, SUM, COUNT, COUNTA

Exploration

Understand the Order of Operations

1. Locate and download the **Chapter12_PowerOfExcel.xlsx** file.

2. Click the **RE1-2** worksheet tab.

3. Examine the sample transaction data below the RE1 heading. In cells C11 and C12 are two different attempts to calculate the amount of sales tax owed for the transactions.

4. In cell **D14**, using your knowledge of the order of operations, select which of the sales tax calculations is correct.

Interpret Errors in Excel

1. Click cell **C19**, then examine the contents.

2. In cell **D19**, using your knowledge of Excel errors, select the option that explains the cause of the error that is being returned in cell C19.

3. Click cell **C21**, then examine the contents.

4. In cell **D21**, select the option that explains the cause of the error that is being returned in cell C21.

IN-DEPTH CASE APPLICATION

Why Do Organizations Use Excel?

Microsoft Excel is one of the most popular software applications in the world and is used by businesses, organizations, and individuals for a variety of data centric tasks.

Data Analysis
In Excel 2016, data can be analyzed either as relational data or as flat data.

1. Open the **Chapter12_PowerOfExcel.xlsx** workbook.

2. To the left of the worksheet tabs are arrows that allow you to navigate to worksheets in the workbook that may be out of view. If necessary, click the next arrow and then click the **ExportQuery** worksheet tab.

The data on the ExportQuery worksheet are the results of a query in the Premiere database. The query combines data from several different tables in the database into one list, considered "flat" data. Although very common, analyzing data in a flat form creates a larger file size and redundancy.

Excel can now easily analyze relational data, a capability introduced in Excel 2010 as a separate download and integrated fully into Excel 2016. The worksheets to the right of the PowerPivotTables worksheet contain tables in Excel that are connected with relationships within Excel's Data Model.

It is easy and common to export data from a database or link a database to a spreadsheet program like Excel for sophisticated analysis.

Questions of interest: Is there a trend in department performance over summer months? What months should Premiere use to define "summer"?

3. Click the **Premiere PowerPivot** worksheet tab.

The Premiere PowerPivot worksheet uses an Excel Power PivotTable to help determine whether there is a time element to how the top-selling categories perform. The PivotTable has been organized to display data on a month-by-month and quarter-by-quarter basis. We are looking at how all of Premiere's departments are selling, but any department could be excluded by using the Department filter located in cell B6. We could also limit the analysis to a particular store location or product brand using the filters in cells B3 and B4. PivotTables allow users to easily organize hundreds of millions of records to easily spot patterns and trends.

Data Visualization

While analyzing data is important, visualizing the data to communicate the analysis is equally important. A chart is the most basic form of data visualization.

1. Click the **Monthly Sales PivotChart** worksheet tab.

2. Click the **Monthly Sales Table & Chart** worksheet tab.

The Monthly Sales PivotChart and Monthly Sales Table & Chart worksheets show some of the charting capabilities.

3. Click the **Premiere Power View** worksheet tab.

Introduced in 2013 and improved in Excel 2016, Excel can create an interactive data visualization dashboard called a Power View report. Power View reports can be useful in revealing patterns, trends, and relationships, also referred to as business intelligence, in large data sets. Interactive data visualization like this was only available in more advanced programs such as SAS JMP and Tableau prior to Excel 2013.

What-If Analysis

Among many reasons to use Excel, one important reason is that it makes what-if analysis easy. When you change a value in a worksheet, Excel can instantly recalculate formulas and functions that refer to that cell.

1. Click the **New Product What-If** worksheet tab.

Premiere Foods wants to take advantage of its growing house brand of products by adding a new homeopathic remedy to the product line. Consumer demand and pricing possibilities are still unclear. This worksheet consists of a simple what-if model that calculates the monthly profit/loss based on several variables.

2. See what-if analysis in action by entering different values in cells **B3** and **B4**.

3. Look over the example on the New Product What-If worksheet, paying attention to the use of cell references in formulas and functions. Identify how many units will need to be sold for Premiere to break even on its new product line. If you need help, hold the mouse pointer

over any cell containing a red triangle in the upper right corner until its comment appears.

4. Save the workbook.

Analyzing Monthly Profits for Premiere Foods

The supermarket business is generally considered to be a low-profit margin industry. On average, the profit margin for a supermarket ranges from 1% to 2%. However, due to changes in demographics and consumer demand, supermarkets that specialize in organic, local, and artisanal foods earn a higher profit margin—between 3.5% and 6%. Analysis of the 2015 revenue and expenses for Premiere Foods has been started on the Profit Analysis worksheet. Use the following steps to complete the analysis.

1. Click the **Profit Analysis** worksheet tab.

Using the AutoFill Feature

2. Select cell **A5**. Notice the Fill handle in the lower-right corner of the cell.

3. Hover your mouse pointer over the fill handle, noticing that the pointer changes shape to a thin black crosshair. Drag the **Fill handle** down to cell A16. Notice that Excel automatically filled each cell with the month name.

AutoFill is a feature that can make entering data that follows a pattern into cells very easy. Excel recognized the data in cell A5 and assumed that the desired result of dragging the fill handle was to list the months in sequential order. By default, Autofill also copies down the formatting, which may or may not be desired. You can modify the behavior of AutoFill by clicking the Auto Fill Options ⊞ button.

4. Click the **Auto Fill Options** button, near the lower-right corner of cell A16, and then select **Fill Without Formatting**.

13	September	20,653.56	39,384.74
14	October		
15	November		
16	December		
17			

- ○ Copy Cells
- ◉ Fill Series
- ○ Fill Formatting Only
- ○ Fill Without Formatting
- ○ Fill Months
- ○ Flash Fill

The revenues for the month of October have not yet been entered into the spreadsheet. Let's assume that the October revenues are the same as the September revenues. The Fill handle can also be used to copy data from multiple cells at once.

5. Select cells **B13:D13**. Drag the **Fill handle** in cell D13 down to D14. Notice that the data and formatting in all three of the selected cells were copied down to row 14.

The monthly expenses for all three Premiere Foods locations are listed in the table to the right of the revenue table. The expenses for the month of October have not yet been entered into the spreadsheet.

6. Based on the expense data in the spreadsheet, in cells **F14:J14** enter reasonable estimates for the various expenses. Notice that after you enter the data into the cells, the formatting differs from the other data.

7. Select **F14:J16**. On the Home tab, in the Number group, click **Comma Style** 🔲 to format the cells with an appropriate style. Since you also formatted the cells for November and December, when data are entered into those cells, they will already be formatted appropriately.

8. Save the workbook.

Analysis of Monthly Expenses

As part of the profit analysis, you have been asked to conduct some additional analysis on the expenses using various mathematical functions.

1. Click cell **F17** and type = (an equals sign). When entering functions or formulas in Excel, an equals sign is required.

2. Type **Av** and notice the tool tip that appears below the cell with various functions that begin with Av. Continue typing until the AVERAGE function is highlighted, or use the down arrow or the mouse to highlight this function.

3. Once the AVERAGE function is highlighted in the tool tip, press **Tab** to insert the function into the cell. The AVERAGE function calculates the average of a range of numbers. In Excel, the numbers are most often contained within a range of cells.

4. Use your mouse to select the range **F5:F16** and then press **Enter**. The average of the monthly utility expenses is calculated. Notice that since you included the empty cells of F15 and F16, the function will automatically update once those values are entered.

5. In a similar fashion, calculate the minimum monthly utility expense amount using the **MIN** function in cell **F18**.

6. In cell **F19**, use the **MAX** function to calculate the maximum monthly utility expense amount.

7. In cell **F20**, use the **SUM** function to calculate the total amount spent on utilities for the year.

8. Select cells **F17:F20**, then drag the Fill handle in cell **F20** across to cell **J20**. Notice that each of the functions was copied across its respective row and the cells referenced in the original functions shifted to the right appropriately so that each column of expenses has the correct calculation.

Some values may be too large for Excel to display correctly, and as a result, you may see a series of pound signs (####).

9. To fix this, the columns need to be resized. Click the line in between two column heading letters to AutoFit the column width to the content.

10. Save the workbook.

Calculating Monthly Profit/Loss

An organization's profit is calculated by subtracting total expenses from total revenue for a particular period of time (e.g., monthly, quarterly, annually).

1. Click cell **K5**. Insert a **SUM** function to calculate the total revenue from all three of Premiere's locations. Then **subtract** from the total revenue the total expenses using another **SUM** function. Be sure to end

each SUM function with a closing parenthesis, as Excel will not do this automatically when the formula contains more than a single function. The result is the total profit earned for the month of January.

2. Drag the **Fill handle** of cell **K5** down through **K16**. If necessary, AutoFit the column so that all values are visible.

3. Save the workbook.

Conducting Analysis on a Sample of Employees

Managers at Premiere Foods are auditing a random sampling of current and former employees. The data are located in columns M-O on the Profit Analysis worksheet. You will use the COUNT and COUNTA functions to answer the questions about the sample in cells M32:M34.

1. Click cell **M32** and type **=COUNTA(M5:M29)** to calculate the number of employees in the sample data.

The data in column M are considered text data. Therefore, the COUNTA function is necessary to determine the number of employees in the random sample. The COUNTA function counts the number of nonblank cells in a range.

Note: Using the range **N5:N29** would also be acceptable.

2. In cell **M33**, type **=COUNT(O5:O29)**.

The dates in column O are considered a type of numerical data. Accordingly, the COUNT function is necessary to determine the number of employees in the random sample who have left the company. The COUNT function counts the number of cells in a range that contain numbers. The function ignores blank cells or cells that contain nonnumeric data.

3. In cell **M34**, use a combination of the **COUNTA** and **COUNT** functions to calculate the number of employees in the random sample who are still employed.

4. Save the workbook.

Diving Deeper into the AutoFill Feature

The AutoFill feature is useful for entering data into a worksheet in a variety of situations, such as filling in months of the year, days of the week, and the like. AutoFill can also be used to extend any basic pattern. Simply type the first two values of the pattern into two adjacent cells, select the two cells, and then drag the Fill handle to repeat the pattern.

1. Click the **Explore AutoFill** worksheet tab.

2. Use your knowledge of the AutoFill feature to fill the desired pattern down each column.

3. Save the workbook.

Understanding How Formatting Changes Meaning

In Excel, how a numeric value is formatted can dramatically change its meaning. For example, the number 0.75 can mean a variety of different things depending on how it is formatted. The following table shows how the value 0.75 is represented with several different formats applied.

Number	Currency	Percentage	Time
0.75	$0.75	75%	6:00 PM

1. On the Explore AutoFill worksheet, examine the values in cells E5:H6. The cells in each row contain the same value with different formatting styles applied.

Using appropriate formatting is crucial in developing clear and concise spreadsheet models that are interpreted correctly by others.

REVIEW PROBLEMS

Review Problem 1

The Review1 worksheet contains monthly sales volume data for Premiere Foods by store location.

1. In cell **G5**, use the appropriate function to calculate the total sales volume for the month of January.

2. Use **AutoFill** to copy the function down to cell **G16**.

3. In cell **D17**, use the appropriate function to calculate the total yearly sales volume for the IL store.

4. Use **AutoFill** to copy the function over to **F17**.

Review Problem 2

The Review2 worksheet contains a model to help you analyze your grade in the course.

1. Use the AutoFill feature to enter the graded item titles into cells **C6:C13**, **C15**, and **C19**.

2. In cells **E5:E16** and **E18:E20**, enter the number of points you have earned on the graded items. If you do not yet know the points earned on the midterm exams, type in estimated values. For other graded items not yet completed, leave points earned blank. Once scores are posted, you can change these values to see more accurate results.

3. Change the points possible values in column D to **0** for any graded items that have not yet been completed.

4. In cells **D22** and **E22**, calculate the total points possible and the total points earned.

5. In cell **E24**, calculate the percentage of points earned by entering a formula to divide the points earned by the points possible.

Conducting a What-If Analysis to Determine Final Grade

1. In cell **D15**, type **200** as the points possible for Lab Practical 2.

2. In cell **D19**, type **80** as the points possible for xP Exam 2.

3. In cells **E15** and **E19**, type in various values for points earned on the final exams to conduct a what-if analysis on your final grade.

What-if analysis is one of several tools used to support decision making in business. How might the results of your what-if analysis influence your behavior in the course? Will you plan to attend office hours or the help lab more often? Will you spend more time practicing with Excel?

Knowledge Check 11

Basic Functions

File Needed

KnowledgeCheck_11.xlsx

Every year, Electronics Products Corp. sends a group of sales reps and interns to the national Consumer Electronics Show (CES) in Las Vegas, the world's largest consumer electronics show. On the CES Expenses worksheet, enter appropriate formulas and functions in the shaded cells to calculate the cost of this trip.

Note: When calculating the duration of the trip (in cells B27 and B28), assume that the group will arrive the day before the show and leave after the show on the last day. Since the show opens on January 6 and ends on January 8, this means that this will be a four-day, three-night trip. Use the dates in cells B2 and B3 to solve for number of days. Then use number of days minus one to solve for number of nights.

Cell Referencing and Named Ranges
Chapter 13

Outline

- Research & Exploration: Research and Define Terms Related to Cell Referencing and Named Ranges, Research the ROUND and INT Functions, Use Different Cell Referencing styles in Functions and Expressions

- In-Depth Case Application: Estimate Final Grade Based on Predicted Exam Scores, Conditionally Format Values, Group Worksheets and Apply Formatting to Several Worksheets at Once, Sum Values from Multiple Worksheets, Create Named Ranges, Calculate Order Quantity and Cost Using Named Ranges

- Review Problems: Practice Grouping Worksheets, Use Different Cell Referencing Styles, Use Various Functions to Summarize Sales, Knowledge Check 12

Objectives

- Create and use named ranges in functions and expressions.

- Use appropriate cell referencing in functions and expressions so that solutions can be copied across columns and down rows.

- Use grouped worksheets to format and calculate expressions across multiple worksheets.

- Understand the difference between the ROUND and INT functions, using each when appropriate.

RESEARCH & EXPLORATION

Research

A cell is the intersection of a column and a row. The default cell referencing in Excel identifies the columns by letters and the rows by numbers. Thus the cell reference A1 refers to the cell marking the intersection of the first column and first row in a worksheet. Another cell referencing style is "R1C1," whereby the row number and column number are identified directly. The cell reference R1C1 is interpreted as row 1 and column 1 and refers to the same location as A1.

A workbook usually has multiple worksheets; cells within the workbook can be referenced using the worksheet name and the cell reference. For example, 'Main Menu'!D1 refers to cell D1 on the Main Menu worksheet in a workbook.

Cell references are used in functions so that if the values in the cell change, the formulas will automatically update and perform the correct calculations. Functions can be written once and then copied or autofilled down or across a worksheet or multiple worksheets. When this is done, cells often need to be absolutely referenced so that the formula always uses the values in those cells when performing the calculation.

Research more about types of cell references, named ranges, and the ROUND and INT functions by reading the following articles:

- Create or change a cell reference

- Using references in Excel formulas

- Using names in Excel formulas

- Select one or multiple worksheets

- ROUND function

- INT function

After researching, you should be able to define the following terms:

- Relative cell reference

- Absolute cell reference

- Mixed cell reference

- Grouped worksheets

- 3D cell references

- Named ranges

- ROUND function

- INT function

Exploration

Navigate to your files, open **Class13-CellReferencing.xlsx**, and then complete the following explorations using the concepts you researched.

Creating a Named Range from a Single Cell

Create a named range referring to cell D1 on the Main Menu worksheet.

1. Select cell **D1** on the Main Menu worksheet.

2. Click the **name box** in the upper left corner of Excel, type **CurrentDate**, and then press **Enter**.

   #### Troubleshooting
   If you ever need to edit or delete a named range, find the Name Manager on the Formulas tab, and then use it to update your named ranges.

Summarizing Sales by Sales Rep and Brand

On the **RE1 worksheet**, the sales revenue for brands of products that Premiere sells are listed for sales representatives Brown and Jones. Find the total sales for each of these sales reps and for each brand.

3. Click cell **D21**, then type **=SUM(D4:D20)**

4. Drag the AutoFill handle of **D21** across to **E21**.

Look at the formula that is now in E21, observing how the cell addresses from the function you entered in D21 changed as the cell content was filled across to E21.

5. Click cell **F4**, then type **=SUM(D4:E4)**

6. Double-click the **AutoFill** handle of **F4** to copy the function down to **F20**.

Look at the formula that is now in F20, observing how the cell addresses from the function you entered in F4 changed as the cell content was filled down to F20.

From your research, you should realize that these examples used relative cell referencing.

Calculating Sales Rep Commission

The **RE2 worksheet** contains the sales data for Premiere product brands sold by three sales representatives: Brown, Jones, and Smith. This worksheet also contains the commission rate that the sales reps earn in D1. Calculate the commission earned by each sales rep. Write one formula in D22 that can be autofilled across to F22.

1. Click in cell **D22**, then type **=D21*D1**

2. Drag the autofill handle of **D22** across to **F22**.

Excel returns a commission amount of "$ -" for Jones and Smith. This is how $0 is shown when cells are formatted as Accounting. Why is Excel calculating a commission of $0 for Jones and Smith? Click in cell **E22** to look at the calculation that Excel is trying to perform. Excel used relative cell referencing, and as the formula was copied across using the autofill handle, the cell reference for the rep total changed to cell E21, as it should have; however, the cell reference for the commission rate changed as well. The commission rate is in cell D1, and that cell must always be referenced even if the formula is copied to another cell or range of cells.

Absolute cell referencing involves marking or anchoring a cell address within a formula/function so that Excel does NOT automatically adjust the column or row number when copying down a row or across a column. Use dollar signs ($) to anchor the column and the row of the cell reference that needs to remain constant (e.g., $A$1).

3. Click in cell **D22**, then create an absolute cell reference to D1 by typing a dollar sign before both the D and the 1. Alternatively, click on D1 in the formula, then press the F4 key on your keyboard to change to an absolute cell reference to cell D1. Your formula should now look like **=D21*$D$1**. Press **Enter**.

4. Copy the formula across to **F22**.

Changing the Rate for Sales Rep Commission

The **RE3 worksheet** contains a small table that will show how the three sales representatives' commissions will change with increasing commission rates. You need to type one formula in **E7** that can be copied both down and across the table to calculate each sales rep's commission based on the differing rates.

Think about the math that needs to occur for this formula to work. Each sales rep's total, in D7:D9, needs to be multiplied by the rates in E6:H6. In E7, you will write one formula, and when you autofill it across, you need the reference to the rate values to change columns, but you want to continue referencing the rep total in column D. When you autofill the same formula down, you need the reference to the rep total to change rows but want to continue referencing the rate values in row 6.

Dollar signs can be used to anchor parts of the cell reference—the column or row, whichever needs to remain constant (e.g., A$1 holds row 1 constant). Anchoring just the column or the row in a cell reference is referred to as mixed cell referencing. You can use the F4 key to toggle through the four possible anchoring configurations.

1. Click in cell **E7**, then type **=D7**

2. Press the **F4 key** on your keyboard three times so that the dollar sign is only in front of the D to keep column D in the formula.

3. Continue the formula: **=$D7*E6**

4. Press the **F4 key** on your keyboard twice so that the dollar sign is only in front of the 6, keeping row 6 in the formula.

5. Your formula should now look like this: **=$D7*E$6**

6. Press **Enter**.

7. Autofill the formula down to **E9** and then across to **H9**.

Referencing Cells on Other Worksheets

At the beginning of this exploration, you created a named range on the Main Menu worksheet for the data in cell D1. Cells on worksheets that are all in the same workbook can be referenced on any worksheet in the workbook.

1. On the **RE3 worksheet**, in cell **A3**, begin a function by typing **=**

2. Click the **Main Menu** worksheet tab.

3. Click cell **D1**.

4. Press **Enter**.

Notice that when you click in cell A3, the formula reads **=CurrentDate**, because Main Menu D1 is the named range called CurrentDate. When named ranges are created and the cell(s) that make up that named range are used in a function, Excel replaces the cell references with the named range text.

IN-DEPTH CASE APPLICATION

Estimating Final Grade

The graded items in K201 are listed in cells **B3:B17** along with the points possible for each item. Below the graded items is a table that will allow you to estimate your final grade based on possible scores on the Excel Exam and on xP Exam 2.

1. In cells **C3:C15**, type in the points earned for each of the graded items for which you have feedback. For those graded items for which you do not have feedback, enter estimated points earned.

2. In cell **D23**, enter a formula that will calculate your final percentage in the class based on the total points earned in C18, the possible scores on the last two exams, which are in cells C23 and D22, and the total points possible in K201, which is in D18. The formula you should type is **=SUM(C18,C23,D22)/D18**

3. To copy the formula across the possible xP Exam 2 scores and down the possible Excel exam scores, the cells referenced need to be anchored as either absolute or mixed cell references.

4. Once you have applied the appropriate cell referencing, fill the cell content across and down to **H28**.

Emphasizing Values

You most likely need to earn a C or better in this course. Apply conditional formatting to D23:H28 so that values <=73% will have a Red fill color and White type.

1. Select **D23:H28**.

2. On the **Home** tab, in the **Styles** group, click **Conditional Formatting**, and then click **New Rule**.

3. In the New Formatting Rule dialog box, click **Format only cells that contain**.

4. Click the **Between** drop-down list, then select **less than or equal to**.

5. In the space to the right, type **.73**.

6. Click the **Format** button, then choose **white** for the type color.

7. Click the **Fill** tab, then choose **red** for the fill color.

8. Click **OK**, then **OK** again.

Working with Grouped Worksheets

Grouping worksheets improves efficiency and consistency throughout the workbook by allowing you to make changes to one worksheet and have those same changes apply to all grouped worksheets.

Use the following steps to group the Quarter 1 Sales through Quarter 4 Sales worksheets:

1. Click the **Quarter 1 Sales** worksheet tab.

2. Hold down the **Shift** key.

3. Click the **Quarter 4 Sales** worksheet tab.

4. Release the **Shift** key.

If you have done this correctly, you should see the text "[Group]" across the top of the Excel workbook, in the title bar. The text in the tabs for these worksheets is also bold. Once the worksheets are grouped, any edits made will be applied to all of the worksheets in the group: if content is added, deleted, or formatted on one worksheet, the changes will occur on every worksheet in the group.

Note: *The Control key can be used to select individual worksheets for a group if the necessary sheets are not in contiguous order.*

Formatting Grouped Worksheets

Fill content and format across the grouped worksheets by using the following steps:

1. Select **A5:D5** on the **Quarter 1 Sales** worksheet.

2. On the **Home** tab of the ribbon, in the **Editing** group, click **Fill** to see the Fill menu, then select **Across Worksheets**.

3. In the Fill Across Worksheets dialog box, make sure **All** is selected so that both the content and the format will be filled, and then click **OK**.

Centering across Selection

With **A5:D5** still selected, format the titles on all of the worksheets simultaneously by choosing to center the title text across the selection of cells.

1. Right-click on the selected cells, then click **Format Cells**.

2. In the Format Cells dialog box, click the **Alignment** tab, click the **Horizontal** dropdown menu, select **Center Across Selection**, and then click **OK**.

Using Formulas and Functions with Grouped Worksheets

Grouping worksheets together not only can save time in formatting but also can save time in writing formulas and functions.

1. Select cell **C7** on any one of the Quarter Sales worksheets, then type **=ROUND(B7,2)**—this ROUND function rounds the sales value in B7 to two digits to the right of the decimal point.

2. Format the cell as **Accounting**.

3. Double-click the **AutoFill handle** in the lower right corner of the cell to copy the function down the column.

4. Click through the other Quarter Sales worksheets, verifying that the ROUND function you just typed has been applied to all four worksheets.

Ungrouping and Customizing Worksheets

1. Ungroup the worksheets by right-clicking any of the worksheet tabs within the group and selecting **Ungroup Sheets**.

2. Customize the titles on each worksheet by changing the quarter number in cell A5 from Quarter 1 to **Quarter 2**, **Quarter 3**, and **Quarter 4** as appropriate.

Summarizing Sales Using 3D Cell Referencing

On the Sales Summary worksheet, in cell **B6**, use the SUM function to add the **rounded sales values** that are in cell C7 on the four **Quarter Sales** worksheets.

1. Click in cell **B6**, then type = SUM(

2. Click the tab for the **Quarter 1 Sales** worksheet.

3. Hold the **Shift** key, then click the tab for the **Quarter 4 Sales** worksheet

4. The four worksheets are now grouped, and the function in the formula bar should now read as follows:
=Sum('Quarter 1 Sales:Quarter 4 Sales'!

5. Click cell **C7 to reference the rounded sales value.**

6. The function in the formula bar now reads as follows:

   =SUM('Quarter 1 Sales:Quarter 4 Sales'!C7

7. Release the **Shift** key.

8. Click at the end of the function in the formula bar, type the closing parenthesis, and then press **Enter**.

   When you press Enter, Excel will take you back to where you began typing the function, Sales Summary B6. The function in cell **B6** should be

   =SUM('Quarter 1 Sales:Quarter 4 Sales'!C7)

9. Format cell B6 as **Accounting**, then double-click the **AutoFill** handle of **B6** to copy the function down the column.

10. Since number of transactions is adjacent to sales values on the Quarter Sales worksheets, autofill the function in B6 across to column **C** to calculate the Total Number of Transactions in cell **C6**.

11. Notice that the Accounting format also autofilled across with the values. Change the format of C6 to **Number** with **0** decimal places.

12. Double-click the **AutoFill** handle of C6 to copy the function down the column.

Managing Inventory

Creating Named Ranges

On the Inventory Management worksheet, create named ranges for the data through the following steps:

1. Select the cell range **A5:I317**.

2. Click the **Formulas** tab, in the Defined Names group, click **Create from Selection**.

3. In the Create Names from Selection dialog box, deselect the Left Column check box, ensure that **Top row** is selected, and then click **OK**.

4. Click the **name box** dropdown in the top-left corner to see the named ranges listed in alphabetical order.

If a created named range needs to be edited or deleted, click **Name Manager**, located on the Formulas tab in the Defined Names group, to view details about the created named ranges.

Calculating Number of Items to Order

The order quantity should be the number of items needed to increase the units in stock to the max units possible.

1. Click cell **H6**, then type the expression **=MaxUnits-InStock**

2. Copy the expression down the column.

   Notice that there are some negative values, which means that Premiere currently has more in stock than it would like. Premiere cannot return items to the wholesaler, nor does having -1 as the value for OrderQuantity make sense. Premiere simply does not need to order any of those products that have negative values for OrderQuantity.

3. To correct the negative values, nest the foregoing expression within the MAX function: **=MAX(MaxUnits-InStock,0)**

4. Autofill the expression down again, noticing that the negative values become 0.

Calculating Total Cost of Ordering Items

Calculate the order total given the order quantity in column H and the wholesale cost in column E:

1. Click in the cell **I6**, then type the expression **=OrderQuantity*WholesaleCost**

2. Format **I6** as **Currency**.

3. Fill the expression down the column.

REVIEW PROBLEMS

Review Problem 1

Calculating Employee Sales for Premiere's Incentive Program

To encourage sales, Premiere Foods has instituted a sales incentive program. Each store employee was assigned a sales goal of 15% more than his or her total sales from the year before. All employees who reached this goal will receive an award of some sort (the higher the sales, the better the award). Your job is to summarize the results of the sales incentive program.

Enter formulas and functions, and format the **Review 1 worksheet**. As you do this, pay close attention to proper cell addressing so that you can copy each formula or function to other cells as necessary.

In cell **H9**, use the appropriate function(s) to calculate the total actual sales in 2015 given the 2015 quarterly sales in the range **D9:G9**.

1. Total 2015 Actual for each employee is the sum of Actual sales for each quarter. Write the function so that it can be filled down the column. Format the cell as **Currency**.

In cell **I9**, use the appropriate function(s) to calculate the 2015 goal for the employee in column B.

2. Use the actual 2014 Sales in column C and the percentage shown in cell C6 to calculate the 2015 goal. The 2015 Goal for each employee is equal to the employee's 2014 Sales multiplied by (1+Goal % Increase).

3. Round the calculation to 2 decimal places, and format the value as **Currency**. Write the function so that it can be filled down the column and so that it correctly calculates the 2015 goal even if the goal percentage changes from what is currently shown.

4. In **J9**, write an expression that calculates the percentage of the goal that was achieved. The percentage reached for each employee is equal to the Total 2015 Actual divided by the 2015 Goal.

5. Round the calculation to 4 decimal places.

6. Format the value as Percentage with 2 decimal places.

7. Write the formula so that it can be filled down the column.

Conditional formatting has been put into place already so that when this calculation is completed correctly, shading will be applied for those employees who met the goal. For example, if the actual 2015 sales in H9 was $17,449.58 and the goal in I9 was $18,538.28, then the percentage of the goal that was achieved was approximately 94.13%. This employee did not reach 100% of the sales goal, so the result will not be shaded. A total of 7 employees met or exceeded the goal.

Review Problem 2

Summarizing Quarterly Sales

Premiere has sales data from 2015 on the four Review 2 Qtr worksheets.

1. Group the worksheets from **Review 2 Qtr1** through **Review 2 Qtr4**.

2. In the cell **'Review 2 Qtr1'!C5**, use the **INT** function to round the employee's sales down to the nearest integer.

3. Format the value as **Currency**. Write the function so that it can be filled down the column.

4. **AutoFill** the function down the column; **ungroup** the worksheets when finished.

Use the Review 2 Sales Summary worksheet to calculate the 2015 goal for these sales representatives and analyze whether they achieved their goals.

1. In cell **C8**, write an expression that calculates a percent increase goal for each employee. Use the percent value from **'Review 1'!C6** and the employee's **2014 Sales** in column B of the Review 2 Sales Summary worksheet.

2. Format the value as **Accounting**. Write the expression so that it can be copied down the column.

3. In cell **D8**, use the appropriate function to calculate the total sales each employee had across all 4 quarters using 3D cell references to **C5** on the Review 2 quarterly worksheets.

4. Format the value as **Accounting**. AutoFill the function down the column.

5. In cell **E8**, use an IF function to return the word Yes or the word No based on the following condition:

If the Actual 2015 Annual Sales in column D is at least the 2015 Goal in column C, then the function should return the word **Yes**. Otherwise, the function should return the word **No**.

6. **Autofill** the function down column E.

7. If you have completed all parts of this problem correctly, the Yes rows will be filled with Background 1, Darker 15% coloring.

The next two problems ask you to use a given image and create formulas to perform calculations. You may find it helpful to input these data on new worksheets in order to construct the formulas and check your work.

To insert a new worksheet to the right of the Review 2 Sales Summary worksheet, click on the **New Sheet** icon, located to the right of the tab

for the last worksheet: ⊕ .

You can then rename the new worksheet by right-clicking on its tab, selecting Rename, and typing Review 3. You can follow this same procedure to create a new worksheet for Review 4.

Review Problem 3

Use the following image to consider the various types of cell referencing needed to perform the calculations for Tax and Total Cost:

	A	B	C	D
1	Sales Tax	7%		
2				
3	Transaction	Price	Tax	Total Cost
4	1	$ 59.99		
5	2	$ 18.29		
6	3	$ 523.25		
7	4	$ 119.99		
8	5	$6,432.12		

Be able to answer the following questions:

1. What formula would you use to calculate the tax in cell C4 so that you could autofill that formula to C5:C8?

2. What type(s) of cell referencing are used in the formula that would calculate tax?

3. What formula would you use to calculate the total cost in D4 so that you could autofill that formula to D5:D8?

4. What type(s) of cell referencing are used in the formula that would calculate the total cost?

Review Problem 4

Use the following image to consider the various types of cell referencing needed to calculate the discounted prices based on the discount rates in column B and the original prices in row 2.

	A	B	C	D	E	F
1				Original Prices		
2			$ 19.99	$ 29.99	$ 39.99	$ 49.99
3	Discount Rates	10%				
4		20%				
5		25%				
6		30%				
7		40%				

Be able to answer the following questions:

1. What formula would you enter in C3 to calculate the discounted price so that you could autofill the formula down and across to F7?

2. What type(s) of cell referencing are used in the formula that would calculate the discounted price?

Knowledge Check 12

File Needed

KnowledgeCheck_12.xlsx

Electronics Products Corporation Product Line Analysis

The KnowledgeCheck_12.xlsx file contains sales revenue data from 2012 for an electronics company. The data are separated by location with a worksheet for each of the three locations: OH Store, IN Store, and Online. Each location's worksheet contains the sales revenue per month per category as well as the total sales for each month, for each category, and overall.

The Category Goals worksheet contains the 2013 Percent Increase Goal values for each category.

Use the data on these worksheets to perform the following tasks.

Insert, Rename, and Fill Across Worksheets

1. Insert a new worksheet to the right of the Online worksheet, then use **Fill Across Worksheets** to transfer the contents of the Online worksheet to it. This new worksheet will eventually calculate monthly averages for each category across the three locations.

2. Name the worksheet **All-Averages**.

Edit New Worksheet and Use 3D Cell Referencing

1. On the **All-Averages worksheet**, edit cell **B1** to clarify the contents of the worksheet.

2. Cell **B3** on this worksheet should contain the average of cell B3 on the OH store, IN store, and Online worksheets.

3. Copy the function in cell **B3** through cell **M12**.

4. On the All-Averages sheet, delete the row and the column labeled Total. (This is row 13 and column N.)

Insert, Rename, and Fill Across Worksheets . . . Again

1. In a similar manner, to the right of the All-Averages sheet, create another worksheet to calculate the range (the difference between the highest and the lowest value) across the three locations. Fill the contents of the All-Averages sheet to this new sheet.

2. Name the new worksheet **Ranges**.

3. Edit cell **B1** to clarify the contents of the worksheet, and in B3, compute the range statistics (the difference between the max and min for each category from each location). Copy the function in B3 through cell M12.

Group Worksheets and Calculate Goals

On the OH Store, IN Store, and Online worksheets, underneath the monthly revenue values for 2012, calculate monthly goals for 2013.

1. Copy the category names from cells **A3:A12**, then paste them to cells **A18:A27**.

2. Cell **B16** should read **2013 Goals**.

3. Cells **B17:M17** should read **Jan, Feb**, and so on to **Dec**.

4. Cell **B18** should calculate the sales goal for January for the Camcorder category on the basis of 2012 revenue for that category and the percent increase goal for that category in 2013, as given on the **Category Goals** sheet. Do this in such a way that you complete all three worksheets at once and so that cell B18 can be copied through cell M27.

5. Format all the 2013 goal values as **Currency**.

6. Ungroup the worksheets.

After completing these steps, go to the course website to answer Koinearning questions.

Conditional Aggregate and Date Functions

Chapter 14

Outline

- Research & Exploration: Research Conditional Aggregate Functions, Practice Date Functions

- In-Depth Case Application: Practice Conditional Aggregate Functions

- Review Problems: Practice Conditional Aggregate and Date Functions

Objectives

- Work with dates using TODAY and DATEDIF date functions.

- Solve problems using conditional aggregate functions (COUNTIF, COUNTIFS, SUMIF, AVERAGEIF).

RESEARCH & EXPLORATION

Research

Research the following Excel functions. Be sure to take advantage of the online Microsoft Support at http://office.microsoft.com.

Excel Functions

- TODAY

- COUNTIF

- SUMIF

- AVERAGEIF

For each function, describe what it does, noting its syntax as well as providing an example of its use:

Function	Definition	Syntax	Example
TODAY			
COUNTIF			
SUMIF			
AVERAGEIF			

Exploration

Calculating Age

Navigate to your K201 files, open Chapter14-ConditionalAggregates.xlsx, and then complete the RE worksheet using the following information.

In Excel, a function called DATEDIF can calculate ages in the units of either years, months, or days. Of course, days can be calculated through simple subtraction as well. Excel sees a date by the **date serial**—the number of days since 1/1/1900. Thus the later the date is in time, the larger the number. Taking tomorrow's date and subtracting today's date would result in a value of 1. However, months differ in the number of days per month. Years differ in the number of days per year because of leap years. Accordingly, DATEDIF is needed for age calculations in months or years.

DATEDIF calculates months and years in whole units and does not round. For example, when calculating a person's age, someone who is 20.9 years old will be 20 years old—this person would not be let into a bar yet where the drinking age is 21.

DATEDIF is the one function that has no support either in the tag or the help. DATEDIF takes the following form:

=DATEDIF(EarlierDate,LaterDate,Units)

The first argument should be a cell reference to the earlier date in time. The second argument should be a cell reference to the later date in time. If the later date in time is today's date, best practice dictates cell referencing to a cell rather than nesting a TODAY() function. The last argument should be "Y", "M", or "D", according to the units needed of years, months, or days. An example could be the following:

=DATEDIF(B8,$C$5,"Y")

where B8 contains the date a person started working at a company, C5 contains today's date, and you want to know how many years the person has been with the company.

Last, DATEDIF differs between Access and Excel. Access will calculate the number of years without regard for the day. For example, a person born on Dec 1, 2015 will be considered a 1-year-old on Jan 1, 2016. Accordingly, do not use this function in Access unless that is what you intend.

1. In the Chapter14-ConditionalAggregates.xlsx workbook, on the RE1 worksheet, click cell **C5**, then type **=TODAY()** and press **Enter**.

2. Right-click cell **C5** to view the cell editing shortcut menu. Select **Format Cells**.

3. In the Format Cells dialog box, select **Date** as the Category and **14-Mar-2012** as the Type. Note you may have to scroll to find the correct type. Click **OK**.

4. Notice cells B8:B137 are the date serial. Select cells **B8:B137**. On the Home tab in the Number group, select the **Short Date** format from the Number Format drop-down menu.

5. If needed, select cells **B8:B137** again. On the Home tab in the Clipboard group, click the ⬚ **Format Painter.**

6. After clicking on the Format Painter, select and drag the paintbrush icon over cells **D8:D137**. Notice the format painter paints only once. To paint more than once, double-click the Format Painter. Once all painting is done, press the Escape key to stop.

7. Click in cell **C8**, then use the DATEDIF function to calculate the age (in years) for Florence Epley by typing **=DATEDIF(B8,$C$5,"Y")**. Autofill the formula down to **C137**.

Troubleshooting
The tag did not show the arguments for the DATEDIF! Unfortunately, DATEDIF does not show in the tag or in the help. You will need to memorize the three arguments.

8. Notice that Age has two decimals and that all decimals are zeros. The DATEDIF automatically returns whole years. Select cells **C8:C137**. On the Home tab in the Number group, click the **decrease decimal** button twice.

9. Click in cell **E8**, then use the appropriate function to calculate the number of months since the member last completed a transaction. AutoFill the formula down to **E137**. Format the values to zero decimals.

When you are finished, save and close the file, then bring your work to the next lab meeting.

IN-DEPTH CASE APPLICATION

Calculating Transaction Age in Weeks

The DATEDIF function allows only years, months, and days as units. What if you want to know how many weeks? You can calculate the number of days—either with the DATEDIF function or with simple subtraction. Then, you can divide the number of days by 7. There are always 7 days in a week, so it can be treated as a constant. However, when the number of days is divided by 7, decimals will be introduced. Units of time should always be expressed in whole units—not rounded. Thus, an integer function is needed to remove the decimal. You cannot just format it to zero decimal places.

1. In the Chapter14-ConditionalAggregates.xlsx workbook, on the Transaction Age worksheet, enter a function in cell **C5** that will always return the current date.

2. Select cells **B8:B137**, then format them to **Short Date**.

3. Select cell **C8**, then enter **=DATEDIF(B8,$C$5,"D")** and press **Enter**. Notice it now returns the number of whole days.

4. Edit cell **C8** to divide by **7** at the end. Notice a decimal is now reintroduced.

5. Edit cell **C8** to put an **INT** function around the calculation. The final formula should be =INT(DATEDIF(B8,$C$5,"D")/7).

6. Select cell **C8**, then format to **2** decimals. Then copy the formula down to cell **C137**.

CRM Training and Using Conditional Summaries

For training in an up-and-coming customer relationship management (CRM) system, you have been asked to identify the number of employees who meet certain criteria.

To do this, you will need the COUNTIF function: =COUNTIF(range, criterion)

The COUNTIF function tells you how many cells in a range meet a given criterion. If the criterion is anything but a simple numeric value or cell reference, it must be placed in quotes. Note the use/nonuse of quotes in the examples at the top of the next page.

=COUNTIF(A1:A25,100) returns the number of cells that contain the value 100.

=COUNTIF(A1:A25,"<100") returns the number of cells that contain a value less than 100.

=COUNTIF(A1:A25,"Local Farmer") returns the number of cells that read Local Farmer.

=COUNTIF(A1:A25,B2) returns the number of cells that are equal to B2.

1. On the CRM Training worksheet, create range names in **B5:E56** on the COUNTIF worksheet, using the **top row** for the names. Then use the range names in appropriate functions to answer the four questions to the right of the table, which appear hereafter.

How Many Employees Are in Division 3?
2. Click in the cell I9, then enter **=COUNTIF(Division,3)**

How Many Employees Have Attained Expert Level?
3. Click in the cell I12, then enter
   =COUNTIF(Proficiency_level,"Expert")

   Notice how Excel replaced the blank space between the words Proficiency and level with the underscore character. Excel does not allow the use of the blank space character within a named range.

How Many Employees Are Not in Division 2?
4. Click in the cell I18, then enter **=COUNTIF(Division,"<>2")**

How Many Employees Have Completed between 10 and 20 Hours of Training?

This problem can be solved in two different ways. You could use a COUNTIF to count the number of employees who worked at least 10 hours and then subtract the number of employees who worked more than 20 hours using another COUNTIF function. However, a more efficient approach would be to use the COUNTIFS function. The **COUNTIFS** function allows for multiple criteria on one or more ranges of cells.

The COUNTIFS Function
=COUNTIFS(criteria_range1,critera1,[criteria_range2,critera2],...)

5. Click cell I15, then enter
   =COUNTIFS(Training_hours_completed,">=10",Training_hours_completed,"<=20")

6. Click cell **I15**, then enter
   =COUNTIFS(Division,1,Proficiency_level,"Expert")

Sales by City Worksheet

To analyze sales, you need to sum up sales by employees, by city, and by large orders. You have the sales numbers, but you will need to use a SUMIF to get the data you need.

The SUMIF function =SUMIF(range,criteria,[sum_range])

The SUMIF function calculates a sum based on a criterion:

- **range:** The data that will be evaluated.
- **criteria:** The criterion used to evaluate the range.
- **sum_range:** The actual cells to sum. If omitted, the range argument will be used in the summation.

What Is the Sum of All Large Orders?

1. Click cell **C4**, then enter **=SUMIF(F7:F4045,">=1500",F7:F4045)**

What Is the Sum of All Orders for Each City?

2. Click cell **J7**, then enter **=SUMIF(C7:C4045,I7,F7:F4045)**

3. Copy the formula down to **J1005**. Notice that some of the values now do not match the correct values. What is causing this problem? The ranges need to have absolute references.

4. Click cell **J7**, then enter **$s** appropriately so the ranges will not change when copied. Recopy the formula down to **J1005**.

You will be using this worksheet on the next few worksheets. You realize using name ranges would be easier than using 3D Cell References with appropriate $s.

5. Select **A6:F4045**, then create named ranges from the selection with the headers in the **Top Row**.

6. Select cell **J7**. Notice the cell references are still there—named ranges did not automatically replace the cell references.

7. Select **J7:J1005**.

8. On the Formulas tab in the Defined Names group, click on the **arrow** next to Define Names. Select **Apply Name**, then click **OK**. Notice cell J7 now uses the new named ranges.

Sales by Rep Worksheet

What Would Be the Sum of All Orders for Each Rep If No Discounts Had Been Given?

Since there are two sum_ranges (Discounts_Given and Discounted_OrderTotals), the solution must include two SUMIF functions.

9. Click cell **C4**, then enter
   =SUMIF(RepName,B4,Discounted_OrderTotals)+SUMIF(RepName,B4, Discounts_Given)

Note: *If named ranges were not created, the solution would consist of 3D cell referencing to the Discounted OrderTotals and would need absolute cell referencing.*

Average Sales by Rep Worksheet
AVERAGEIF(range, criteria, [average_range])

The AVERAGEIF function calculates an average based on a criterion. Its arguments are identical to the arguments used in the SUMIF. The only difference between SUMIF and AVERAGEIF is that the former calculates a sum and the latter an average.

What Was the Average Discount Given by Each Rep?

Calculate the average of the Discounts_Given by each representative shown in column B. **Round** the calculation to **2** decimal places.

10. Click **C4**, then enter
    =ROUND(AVERAGEIF(RepName,B4,Discounts_Given), 2)

11. Notice the value is rounded, not formatted, to two decimals. Format cell C4 to two decimals, then copy it down to **C84**. Note the correct value column still has four decimals to show the change in value.

When you are finished, save and close the file, then bring your work to the next lab meeting.

REVIEW PROBLEMS

Review Problem 1

Determine Ages and Length of Employment for a Banquet

1. On the Review1 worksheet, click cell **D9**, then write a function that calculates the difference between 2 dates in years. Use the birthdate in column C as the early date and the Today() function as the later date. Write the function so that it can be copied down column D. Format to 0 decimals, then copy the formula to column D.

2. Similarly, write a function in F9 that calculates how many years each employee has been employed. Format to 0 decimals, then copy the formula down column F.

3. Any employee who has worked at least 25 years qualifies for a gold watch at the next company banquet. Click in cell **D6**, then write a function that will count the number of employees who qualify.

4. Click cell **F6** and write a function that will calculate the combined number of years worked by employees older than 50.

Review Problem 2

Premiere's Sales Incentive Program

1. On the Review2 worksheet, click in cell **F5**, then enter a function that will return the number of employees from the Illinois store whose sales are being tracked for an incentive program. Do this in such a way that your solution can be copied to cell **G5**. Similarly, complete **H5:K5**.

2. Click cell **F6**, then enter a function that calculates the average of the values in column K for the Illinois store only. Enter your solution in such a way that it can be copied to cell **G6**. Similarly, complete **H6:K6**.

3. Click in the cell **F9**, then enter an expression that calculates the number of employees who met or exceeded the goal.

4. Format the worksheet as outlined hereafter.

5. Without merging cells (right-click and choose Format Cells... for this), center cell **A2** across columns **A** through **K**. For cells A2:K2, format the text as **14 point, dark red, Georgia**, then apply an **Aqua Accents 5, Lighter 80%** fill color.

6. Using Format Cells, add the **thickest** border, colored **dark red**, to cell **B8**.

7. Right-align **E5:E6** and **E9**.

8. Merge & Center the range **F3:G3** and **H3:K3**.

9. Format all sales values as **currency** with **0** decimal places displayed.

10. Format all percentage values as **Percent** with **1** decimal place displayed.

You should be able to answer the following questions:

1. Describe how the COUNTIF, SUMIF, and AVERAGEIF functions follow (or don't follow) the IF-THEN-ELSE logic introduced during the first half of the semester (i.e., the IIF function in Access).

2. On the Sales by City worksheet, are the data values in column I of the Sales by City worksheet unique, or do the same data values occur many times?

3. On the Sales by City worksheet are the data values referred to as OrderCityState in the solution in J7, =SUMIF(OrderCityState,I7,Discounted_OrderTotals), unique, or do the same data values occur many times?

Financial Analysis

Chapter 15

Outline

- Research & Exploration: Research Financial Terms, Practice Financial Functions

- In-Depth Case Application: Conduct Financial and Loan Analyses

- Review Problems: Practice Financial, Loan Analyses, and Konwledge Check 13

Objectives

- Understand the time value of money.

- Use the NPER, PMT, PPMT, and IPMT functions to conduct a loan analysis.

- Use the PV, FV, and RATE functions to conduct a financial analysis.

RESEARCH & EXPLORATION

Research

Research the following key terms and Excel functions to complete the Exploration section, being sure to take advantage of the Excel tutorials online at http://ittraining.iu.edu/ and of online Microsoft Support, available at https://support.office.com/:

- Time value of money

- Amortization schedule

- Excel functions: RATE, PMT, PPMT, IPMT

You should be able to answer the following questions:

Summarize what is meant by the time value of money.

What is an amortization schedule?

What does the RATE function calculate?

In the context of a loan, what does the PMT function calculate?

A loan payment comprises a _____ payment and an _____ payment.

Exploration

Navigate to your K201 files, open **Class15-FinancialAnalysis.xlsx**, and then complete the RE worksheet(s) using the following information.

Calculating Interest Rate

Purchasing equipment on credit is commonplace in businesses of all sizes. The CTO (chief technology officer) of Premiere Foods has just purchased new computer equipment for the accounting department.

Use the RATE function to calculate the annual interest rate (APR) that Premiere would be paying for this purchase if it makes only the minimum payment for 30 months.

The RATE function is RATE(NPER,PMT,PV,[FV],[TYPE]):

- **NPER:** The total number of payments. For example, a 5-year monthly loan would have a NPER of 60.

- **PMT:** The amount of the regularly occurring payment. If the amount owed every month on a car loan is $500, the PMT is $500.

- **PV:** The present value—the total amount that a series of future payments is worth now. For example, if you take out a loan for $10,000, the present value is $10,000.

- **[FV]:** An optional argument of future value, or a cash balance you want to attain after the last payment is made. If omitted, FV = 0.

- **[Type]:** An optional argument equaling a 0 or a 1. A value of 1 represents the payment being made at the beginning of the payment period. A value of 0 represents the payment being made at the end of the payment period. If omitted, TYPE = 0. If not specified in a problem, assume that TYPE = 0.

When using financial functions, arguments that represent dollar values can be positive or negative, depending on the cash flow. Because of this, it is important to know from whose perspective the problem is being done. Once you identify the perspective, then dollar amounts that come out of that person's account are negative—money being spent. Dollar amounts that enter that person's account are positive—money being received.

1. In the Chapter15-FinancialAnalysis.xlsx workbook, on the RE1 worksheet, in cell **B7**, type **=RATE(B6,-B5,B4)**

   Cell B6 is the number of months to pay on the loan, so NPER=B6 (value of 30).

   The next two arguments represent dollar values: PMT and PV. Remember, dollar amounts can be positive or negative, depending on the cash flow. This problem is being done according to the perspective of Premiere, not the bank.

   The PMT is the regularly occurring payment that Premiere must pay, so it comes out of Premiere's bank account. Thus the PMT must be a negative B5.

The PV is the present value of this loan or, in this case, the purchase amount. Premiere will receive this amount in Premiere's bank account to then use to pay for the computers. Thus the money flows from the bank into Premiere's bank account; PV is a positive B4.

2. Excel returns 1%. Format the result as **Percentage** with 2 decimal places. It returns a rate of 1.22%. Since the PMT argument is a *monthly* argument, the RATE function returns the *monthly* rate. Financial functions will always return a value corresponding with the time interval used by the PMT argument. However, Premiere wants to know the *annual* interest rate.

3. Edit the formula in cell B7 to multiply the RATE function by 12:
=RATE(B6,-B5,B4)*12
This returns the annual percentage of 14.63%.

Evaluating Loan Options

Premiere Foods is looking to invest in a new location and has been offered two loan options from a bank. Being able to determine which option is the better deal could save Premiere hundreds or even thousands of dollars over the course of the loan.

To do this calculation, you will use the PMT function. Remember that PMT is a regularly occurring payment. Although it was an argument of the RATE function in the foregoing problem, it is also a function.

1. Go to the **RE2** worksheet. In cell **B6**, calculate the amount needed to finance for loan option 1. When taking out a loan, the amount you finance does not include your down payment. Accordingly, subtract the Down Payment from the Purchase Price.

2. In cell **B9**, type **=PMT(B7/4,B8*4,-B6)** to calculate the quarterly payment amount required to pay off loan option 1.

   Since this is a quarterly payment, the first argument of RATE must be divided by 4. The PMT wants the RATE per payment. The Rate in cell B7 is an APR, or annual rate. Thus cell B7 is divided by 4.

   Also, the Term is in years. However, due to the quarterly payment, Premiere will make 4 payments per year. Accordingly, cell B8 is multiplied by 4.

For this problem, track cash flows from the bank's perspective, not Premiere's. The amount being borrowed is coming out of the bank's account into Premiere's account—so the PV argument is negative.

The PMT function returns a positive value, because when Premiere makes each quarterly payment, the bank will receive the money back into the bank's account.

3. In cell **F6**, calculate the amount needed to finance for loan option 2.

4. In cell **F9**, type **=PMT(F7/12,F8*12,-F6)** to calculate the monthly payment amount required to pay off loan option 2.

1. In cell **B13**, select the loan that is the better deal for Premiere Foods. If needed, calculate how much Premiere will pay over one year for both options.

In-Depth Case Application

Creating an Amortization Schedule

Part of your research was to define an amortization schedule. An amortization schedule shows the details of each periodic payment made throughout the life of a loan. Each payment comprises a principal payment and an interest payment.

The Principal Payment function (PPMT) calculates how much of each payment is applied toward the principal (the amount owed). The Interest Payment function (IPMT) calculates how much of each payment is applied toward the interest that accrues each period.

The PPMT and IPMT functions use the same arguments as PMT, with one addition: the second argument, **per**. This represents the payment number. For a three-year loan that is paid down monthly, you will have payment numbers from 1 through 36. Unlike PMT, both PPMT and IPMT need to know where you are in the repayment schedule—that is, which payment is currently being made.

PPMT/IPMT(rate, per, nper, pv, fv, type):

- **rate:** The per period interest rate.
- **per:** The specific period in which a payment is being made.
- **nper:** The total number of payment periods.
- **pv:** The amount of money borrowed.
- **fv:** The amount of debt you want remaining after your last periodic payment. The default is 0.
- **type:** Either a 0 or a 1 to indicate when periodic payments are made. The default value is 0, indicating the end of the period. A value of 1 indicates the beginning of the period.

Loan Amortization Worksheet

Loan 2 from the RE2 worksheet is the better deal for Premiere Foods, which will save more than $700 over the course of the loan. On the Loan Amortization worksheet, you will create an amortization schedule to see the details of each monthly payment.

ALL amortization tables in K201 should be done from the bank's perspective when determining cash flows (negative vs. positive).

1. In the Chapter15-FinancialAnalysis.xlsx workbook on the Loan Amortization worksheet in cell **B6**, calculate the amount needed to finance by subtracting the down payment from the purchase price.

2. In cell **B9**, use the PMT function to calculate the equal monthly payment amount required to pay off the loan.

3. In cells **A12:A71**, type payment numbers **1** through **60** for each of the payments Premiere Foods will make.

4. In cell **B12**, reference the loan amount in cell **B6** as the beginning balance before the first payment is made.

5. In cell **C12**, use the **PPMT** function to calculate the amount of the first payment that will go toward the principal. Be sure to use appropriate absolute, relative, and/or mixed cell references so that you can copy the formula down. Also, since the present value of the loan amount is a cash outflow for the Bank, make the pv argument negative.

6. In cell **D12**, use the **IPMT** to calculate the amount of the first payment that will go toward the interest that accrued during the first month. Be sure to use appropriate absolute, relative, or mixed cell references so that you can copy the formula down. Also, since the present value of the loan amount is a cash outflow for the Bank, make the pv argument negative.

7. In cell **E12**, calculate the balance owed after the first payment is made by subtracting the principal payment from the beginning balance. *You DO NOT deduct the interest payment from the amount owed.*

8. In cell **B13**, reference the ending balance in cell **E12** as the beginning balance before the second payment is made. Drag the **AutoFill** handle down to **B71**.

9. Drag the **AutoFill handle** of cell **C12** down to **C71**.

10. Drag the **AutoFill handle** of cell **D12** down to **D71**

11. Drag the **AutoFill handle** of cell **E12** down to **E71**.

The amortization schedule is now complete. You can verify the accuracy of the amortization schedule by confirming the following:

- The ending balance of the final payment is $0.00.
- The principal payment amount continues to get larger after each payment.
- The interest payment amount continues to get smaller after each payment.
- The principal payment plus the interest payment always equals the period payment of the PMT function.
- The sum of all principal payments is equal to the amount financed.

Total Interest Paid

Interest is the primary cost of borrowing money. Calculating the total amount of interest paid over the life of the loan is helpful in determining how much the loan actually costs.

12. In cell **D73**, calculate the total interest paid by summing all the interest payments made.

Paying More Than the Minimum Payment

When paying off a loan, you should pay more than the minimum payment whenever possible. Making additional payments earlier in the loan holds more value than making those same additional payments toward the end of the loan. This is a good example of the time value of money. Paying more money at the beginning reduces the amount owed earlier, so the interest is accruing on a smaller balance.

To the right of the amortization schedule you just completed is a table that will allow you to incorporate additional payment amounts and calculate a new beginning balance, interest payment, and ending balance.

13. In cell **G12**, type **500** as the additional amount paid at the end of the first month.

14. Scroll down to cell **I74**, noticing that there is $164.71 in total interest savings.

15. Delete the value in cell **G12** and in cell **G70**, type **500** as the additional amount paid at the end of month 59.

    Notice that the same amount paid at the end of the loan results in only $2.79 in total interest savings.

Calculating the Present Value of an Investment

Would you rather receive $1,000 in 5 years or receive $500 today? Being able to calculate the present value of that future $1,000 can help you make good investment decisions by determining if you can make more than that amount within the same time period by investing elsewhere.

The basic and most common equation to calculate present value is

$$PV = \frac{FV}{(1+i)^n}$$

where *FV* is the future value that is to be received, *i* is the periodic interest rate, and *n* is the total number of periods during the time period of the investment.

This equation assumes that the investment results in one lump sum of money at the end of the period.

Let's assume that the effective annual interest rate of a guaranteed investment is 5%. When you plug the values into the equation, you get $1,000/(1+.05) ^5. The result is that the $1,000 five years from now is worth $783.53 today, which is a better deal than $500.

The PV Function

The PV function can easily calculate the present value of either lump sum investments or investments involving equal periodic payments.

The PV function contains the following arguments: rate, nper, pmt, fv, and type.

PV(rate, nper, pmt, fv, type):

- **rate:** The per period interest rate. If the investment offers a 6% annual rate but makes payouts every month, then the rate would be 6%/12.
- **nper:** The total number of payment periods.
- **pmt:** Used with investments that return periodic payments of equal value and do not change. If omitted, then a future value is required.
- **fv:** Used with investments that result in a lump sum payout.
- **type:** Either a 0 or a 1 to indicate when periodic payments are received. The default value is 0, indicating an end-of-period payout. A value of 1 indicates a beginning-of-period payout.

Calculating the Future Value of an Investment

The value of money fluctuates over time. $500 today will not be worth the same in five years. This is because that money can be invested, and that value can increase or decrease with interest. Also, what you can buy with $500 today may not be the same amount you will be able to buy in five years, thanks to inflation.

The basic equation to calculate future value is

$$FV = PV * (1 + i)^n$$

where PV is the amount you are investing, i is the periodic interest rate, and n is the total number of periods.

This equation assumes a lump sum investment amount and a constant, compounding interest rate. It does not account for any deposits (payments) that could be made over the life of an investment such as in a retirement fund.

The FV Function

The FV function can easily calculate the future value of an investment consisting of a lump sum amount or equal periodic payments or both.

The FV function contains the following arguments: rate, nper, pmt, pv, and type.

FV(rate, nper, pmt, pv, type):

- **rate:** The per period interest rate.
- **nper:** The total number of payment periods.
- **pmt:** Used with investments that involve periodic payments of equal value and do not change. Since it is an outgoing cash flow, this amount is entered as a negative value. If omitted, then a present value is required.
- **pv:** Used with investments that require a lump sum at the beginning. Since it is an outgoing cash flow, this amount is entered as a negative value.
- **type:** Either a 0 or a 1 to indicate when periodic investment payments are made. The default value is 0, indicating an end-of-period payment. A value of 1 indicates a beginning-of-period payment.

The NPER Function

The NPER function calculates the total number of periods in an investment or loan. It can be used in a variety of ways. For example, NPER can be used to calculate how long it will take you to pay off a loan, assuming a constant interest rate and equal periodic payments. The function can also be used to calculate how long you can withdraw from a retirement account, assuming a constant interest rate and equal periodic withdrawal amounts.

The NPER function contains the following arguments: rate, pmt, pv, fv, and type.

NPER(rate, pmt, pv, fv, type):

- **rate:** The per period interest rate.
- **pmt:** The periodic payment or withdrawal amount.
- **pv:** The amount of money in the investment.
- **fv:** The amount of cash balance you want to attain after the last payment or withdrawal is made.
- **type:** Either a 0 or a 1 to indicate when periodic payments or withdrawals are made. The default value is 0, indicating the end of the period. A value of 1 indicates the beginning of the period.

Investment Analysis Worksheet

Go to the **Investment Analysis** worksheet to practice using the NPER, FV, and PV functions.

College Fund
The CEO of Premiere foods has been putting money into a college fund for his daughter. This fund will be used for various expenses so that she can focus on her college experience and not have to worry about having a job. He wants to make sure that the $60,000 will last at least 5 years if his daughter is allowed to withdraw $1,000 a month from the account.

1. In cell **B8**, use the NPER function to calculate the total number of periods that his daughter can withdraw $1,000 from the account.

Note: *Consider the direction of the cash flow for the pmt and pv arguments. If we examine the cash flows from the perspective of the account, then the monthly $1,000 withdrawal from the account (pmt) is a negative cash outflow. The pv is the amount the account is worth today and is a positive cash inflow of $60,000.*

2. Divide the result of the NPER function by 12 to calculate the number of years the money will last.

3. Format the result as **Number** with **2** decimal places.

Retirement Savings

Using the FV function, you can calculate how much money you will have at retirement based on an initial deposit and equal periodic payments. In this example, you have the opportunity to earn a 4% APR in a retirement account. You are able to deposit $5,000 today and then make monthly deposits of $500 at the end of each period, until you reach your desired retirement age.

16. In cell **B16**, enter your current age.

17. In cell **B17**, enter your desired retirement age.

18. In cell **B18**, calculate the total number of payments you will make during the period. Use *(Retirement Age - Current Age) *12.*

19. In cell **B20**, use the **FV** function to calculate how much money you will have in the account once you reach your desired retirement age.

Note: *Consider the direction of the cash flow for the pv and pmt arguments. Both are negative cash outflows from the investor's pocket into the account.*

Personal Savings

How much would you need to invest today to have $12,000 in 5 years? The PV function can calculate the initial amount required based on a constant interest rate (rate of return) for the investment. In this example, you can earn 4.5% compounded annually.

20. In cell **F8**, use the **PV** function to calculate the amount required to have 12,000 in 5 years.

Note: *Since there is no recurring (periodic) payment with this investment option, the pmt argument should be 0. The fv argument should be positive, because it will be an incoming cash flow into the investor's pocket.*

REVIEW PROBLEMS

Review Problem 1

Premiere Foods is considering a loan to renovate its IN store and needs your help with the loan analysis. The estimated cost of the renovation is in cell B3. The amount of capital that Premiere Foods has for the renovation is in cell B4.

1. In the Chapter15-FinancialAnalysis.xlsx workbook on the Review1 worksheet in cell **B5**, calculate the amount that needs to be financed to fund the renovation.

2. In cell **B7**, use the **RATE** function to calculate the annual percentage rate (APR) for the loan. Don't forget to multiply the result of the RATE function by 4.

3. Within the range **A12:E31**, create an amortization schedule to see the details of each of the 20 quarterly payments Premiere Foods will make over the course of the 5-year loan.

4. In cell **E8**, calculate the total amount of interest that Premiere Foods will pay for the loan.

Review Problem 2

One way to determine the value of an investment is to compare it to an alternative investment option, such as a risk-free savings account or a government bond. The rate earned from an alternative risk-free investment is used to discount the future value of the investment options. If the Present Value of the investment is more than the investment amount, then it should be considered. If it's not, then the alternative, risk-free option would be the better way to invest. This worksheet contains information about two different investment options.

Option 1: Invest $150,000 today and after 5 years, receive a one-time payout of $175,000. Alternatively, the $150,000 can be invested in a risk-free savings account earning 2.5% interest annually. Use the PV function to determine whether you would have to pay more or less than $150,000 if the alternative risk-free option is pursued.

Option 2: Invest $200,000 and after 3 years, receive a one-time payout of $220,000. Alternatively, the $200,000 can be invested in a risk-free savings account earning 3.5% interest annually. Use the PV function to determine if you would have to pay more or less than $200,000 if the alternative risk-free option is pursued.

Evaluate each of the two investment options using the PV function. For each investment option, use the Alternative guaranteed rate that you could earn if you invested your money elsewhere and assumed no risk to discount the future incoming cash flows referred to as investment payouts. Remember: under all the options, no regularly occurring payment exists.

Note: *Similar to the Personal Savings problem completed in class, there is no periodic payment with either investment option, so the pmt argument should be 0.*

To determine which is the better investment, compare each investment amount to the present value. As already stated, if the Present Value of the investment is more than the investment amount, then the investment should be considered good—you do not have to invest as much money today as the alternative investment with the guaranteed rate wants you to invest. Yet you receive the same payout after the term ends.

Review Problem 3

Joan Harris, one of the managers of Premiere Foods, is considering a small personal investment. She has $3,000 a year to invest and is considering two options.

Option 1: Joan makes two $1,500 deposits a year for 10 years and earns 5.5% interest.

Option 2: Joan makes monthly deposits of $250 for 10 years and also earns 5.5% interest.

Use the FV function to determine how much money Joan will have at the end of the 10 years for each option.

Note: *When solving for the rate argument, be sure to calculate the periodic rate for each investment based on the frequency of deposits.*

Knowledge Check 13

File Needed

KnowledgeCheck_13.xlsx

Loan Analysis

Julie Peterson, owner of Your Best Alloys, a custom-designed jewelry store, has taken out a loan for $50,000, primarily to pay for new soldering torches and tips, a new rolling mill, centrifugal casting equipment, and a new buffing machine. She has asked you to complete an amortization schedule so that she can track her monthly repayment of this loan. Julie will make her monthly payments at the end of each month.

Loan details are provided on the **Loan** worksheet in cells **B3:B5**, and an amortization schedule has been started for you. Complete the amortization schedule for this loan.

Investment Analysis

Julie is also considering a small short-term investment. On the **Investment** worksheet, use the appropriate function to calculate the Present Value of the investment to determine if it is worth the money.

The investment opportunity that Julie is considering will require a one-time investment of $20,000. Every year for 5 years, Julie will receive a payment of $2,500. At the end of 5 years, she will also receive a lump sum of $10,000. This would mean that at the end of the 5 years, Julie's $20,000 investment will return a total of $22,500. Is this a good opportunity?

To determine this, Julie will need to compare this option to an alternative no-risk investment option. With this second option, Julie would instead deposit the $20,000 into a savings account that earns 3.5% interest for the same period with no risk of losing any money.

In cell C13, use the PV function to determine the present value of the future incoming cash flows of the investment. You will use the interest rate that Julie would be giving up if she chose this investment opportunity rather than a no-risk savings account to discount those potential future cash flows.

After completing these steps, go to the course website to answer Koin-earning questions.

Logical Functions

Chapter 16

Outline

- Research & Exploration: Research Conditional Formatting, Explore Use of Conditional Formatting and IF Statements

- In-Depth Case Application: Work with Basic IF, AND, and OR Functions, Work with Nested IFs

- Review Problems: Practice Using IF, AND, and OR Functions, Practice Using Nested IF Functions, Knowledge Check 14

Objectives

- Implement conditional formatting.

- Solve problems using the IF function.

- Solve problems using the AND and OR functions.

- Identify instances when nested IF functions are necessary.

- Solve problems using nested IF functions.

RESEARCH & EXPLORATION

Research

Use your favorite online search engine to research conditional formatting in Excel. Aim to understand what conditional formatting is and why it is useful.

Remember that you can also take advantage of the Excel 2016 tutorials available through Microsoft Support at http://office.microsoft.com.

Exploration

Conditional Formatting

Navigate to the **RE1** worksheet in the Chapter16_LogicalFunctions.xlsx file. Suppose you are managing Premiere's product categories and want to quickly draw the CEO's attention to different levels of performance among the categories. It would be helpful to apply special formatting to high and low sales revenue values so that they stand out on the worksheet. You decide on the following formatting scheme for the Sales Revenue column:

Product Category	Sales Revenue
Baking Mixes	$2,000.00
Books and Brochures	$9,729.32
Baking supplies	$6,484.86
Breads	$10,000.00
Broths	$181.53
Broth Powders	$3,067.59
Bath	$16,418.75
Butters	$2,665.32
Organic Coffee	$11,455.32
Organic Cheese	$1,828.04
Cheese Substitutes	$2,385.02
Wisconsin Cheese	$4,355.71
Canned Fruits and Vegetables	$8,632.92
Condiments	$13,078.99

You could go through the column one cell at a time and manually apply the correct formatting to each cell, but this would be time-consuming and tedious, and if the data set contained thousands of entries, such an approach would be completely impractical. Instead, use conditional formatting to automate the process. As you discovered in your research, conditional formatting is formatting that is applied to a cell based on whether its value meets a specified criterion.

Here are the formatting rules for the Sales Revenue values:

- Sales less than $2,000 should appear in bold white type and red fill.

- Sales between $2,000 and $10,000 should appear in bold blue type.

- Sales greater than $10,000 should appear in bold green type.

Use the following process to apply this conditional formatting:

1. Select cell **C6**.

2. While simultaneously holding down **Ctrl** and **Shift**, momentarily press (do not continue to hold) the **Down Arrow** key. This will select the entire range **C6:C72** for you.

3. Release the **Ctrl** and **Shift** keys.

4. On the **Home** tab, in the Styles group, click **Conditional Formatting**.

5. Select **New Rule**. Then in the "New Formatting Rule" dialog box, under the "Select a Rule Type" heading, select **Format only cells that contain**.

6. Use the fields under the "Edit the Rule Description" heading to specify the first condition (revenue values less than $2,000).
Note: You do not need to type the dollar sign or comma when you specify $2,000. It is recommended that when in Excel you type all numeric values, even financial values, as plain numbers. Let cell formatting settings handle the display of dollar signs and the like.

7. Click **Format**, then specify the desired formatting for values that meet the condition.

8. Click **OK**, then click **OK** again. You should see the formatting rule take effect immediately.

9. Repeat the steps above to apply the two remaining conditional formatting rules.

Troubleshooting

If your formatting does not match the picture in column F, then double-check your rules. The Conditional Formatting Rules Manager can display all rules created in a selection of cells or across an entire worksheet, allowing you to edit or delete rules as desired. To manage your rules, click the **Conditional Formatting** button as above, then select **Manage Rules**.

For this problem, remember the difference between math operators like "greater than" and "greater than or equal to". In Excel, the "between" operator includes the two endpoints.

In conditional formatting, Excel checks whether the specified condition (e.g., that the cell's value is less than 2000) is TRUE or FALSE and applies the specified format if the condition being evaluated is TRUE. This operation modifies the appearance of a cell but does not change the cell's underlying value. What if we needed to output different values in a cell—not just change its format—based on whether some condition was TRUE? For that, we cannot use conditional formatting. We must use a function.

The IF Function

The IF function outputs one of two user-supplied values depending on whether a user-supplied condition is TRUE or FALSE. The IF function has three arguments:

IF(logical_test, value_if_true, value_if_false)

logical_test

This is the condition you want Excel to evaluate as being either TRUE or FALSE. This should contain some type of comparison operator (e.g., =, <>, <).

value_if_true

This is the result you want Excel to output if the logical test is TRUE. This output can be a cell reference, formula, function, number, or text string. If the output you want is text, then you must use double-quotes around this argument. Do not put quotes around numeric values.

value_if_false

This is the result you want Excel to output if the logical test is FALSE. Again, this output can be a cell reference, formula, function, number, or text string. If the output you want is text, then you must use double-quotes around this argument. Do not put quotes around numeric values.

Notice that these three arguments follow a basic IF-THEN-ELSE structure. If the logical test is TRUE, then the value_if_true will be the output of the function. Else (i.e., if the logical test is FALSE), the value_if_false will be the output.

=IF(logical_test, value_if_true, value_if_false)

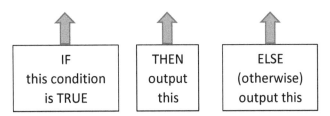

| IF this condition is TRUE | THEN output this | ELSE (otherwise) output this |

Logical Tests

As you have already learned, the first argument of the IF function is a logical test for Excel to execute. To use the IF function properly, you must be able to write logical tests that accurately describe the condition you need to evaluate.

For example, say we are evaluating whether a payment amount meets or exceeds the minimum payment due. For this, we would use the following logical test:

payment amount >= minimum payment

If we replaced the placeholding words "payment amount" and "minimum payment" with actual numeric values, we might end up with something like this:

50 >= 100

The result of any logical test is either TRUE or FALSE. For the example numbers used here, our logical test evaluates to FALSE. That is, the statement "50 is greater than or equal to 100" is FALSE.

Logical tests are not limited to numeric values only. You can also use text in a logical test. For example, writing

B7 = "Paid"

as a logical test would evaluate whether it is TRUE or FALSE that cell B7 contains exactly the word "Paid" and no other characters.

Imagine This!

Imagine you are Premiere's human resources director and are looking at employee records. How would you write the following logical tests using a combination of placeholding words, numbers, and comparison operators (example: monthly income >= 3 * rent payment)?

- Employees must be at least 16 years old.

- The number of people in each department must be greater than 3.

- Overtime pay rate must not exceed 1.5 times the regular pay rate.

Practice Writing IF Functions

Navigate to the **RE2** worksheet. On this worksheet, you are in charge of determining product placement for brands of bread in the upcoming month. If sales of a brand of bread were at least 110% of sales projected last month, it will be given premium end-cap shelf space, indicated by the word **Yes** in column F. Otherwise, the cell in column F should be blank.

To solve this problem, you need the IF function. To approach such a problem, some people like to think through the IF-THEN-ELSE structure verbally:

IF actual sales/projected sales >= 1.1

THEN output the text "Yes"

ELSE output ""

Others prefer to sketch a flowchart:

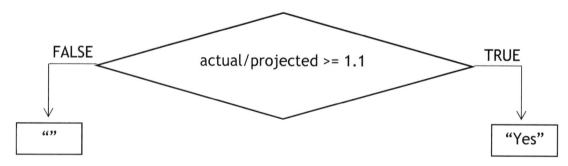

You might find a different way of outlining or sketching the problem. Regardless of the specific approach you choose, it is important to have *some* method that works, because these problems can become complex. Make it a habit to outline or sketch the logic for the problem on paper before you type anything in Excel.

1. Once you understand the logic for the problem, enter the solution in cell **F6**.

2. **AutoFill** the solution down to **F18**.

More IF Function Practice

Navigate to the **RE3** worksheet. Hourly employees of Premiere Foods are paid their hourly rate for time worked up to and including 40 hours. For time worked in excess of 40 hours, employees are paid 1.5 times their hourly rate. Calculate the total gross pay for each employee, using the ROUND function to round their pay to the nearest penny.

You will have two different calculations (outputs) for total gross pay: one for those who worked 40 or fewer hours, and another for those who worked more than 40 hours.

1. Using one of the methods above, outline or sketch the logic for the problem.

2. Enter an appropriate formula in **F6**.

3. Make sure cell **F6** is formatted as **Currency**.

4. **AutoFill** the solution down to **F87**.

Be sure to save your file when you are finished with this exercise.

IN-DEPTH CASE APPLICATION

Evaluating Training Status and Hours Remaining

Navigate to the **CRM Training** worksheet. To attain Expert status on Premiere's custom-designed customer relationship management (CRM) software, an employee needs to complete at least 20 hours of training seminars. Until then, employees have User status.

On this worksheet, we want to list each employee's status (**Expert** or **User**) and calculate the remaining number of training hours each employee must complete to reach Expert status:

1. Enter an appropriate formula into cell **E6** to output the employee's status. Be sure to refer to cell **F3** in your logical test. Referring to cell **F3** will allow Premiere to easily adjust the model if the required number of hours were to change.

2. **AutoFill** the solution down to **E56**.

3. Enter an appropriate formula into cell **G6** to calculate the remaining number of hours each employee must complete to reach Expert status. If an employee is already an expert, the output should be 0.

4. **AutoFill** the solution down to **G56**.

The AND Function

In the previous exercise, only one condition needed to be TRUE for an employee to reach Expert status, but often, more than one condition must be met for a certain output to apply. For example, what if reaching Expert status required completing 20 hours of training *and* passing a proficiency test? In that case, two logical tests would be required: one to verify that the number of training hours is sufficient and one to verify that the proficiency test has been passed.

The IF function on its own can only accommodate a single logical test; we cannot simply insert additional logical tests inside the IF when we are dealing with multiple conditions. Instead, we place another function *inside the IF function* to group the multiple logical tests.

When multiple conditions must all be TRUE for a particular output to apply, we use the AND function inside the IF. The AND function has the following syntax:

AND(logical1, logical2, logical3,...)

Be careful to follow this syntax exactly. All of the logical tests go inside the parentheses and are separated by commas. Each argument must be a *complete* logical test and must include its own comparison operator. Do not attempt to combine multiple logical tests that contain the same number or cell reference.

NO!　=AND(A1>2, <4)

NO!　=AND(2<A1<4)

NO!　=AND(2<3<4)

YES!　=AND(A1>2, A1<4)

The AND function evaluates all of the logical tests (up to 255) that you specify in its arguments. If *all* of its logical tests evaluate to TRUE, then the AND function itself evaluates to TRUE. If one or more of the logical tests evaluate to FALSE, then the AND function evaluates to FALSE.

If you have multiple conditions that all must be TRUE for a particular output to apply within your IF function, then place those conditions (logical tests) within an AND function, using that AND function as the first argument of your IF function:

=IF(AND(A1>2, B1>3, C1>4),　"Yes",　"No")

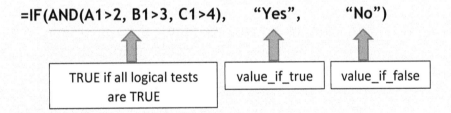

| TRUE if all logical tests are TRUE | value_if_true | value_if_false |

The OR Function

Now suppose that to reach Expert status, an employee could choose *either* to complete 20 hours of training *or* to pass a proficiency test. In this case we would still have two logical tests: one to verify that at least 20 training hours have been completed and one to verify that the proficiency test has been passed.

Again, we cannot simply put multiple logical tests inside our IF function without the help of another function to group those tests. However, in this case we cannot use AND: that would require both conditions to be TRUE, but here only one of the conditions—not both—needs to be TRUE for the employee to gain Expert status. Fortunately, Excel also has an OR function. The OR function has the following syntax:

OR(logical1, logical2, logical3,...)

The OR function follows the same syntax rules as the AND function and can also accommodate up to 255 logical tests. The OR function evaluates to TRUE if *at least one* of its logical tests is TRUE. The OR function will evaluate to FALSE only if *all* of its logical tests are FALSE.

If you have multiple conditions and at least one—but not necessarily all—must be TRUE for a particular output to apply within your IF function, then place those conditions (logical tests) within an OR function, using that OR function as the first argument of your IF function:

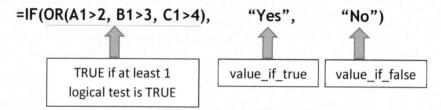

=IF(OR(A1>2, B1>3, C1>4),   "Yes",   "No")

| TRUE if at least 1 logical test is TRUE | value_if_true | value_if_false |

Summary: IF with AND or OR

When you have multiple logical tests that must be evaluated to determine the output of your IF function, think about how those logical tests or conditions relate to each other. If all conditions must be TRUE for an output to apply, then place the associated logical tests inside an AND function, making that AND function the first argument of your IF function. If at least one (but not necessarily all) of the conditions must be TRUE for an output to apply, then place the associated logical tests inside the OR function, using that OR function as the first argument of your IF function.

Calculating Employee Bonuses

Navigate to the **Employee Bonuses** worksheet. Premiere's newer managers receive a year-end bonus of 5% of their salary for meeting managerial development training goals. To qualify, a manager must have been with the company for no longer than three years and must have met or exceeded the training goal in each of the four quarters.

1. Nest the appropriate function inside an IF function to return the bonus amount in cell **K10**. If a manager receives no bonus, insert a bonus amount of **$0** (do not type the dollar sign).

2. Format **K10** as **Currency**.

3. **AutoFill** the solution down to **K34**.

Determining Product Placement

Navigate to the **Product Promotions** worksheet. Premiere is running a promotion on Generic House and Jason brand products this month. Any product from either of these brands should be given premium end-cap shelf space. Premiere also wants to feature best-selling products regardless of brand, so any product whose sales reached at least 110% of sales projected last month (regardless of brand) should also be placed on the end cap.

1. In cell **G8**, nest the appropriate function inside an IF function to return either the word **Yes** or a **blank**.

2. **AutoFill** the solution down to **G39**.

Nested IF Functions

The IF problems we have seen so far have involved only two outputs. If the first argument (the logical test) of the IF evaluated to TRUE, then Excel outputted the value_if_true argument. Otherwise, Excel outputted the value_if_false argument. The following flowchart represents this usual two-output scenario (for example, Output A and Output B):

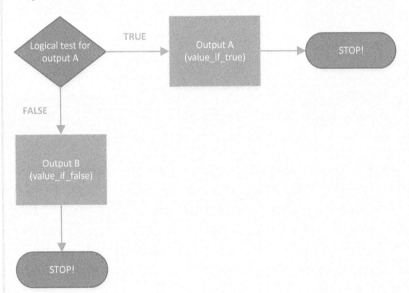

What if a problem involves more than two possible outputs? For example, what if we have Output A, Output B, and Output C? Think about how you would solve such a problem outside of Excel: You might first determine whether the condition that leads to Output A is TRUE or FALSE. If it's TRUE, then you would choose Output A. But if that condition is FALSE, then instead of having a single value_if_false to which to default, you would still have two more outputs (B and C) between which to decide. To decide between Output B and Output C, you would need to perform one more logical test to see whether the condition leading to Output B is TRUE. If that condition is TRUE, then you would choose Output B. If it's FALSE, then you don't need any more logical tests, because there is no decision to make. You only have one possible output remaining in such a case—Output C. That process is represented by the following flowchart:

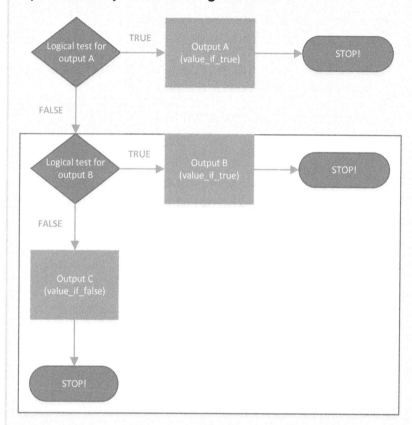

Notice that you have essentially taken the value_if_false from the original IF function and replaced it with another IF function! The large boxed region in the flowchart above demonstrates this replacement. This is the method for solving IF problems that have more than two outputs: keep using an IF function to replace the value_if_false argument of the preceding IF function until you have only one possible output remaining. Doing so is called "nesting" IFs.

To determine how many IF functions you need, subtract 1 from the number of possible outputs. In the example above, we had three possible outputs and thus needed two IF functions. For four outputs, we would need three IF functions—and so forth.

For a more concrete example, consider the following problem.

All incoming university students are required to take a mathematics placement exam. This test helps determine the math course in which a student should enroll. Course recommendations correspond to the following placement test scores:

Score Range	Recommended Course
0-30	Math I
31-50	Math II
51-80	Math III
80-100	Other

Always start a nested IF problem by determining how many IF statements you need. With four outputs here, we need three IFs. Here is one possible solution to this example:

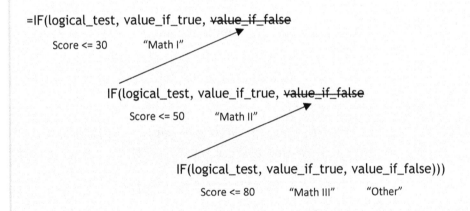

Consider a score of 25. If you were solving this problem without Excel, you would likely first ask, "Is this score between 0 and 30?" If it is, you would immediately know to recommend Math I. Would you bother to go on asking whether the score is between 31 and 50, 51 and 80, and so on? No. You've already determined what the recommendation should be.

Now consider a score of 75. Again, without Excel, you would start by asking, "Is the score between 0 and 30?" In this case, it is not, so you would not recommend Math I. You would then proceed to the next logical test and ask, "Is this score between 31 and 50?" Again, it is not, so you would not recommend Math II. You would need to proceed to the next logical test: "Is this score between 51 and 80?" It is, so you would recommend Math III.

Excel follows this same process. It runs through the IF functions in order of occurrence in your formula, from left to right. The instant one IF function's logical test argument evaluates to TRUE, Excel outputs the value_if_true for that IF function, and evaluation stops there. The remaining logical tests are not evaluated; there is no need.

Distributing Coupons

Navigate to the **Member Coupons** worksheet. In advance of Member Appreciation Day, Premiere's Bloomington store would like to e-mail special coupons to its members. The longer a customer has been a member, the larger the coupon he or she receives:

- Members who have been enrolled for at least 10 years receive a 60% off coupon.

- Members who have been enrolled for 5 to 9 years receive a 40% off coupon.

- Members who have been enrolled for 2 to 4 years receive a 25% off coupon.

- Members who have been enrolled for fewer than 2 years receive a 10% off coupon.

1. In cell **F6**, use the nested IF syntax outlined above to enter a formula that will return the coupon that this member should receive.

2. **AutoFill** the solution down to **F40**.

3. In cell **J6**, enter a formula to calculate the percent of the members on this worksheet who received the 60% off coupon.

4. Format **J6** as Percentage, then **AutoFill** the solution down to **J9**.

Remember to save your file.

REVIEW PROBLEMS

Review Problem 1

Navigate to the **Review1** worksheet. Any salesperson who sells more than $12,000 worth of merchandise receives a $500 bonus on top of base salary. Otherwise, total pay is the same as base salary.

1. In cell **F8**, enter an appropriate solution to return each salesperson's Total Pay.

2. **AutoFill** the solution down to **F58**.

Review Problem 2

Navigate to the **Review2** worksheet. Determine whether each employee is eligible for normal retirement. To qualify for normal retirement, an employee needs to be at least 65 years old or needs to have worked for at least 30 years.

1. In cell **I6**, enter an appropriate solution to return the letter **Y** if the employee qualifies; otherwise **N** should appear.

2. **AutoFill** the solution down to **I56**.

Review Problem 3

Navigate to the **Review3** worksheet. Calculate this month's commission rate for each sales rep according to the following conditions:

- A rep with sales less than $10,000 earns a rate of **0**.

- A rep with sales of at least $10,000 but less than $25,000 earns a rate of **.05**.

- A rep with sales between $25,000 and $40,000 earns a rate of **.07**.

- A rep with sales of more than $40,000 earns a rate of **.1**.

1. In cell **F5**, enter an appropriate solution to return each salesperson's commission rate.

2. **AutoFill** the solution down to **F28**.

Knowledge Check 14

This Knowledge Check will test your understanding of IF statements, the PMT function, conditional aggregate functions, and conditional formatting. Solve the following problems in the KnowledgeCheck_14.xlsx file.

Monthly Payment Calculations

Bank Seven's loan terms reward repeat borrowers who are in good standing by giving them a lower interest rate. Based on this information and the rates given in cells D3 and D4, find the monthly payments for the borrowers in the table. Enter a formula in cell **G7** that meets the stated conditions so that it can be copied to cells **G8:G34**.

Loan Summaries

Once you have calculated all of the monthly payments, enter functions in cells **J3**, **J4**, **J7**, and **K7** to calculate the statistics indicated. The functions in cells **J7** and **K7** should be entered so that they can be copied to **J8:J10** and **K8:K10**, respectively. Finally, format cells **J7:K10** so that any cell with a percentage greater than 35% will appear in red type.

After completing these steps, go to the course website to answer Koin-earning questions.

Compound Nested IFs
Chapter 17

Outline

- Research & Exploration: Using Compound AND and OR Functions within IF Statements

- In-Depth Case Application: Compound ANDs and ORs within IF and Nested IF Statements

- Review Problems: Use Compound ANDs and ORs within IFs and Nested IFs, Knowledge Check 15

Objectives

- Understand when compound AND and OR functions are needed.

- Solve IF problems involving compound AND and OR functions.

- Solve IF problems involving both nested IFs and compound AND and OR functions.

RESEARCH & EXPLORATION

Research

In this chapter, we will use AND and OR functions inside each other and inside IF functions. We will refer to ANDs and ORs nested inside each other as a *compound AND and OR* configuration. When compound ANDs and ORs are used in conjunction with nested IF statements, we will refer to this as a *compound nested IF* configuration. Read the following article on Microsoft's website to become familiar with the use of compound ANDs and ORs on their own and within IF functions:

http://support.office.com/en-us/article/Use-AND-and-OR-to-test-a-combination-of-conditions-0084efde-35e7-41aa-8909-2fa0c101ae0c.

Exploration

The article introduced you to combining the AND function and the OR function to describe more complicated real-world situations. It is important to understand exactly how these two functions work together outside the IF function before you attempt to use them inside the IF. When would you need to use an AND within an OR or an OR within an AND? Let's look at two scenarios.

AND within OR

Examine the following diagram. Here we have two main conditions, Condition 1 and Condition 2. Suppose that we need at least one (not necessarily both) to be TRUE. In this case, these two main conditions should be grouped by the OR function. However, suppose that Condition 1 is actually composed of two subconditions, 1A and 1B, and that both of these subconditions must be simultaneously TRUE. The subconditions would hence need to be placed within the AND function.

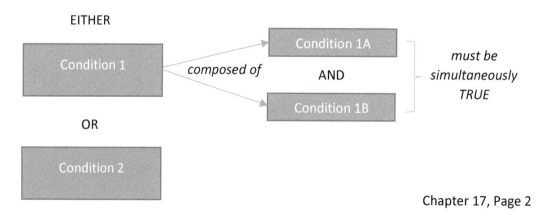

Sketched with Excel functions, this becomes

=OR(AND(Condition 1A, Condition 1B), Condition 2)

Why does the OR appear on the outside here? The function on the outside describes the highest-level relationship—how Condition 1 and Condition 2 are related. In this case, it's an either/or scenario.

In words, we could say,

"*EITHER* Condition 1A *AND* Condition 1B must be TRUE, *OR* Condition 2 must be TRUE, to get an overall TRUE outcome."

OR within AND

Now examine a different diagram. In this scenario, we have two main conditions, Condition 1 and Condition 2, both of which must be TRUE—so these two main conditions should be placed within the AND function. Again, say that Condition 1 is actually made up of two subconditions, Condition 1A and Condition 1B, but this time, we need at least one (not necessarily both) of these subconditions to be TRUE. In this case, Conditions 1A and 1B should be placed inside the OR function.

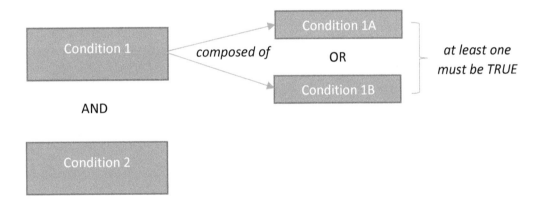

Sketched with Excel functions, this becomes

=AND(OR(Condition 1A, Condition 1B), Condition 2)

Why does the AND appear on the outside here? The function on the outside describes the highest-level relationship—how Condition 1 and Condition 2 are related. In this case, it's a both-and scenario.

In words, we could say,

"*EITHER* Condition 1A *OR* Condition 1B must be TRUE, *AND* Condition 2 must be TRUE, to get an overall TRUE outcome."

Understanding Compound ANDs and ORs in Excel

Navigate to the **RE1** worksheet in the Chapter17_CompoundNestedIFs.xlsx file. Cells A5, B5, and C5 contain specific numbers, Column E shows the contents of three compound AND and OR formulas, and Column F shows the corresponding outputs of the example formulas. Let's examine how Excel arrives at each of the outputs in Column F. Remember that the output of any AND or OR function, or any nested combination thereof, is either TRUE or FALSE rather than a number or text.

1. Select cell **F5**.

2. Click the **Formulas** tab in the Ribbon, and then, in the Formula Auditing group, click **Evaluate Formula**.

3. In the Evaluate Formula box that pops up, notice the underlined cell reference. Click the **Evaluate** button. Excel will replace the underlined cell reference with the value contained in that cell.

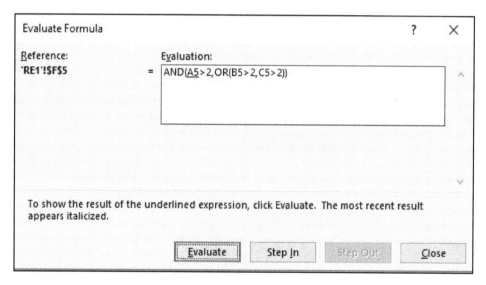

4. Continue clicking the **Evaluate** button while watching the results of the underlined expressions until you reach the final output of the formula.

5. Click the **Close** button in the Evaluate Formula box.

6. Repeat Steps 2 through 5 after selecting cell **F6** and again after selecting cell **F7**.

As you can see, the Evaluate Formula utility is very useful for understanding what is happening at each step in a particular calculation. This can come in handy when you need to troubleshoot errors and other unexpected results.

Interpreting Compound ANDs and ORs within an IF

Using your understanding of how the ANDs and ORs worked together on the RE1 worksheet, think about the results of placing these same compound ANDs and ORs into an IF function.

- Explain what the following statement means:

  =IF(AND(A1 > 2,OR(B1 > 2,C1 > 2)),"Yes","No")

- Does the following statement mean anything different from the foregoing one? If so, what does this one mean?

  =IF(AND(OR(B1 > 2,C1 > 2),A1 > 2),"Yes","No")

- Explain what the following statement means:

  =IF(OR(AND(B1 > 2,C1 > 2),A1 > 2),"Yes","No")

Building IF Statements with Compound ANDs and ORs

Navigate to the **RE2** worksheet. All employees in Division 3 or 4 who have completed fewer than 12 hours of training must attend an upcoming software training session. The output **Y** should appear in such cases; otherwise, **N** should appear.

Here is one recommended method for solving this or any other complicated IF problem.

1. Think through the situation:

IF	Division = 3 OR Division = 4
	AND
	Training Hours < 12
THEN	output "Y"
ELSE	output "N"

2. Write all the individual comparison statements leading to the value_if_true output in terms of their cell references:

D6 = 3	(Division = 3)
D6 = 4	(Division = 4)
E6 < 12	(Training hours < 12)

3. Determine and sketch how these conditions are related. Conditions that must be TRUE at the same time should be placed

inside the AND function. When at least one condition—but not necessarily all conditions—in a group must be TRUE, these conditions should be placed inside the OR function:

$$
\left.\begin{array}{l}
D6 = 3 \\
D6 = 4
\end{array}\right\} OR \\
\left.\begin{array}{l}
\\
E6 < 12
\end{array}\right\} AND
$$

4. Write the Excel formula on paper. This could be written in two equivalent ways:

    =IF(AND(OR(D6 = 3, D6 = 4), E6 < 12), "Y", "N")

    =IF(AND(E6 < 12, OR(D6 = 3, D6 = 4)), "Y", "N")

Notice that in this example, the OR function is inside the AND function. The AND is on the exterior because both the Division requirement and the Training Hours requirement must be met simultaneously to achieve the **Y** output. It is not the case that either the Division requirement is met or the Training requirement is met to get the **Y**.

Since the Division requirement consists of two alternative options, either of which is adequate, we need the OR for just the Division component. We thus end up with OR inside AND.

5. Enter the solution in cell **F6**.

6. **AutoFill** the solution down to **F56**.

Now navigate to the **RE3** worksheet. Any employee who is eligible for either early or normal retirement and who has worked at least 15 years qualifies for a bonus of **$1,000.00**. Otherwise, the employee receives a **$0.00** bonus.

1. Think through the problem and sketch a solution on paper.

2. Use your sketch to enter a formula for the bonus in cell **K6**. Remember not to put quotation marks around numeric values.

3. **AutoFill** the solution down to **K56**.

IN-DEPTH CASE APPLICATION

Determining Employee Retirement Eligibility

Navigate to the **Employee Retirement** worksheet. We will determine whether each employee is eligible for normal retirement at the end of the fiscal year. There are three independent ways to qualify:

- Be a member of Group 1 and have worked for at least 25 years   OR

- Be at least 65 years of age   OR

- Have worked for at least 30 years

If the employee qualifies, **Y** should be the output in Column I. Otherwise, **N** should appear.

To begin, think through the problem, sketching it on paper. You have already seen one method for sketching the logical tests leading to the value_if_true output. Here is an example of another technique.

1. List all conditions from the problem statement on one line and separated by commas. As you do this, translate the words from the problem statement into cell references:

   > D7 = 1,   H7 >= 25,   F7 >= 65,   H7 >= 30

2. Determine how these conditions are related. Must any of them be TRUE at the same time? Is there an either/or scenario among any of them? The first bullet point in the problem statement says "be a member of Group 1 and have worked for at least 25 years." This a simultaneous requirement—not an either/or scenario—so place the AND function with its parentheses around those two conditions:

   > AND(D7 = 1, H7 >= 25), F7 >= 65, H7 >= 30

3. You can treat the entire contents of the AND function as a SINGLE condition. This means we essentially have three conditions now, matching our three bullet points from the problem statement:

   > AND(D7 = 1, H7 >= 25), F7 >= 65, H7 >= 30

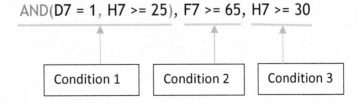

4. Ask how Condition 1 relates to Condition 2. Must they be TRUE at the same time? No, it's an either/or scenario, and the same applies to Condition 3. Either Condition 1 or Condition 2 or Condition 3 being TRUE will yield the **Y** output, so all three of these conditions (one of which already contains the AND function) go inside the OR function. Add the OR to the sketch:

> OR(AND(D7 = 1, H7 >= 25), F7 >= 65, H7 >= 30)

5. The foregoing line now becomes the first argument inside the IF function. It comprises the entirety of the logical test leading to the **Y** output. To be meticulous, insert the IF—with its equals sign, parentheses, and other arguments—into your sketch. Don't forget to put a comma after the logical test argument (that is, the OR function):

> =IF(OR(AND(D7 = 1, H7 >= 25), F7 >= 65, H7 >= 30), "Y", "N")

After you have completed the sketch on paper, return to your Excel file.

1. In cell **I7**, enter a formula to output **Y** or **N** as appropriate.

2. **AutoFill** the solution down to **I57**.

Sketching Nested IFs with Compound ANDs and ORs

The previous examples involved only one IF function. However, you will also encounter situations that require both nested IFs and compound ANDs and ORs (compound nested IFs). Here is one method for approaching these types of problems:

1. Count the possible outputs and subtract 1. This is the number of IF functions needed.

2. Sketch a template for just the IF structure. Do not worry about compound ANDs and ORs yet. Your template might look something like the following for three outcomes and two IF functions:

=IF   (_____,

           Logical test for Output1

_____,

           Output1 (value_if_true)

   IF   (_____,

            Logical test for Output2

_____,

           Output2 (value_if_true)

_____))

           Output3 (value_if_false—

           if all logical tests are false)

Be sure that at the very end of the template you include one closing parenthesis for each IF function used. Also note that since we are nesting functions inside each other, the equals sign appears only once, at the beginning of the structure.

3. Fill in the outputs. These are often more straightforward than the logical tests.

4. Using your favorite technique, sketch the logical test for each value_if_true output, then plug it into the appropriate space in the IF template.

5. Enter the formula in Excel. Use the function tool tip to guide you through each function's arguments as you type.

Allocating Customer Rewards

Navigate to the **Customer Rewards** worksheet. Premiere rewards its best customers with two levels of free product offers:

- Any customer with A or B status whose last invoice totals at least $300 will receive the **Premium** offer.

- Any customer with A or B status whose last invoice totals at least $200, or any customer of any level whose last invoice totals at least $350, will receive the **Select** offer.

- All other customers receive **None**.

The formula that you write should return **Premium, Select,** or **None** as appropriate.

1. Think through the situation.

   IF the customer has status A or B AND last invoice >=300

   THEN "Premium"

   ELSE IF the customer has (1) status A or B AND last invoice >=200; OR (2) last invoice >=350 regardless of status

   THEN "Select"

   ELSE "None"

2. Sketch a template for the IF structure, filling in the three outputs.

3. Group the conditions that lead to the first output ("Premium"):

   Condition 1: D7="A"
   Condition 2: D7="B" } OR
   Condition 3: E7>=300 } AND

4. Group the conditions that lead to the second output ("Select"):

   Condition 1: D7="A"
   Condition 2: D7="B" } OR
   Condition 3: E7>=200 } AND
   Condition 4: E7>=350 } OR

5. Add the sketches for these logical tests into your IF template.

6. Use your sketch to enter the solution in cell **F7**.

7. **AutoFill** the solution down to **F53**.

REVIEW PROBLEMS

Review Problem 1

Navigate to the **Review1** worksheet. Any employee who is eligible for either early or normal retirement and who has worked for at least 40 years has a rank of **Premiere**; any employee who is eligible for either early or normal retirement and who has worked for at least 25 years has a rank of **Superior**; all others have a rank of **Valued**.

1. Use your preferred compound nested IF problem-solving method to enter a formula for Rank in cell **K7**.

2. **AutoFill** the solution down to **K57**.

Review Problem 2

Navigate to the **Review2** worksheet. Calculate the number of vacation and family leave days allocated to each Premiere Foods employee. Here is the leave policy:

Vacation Days

- 17 days for full-time employees who have worked more than 5 years

- 12 days for full-time employees who have worked more than 1 year

- 7 days for full-time employees who have worked no more than 1 year or for part-time employees who have worked more than 3 years

- 0 days for all other employees

Family Leave

- 5 days for full-time employees who have worked more than 1 year

- 3 days for full-time employees who have worked no more than 1 year or for part-time employees who have worked more than 2 years

- 0 days for all other employees

1. Sketch the problem on paper; then return to your Excel file.

2. In cell **D4**, enter a formula that calculates Vacation Leave.

3. **AutoFill** the solution down to **D105**.

4. In **H4**, enter a formula that calculates Family Leave.

5. **AutoFill** the solution down to **H105**.

Review Problem 3

Navigate to the **Review3** worksheet.

1. In **Column C**, use the appropriate function to calculate the total number of employees eligible for the different vacation and family leave plans. (Hint: An employee who is eligible for the 17-day vacation leave will have the value 17 in Column D of the Review2 worksheet.) Write solutions in **C4** and **C13**, then **AutoFill** them through **C7** and **C15**, respectively.

2. In cells **C8** and **C16**, calculate the total number of employees based on the number of employees in each leave plan.

3. In **Column D**, use the appropriate function to calculate the total number of leave days per plan. This result depends on the number of days in the plan and the number of employees eligible for that specific plan. Write solutions in **D4** and **D13**, then **AutoFill** through **D7** and **D15**, respectively.

4. In cells **D8** and **D16**, calculate the total number of leave days based on the total number of days in each leave plan.

5. In **Column E**, use the appropriate function to calculate the number of vacation and family leave days already used by employees under each plan. Write solutions in **E4** and **E13**, then **AutoFill** through **E7** and **E15**, respectively.

6. In cells **E8** and **E16**, calculate the total number of days used based on the number of days used in each plan.

7. In **Column F**, use the Total Days and Days Used results to calculate the number of vacation and family leave Days Remaining for employees under each plan. Write solutions in **F4** and **F13**, then **AutoFill** through **F7** and **F15**, respectively.

8. In cells **F8** and **F16**, calculate the total number of vacation and family leave days remaining.

Knowledge Check 15

This Knowledge Check will test your understanding of nested IFs and compound ANDs and ORs. Solve the following problems on the **Ordering** worksheet in the KnowledgeCheck_15.xlsx file.

Number to Order

Column G should return the number of each item to order according to the following conditions:

- For items with an average rating of at least 3.5 that will be part of an upcoming promotion (see cells **C12**, **C13**, and **C14** on the **Promotions** worksheet) and of which there are fewer than 50 in stock, the number to order should be enough to bring stock back up to 50 after customer orders have been met.

  Hint: To determine how many to order to bring stock back up to 50, take 50, add the number of customer orders, and then subtract the number already on hand.

- For other items with an average rating of at least 3.5 of which there are fewer than 20 in stock, order enough to bring stock back up to 20 after customer orders have been met.

- For the remaining items, if there are more orders than stock, order just enough to fill the customer orders.

- For all other items, order 0.

In cell **G5**, enter a formula that satisfies the foregoing conditions. **AutoFill** the formula through cell **G46**.

Order Date

Column H should return the date by which the order should be placed based on the following conditions:

- If there are currently not enough units on hand to fill customer orders, this should be today's date.

- If the product is part of a current promotion (see cells **C5**, **C6**, and **C7** on the **Promotions** worksheet) and there will be 5 or fewer units on hand after current customer orders have been met, this should be 3 days from today.

- Otherwise, this should be 7 days from today.

In cell **H5**, enter a formula that satisfies the foregoing conditions. **AutoFill** the formula through cell **H46**.

Rush Delivery

Column I should indicate whether rush delivery should be requested from the manufacturer:

- If the manufacturer does not offer rush delivery (cells **C3**, **C4**, **C5**, and **C6** on the **Rush Delivery** worksheet indicate which manufacturers do), the output should be **N/A**. (Hint: The "not equal to" operator may be useful here.)

- Otherwise, if there will be 2 or fewer units on hand after customer orders have been met, the output should be **Yes**.

- In all other cases, the output should be the text **No**.

In cell **I5**, enter a formula that satisfies the foregoing conditions. **AutoFill** the formula through cell **I46**.

After completing these steps, go to the course website to answer Koin-earning questions.

Data Retrieval: VLOOKUP, HLOOKUP, MATCH

Chapter 18

Outline

- Research & Exploration: Named Ranges, VLOOKUP, HLOOKUP, and MATCH Functions

- In-Depth Case Application: Working with VLOOKUP, HLOOKUP, and MATCH Functions

- Review Problems: Practice Data Retrieval Functions, Knowledge Check 16

Objectives

- Create named ranges for use with data retrieval functions.

- Return values using the VLOOKUP function with an exact match and a range.

- Return values using the HLOOKUP function with an exact match and a range.

- Return position or rank using the MATCH function.

- Dynamically return values using a combination of functions.

- Create an in-cell drop-down list.

RESEARCH & EXPLORATION

Research

Research the following Excel functions. Be sure to take advantage of the Excel tutorials online and Microsoft Support at http://office.microsoft.com. You should be able to describe the purpose of these functions.

- Lookup and Reference functions

- Excel functions: VLOOKUP, HLOOKUP, MATCH

Exploration

Navigate to your K201 files, open **Class18-RetrievalFunctions-LOOKUPS.xlsx**, and then complete the RE worksheet(s) using the following information.

Why Use a VLOOKUP?

In the Class18-RetrievalFunctions-Lookups.xlsx workbook, on the RE1 worksheet, look at the expression in **C4**. That is a long IF statement! If the table in F5:I19 increased much more in size, you would not be able to use an IF at all. However, a VLOOKUP can easily handle a large table of data.

The VLOOKUP function takes a value, locates it in the leftmost column of a table, and returns a value in the same row from a column that you specify.

Consider the **Vertical table—Exact match** on the RE1 worksheet. If you are looking for the symbol "MSFT", look down column F until you find exactly "MSFT". Once you find "MSFT", you can retrieve the Company Name from the third column of the table.

Many of the lookup tables that you encounter will be organized vertically—data are arranged in vertical columns. To retrieve values from a vertically organized table, use the VLOOKUP function (vertical lookup).

VLOOKUPs can only return a value that is to the right. If you wish to return a value that is to the left, other functions must be used. If you know the Phone Number, you cannot use VLOOKUP to return the Symbol, because it is to the left of the phone number. You could move the Symbol data to the right of the phone number, but in K201, you will assume that our client does not want us to move the data.

Named Ranges and VLOOKUP

Before using the VLOOKUP function, it's a good idea to name the range of data that you want to use as a table. In an earlier chapter, you created named ranges for columns of data. For a VLOOKUP function, we will give the entire table one name.

If you make a mistake with your named range, click the **Formulas tab** on the Ribbon and then, in the Defined Names group, click **Name Manager**. The Name Manager can help you delete, edit, or create a named range.

Named ranges contain absolute referencing so that no dollar signs are needed to lock in a cell before autofilling. Also, named ranges can make complicated expressions easier to read.

1. Select **F5:I19**.
2. Create a named range by clicking the **Name Box**, type **Company**, and press **Enter**.

In C11, use the VLOOKUP function to return the full company name that corresponds to the symbol MSFT in B11.

VLOOKUP Arguments

- **lookup_value:** The value you are locating—MSFT or the value in B11.

- **table_array:** The table where you are looking for MSFT—F5:I19 or the **Company** named range.

- **col_index_num:** The number of the column in the table of data you want to return values from—not 1, which is the first column, Symbol; not 2, which is the second column, Phone Number; but 3, which is the third column, Company Full Name.

- **range_lookup:** Are you looking in a range? No, we want to exactly match "MSFT", so we would use False. A lookup value that is a text data type will always be an exact match!

3. In cell **C11**, type **=VLOOKUP(B11,Company,3,FALSE)** and then press **Enter**.

4. **AutoFill** the expression down the column.

Notice that Excel returned a #N/A in cell C22 for the Symbol of PPP. This is because there is no PPP symbol in our table, so this is a correct result. If you change the symbol in **B22** to **PFE**, Pfizer Inc will be returned.

VLOOKUP—Table_Array

In a VLOOKUP, Excel looks up a value in the first column of the table_array that you defined. If you know the Phone Numbers and wish to return the Company full name, the table_array argument must start in column G instead of column F.

5. In cell **C26**, type **=VLOOKUP(B26,G5:I19,2,FALSE)**, then press **Enter**.

6. **AutoFill** your expression down to the next cell. Notice that you receive an error. Some of the cells need an absolute cell reference. In cell **C26**, add absolute references to the range **G5:I19**. Then Autofill to the next cell.

HLOOKUP and the Range Argument

Named ranges can help make our expressions easier to read, especially when multiple spreadsheets are used. Because named ranges automatically use absolute cell references, referencing errors may occur less often.

1. On the RE2 worksheet, select cells **E4:K5**.

2. In the Name Box, type in **Price** to name the range.

VLOOKUP and HLOOKUP—Range Argument

The last argument in the VLOOKUP or HLOOKUP asks if you are looking up a value in a range.

In the previous problems, you were always looking for an exact match or always using FALSE for the fourth argument. Sometimes we want Excel to look within a range of values, like 0-999 or 1000-1499, instead of finding an exact match like "MSFT". These types of tables can be confusing, since the value listed in the table is only the lowest value in the range. For example, we would list only 0 to represent the range 0-999. We would list only 1000 to represent the range 1000-1499. For a

VLOOKUP range_lookup, always start with the lowest number. In K201, these tables will be set up for you.

On the RE2 worksheet, Premiere needs an order price for a type of vitamin. The greater the quantity ordered, the less the supplier charges per item—a large quantity discount. This time, the data are arranged horizontally in rows instead of vertically as they were in the prior two problems.

In F4, the 0 represents the range 0-999.

In G4, the 1000 represents the range 1000-1499.

In H4, the 1500 represents the range 1500-1999.

In I4, the 2000 represents the range 2000-2499.

In J4, the 2500 represents the range 2500-2999.

In K4, the 3000 represents the range 3000 and beyond.

This time, for the fourth argument, range_lookup, "Are you looking in a range?", you would type or select TRUE, since you are looking in a range. Note that the range argument is optional. If none is specified, then Excel assumes a TRUE, or range. Best practice dictates always specifying this argument as if it is required.

1. In **C6**, type **=HLOOKUP(B6,Price,2,TRUE)**

While typing in the foregoing expressions, you can type in the named range or use the **F3** or **F5** keys. The F3 key will list named ranges. The F5 key will list named ranges and take you to that named range, which is useful when working with multiple worksheets.

2. Notice that the result does not carry the format from the table over. Format cell **C6** to **Accounting**.

Test your results by trying different order quantities.

Note: *Use an HLOOKUP if your reference table is set up in horizontal rows, but use a VLOOKUP if your reference table is set up in vertical columns.*

The Match Function

The MATCH function returns the position or rank of a value from **one** column or **one** row of data. Match by itself is rarely used, as there are not many situations in which you need to know the position of an item in a list.

At Premiere, employee points are earned for many different things such as seniority, working a last-minute shift, and excellent performance. Points are used in determining schedule preferences, raises, and many other situations. A high employee point total is advantageous. Employees will come in and want to know their point rank and how many points away they are from the highest pointholder. You will use MATCH and VLOOKUP to find this information.

MATCH Arguments

- **lookup_value:** value you are locating—F6 or the Employee's name.

- **lookup_array:** column or row where you are looking for the position rank of the Employee's name—B4:B25

- **match_type:** exact match or 0

1. In cell **F7**, type **=MATCH(F6,B4:B25,0)**

   Note that the employees have already been sorted with the highest point total at the top and the lowest at the bottom. Without this sort, the function would not mean anything in this example. The match function simply tells you that Sanders, Jim is the twelfth cell down on the list. It does not return the fact that Sanders, Jim has 46 points. You need a VLOOKUP to return that value.

   A common mistake is to select a whole table of data for the MATCH function. While this is necessary for the VLOOKUP or HLOOKUP functions, the MATCH function can use only one row or one column of data.

   MATCH includes blank and empty cells in its determination of position or ranking. If you delete Pearce, Kara in B10, Jim Sanders is still shown as being twelfth in the list.

2. Jim wants to know how many points away he is from the top employee. In cell **F8**, type **=MAX(C4:C25)-VLOOKUP(F6,B4:C25,2,FALSE)**

While the MATCH function by itself is very simple, the MATCH function is very useful when used within other functions.

IN-DEPTH CASE APPLICATION

Graded Items

You are working for an instructor who keeps his gradebooks in Excel. The table on the Graded Items worksheet shows the grades of the students. The instructor would like you to come up with a way to help protect students' confidentiality when reviewing grades with students. He doesn't want to have to open the gradebook to this worksheet; he would rather have a separate worksheet on which he can enter one student's user ID and view grades for just that student.

1. In the Chapter18-RetrievalFunctionsLOOKUPs.xlsx workbook, on the Graded Items worksheet, name the range **B3:G17** on this sheet **StudentResults**

MATCH Review

2. In **C20**, return the position of cfoster in the list of usernames.

3. In **C21**, return the position of Final grade in the range **B2:G2**.

Note: *The first MATCH function returned the row in which all cfoster's grades could be retrieved. The second MATCH function returned the column number in which the final grade is stored in the table.*

Grade Retrieval Worksheet

In this problem, you will see how the MATCH function combined with another function can make a dynamic spreadsheet.

1. Name the range **G2:S4** on the Grade Retrieval worksheet **Scale**.

2. In **C6**, type **=VLOOKUP(B3,StudentResults,6,FALSE)** to return the Final Grade percentage for cfoster using the value in B3. Format the result as **Percentage**.

3. The faculty member wants to be able look at other grades besides the Final Grade. Notice that the formula in cell C6 has a hardcoded column index number of 6 that forces it to always return the Final Grade. Edit the function to nest the match function in for the col_index_num argument. Then the match will do the work of figuring out the column index number.

4. In **D6**, use the appropriate LOOKUP function to return the Letter Grade equivalent of the percentage retrieved by the function in cell C6.

Test Your Functions

5. Click cell **B3**, then type **rstone** to test that your functions return the correct values.

6. Enter your own **username** into cell B3. Both your functions should return #N/A. Enter **cfoster** again.

Create In-Cell Drop-Down Lists

In **B3**, create a drop-down list of the usernames of the students:

1. Select cell **B3**.

2. Click the **Data** tab in the Ribbon; in the Data Tools group, click the arrow next to **Data Validation**, then click **Data Validation** again.

3. In the **Allow** box, select **List**.

4. Click in the **Source** box. Click on the **Graded Items** worksheet tab. Select cells **B3:B17**.

5. Click **OK**.

6. Click on cell **B3**, then try out your drop-down list.

7. Also create a drop-down list for **B6** so that different assignments can be selected. Use the range **C2:G2** on the **Graded Items** worksheet as the source.

Supervisor Schedule

The table of data contains a schedule of supervisors on duty for each product department. How could you get Excel to tell you, for any combination of (1) time of day and (2) product department, which supervisor is available to answer questions, handle problems, and meet with reps from various brands?

1. Name the range B6:H19 **schedule**, then continue to the next worksheet.

Company Rep Visits

On the Company Rep Visits worksheet, you have dates and times when reps have scheduled visits to give out free samples at the store. Column E should return the name of the supervisor who is available to meet with each rep.

Because the result depends on both the time when the rep will arrive and the product department in question, K201 refers to this type of problem as a "double lookup."

1. A VLOOKUP function can locate the appropriate time in the **schedule** table, but what should the column index number be?

2. For now, enter a **VLOOKUP** function, then use **4** as the column index number. Fill this down to cell **E7**. The names returned will be supervisors for Perishable products (column 4). Verify the correct supervisor for cells E5 and E7. Notice that cell E6 is incorrect: it returns the supervisor for Perishable Foods instead of for Personal Hygiene.

3. In cell **F5**, enter the MATCH function using the product department from cell **D5** to find out what column number the category occupies in the range **B5:H5** on the Supervisor Schedule worksheet. (Recall that the lookup array for a MATCH function must be a **single** column or row.) You should see that Perishable Foods occupies column 4, Personal Hygiene occupies column 5, and so forth.

4. Delete the contents of column **F**—you want column E to contain the entire solution rather than relying on a MATCH function in another column.

5. Finally, return to your function in cell **E5**, editing it so that it returns the supervisor name from the appropriate column. Remember: cell E5 should contain the entire solution.

6. When you are finished, fix the problem of the #N/A errors as well by nesting in an IF, IFERROR, or IFNA function.

REVIEW PROBLEMS

Review Problem 1

1. Name the vertical table **BonusRates**.

2. Name the horizontal table **CommissionRates**.

Review Problem 2

1. **Column E** should return the commission earned, rounded to the nearest **penny**.

2. **Column G** must consider the following conditions to calculate the bonus earned:

   - For those with sales of at least **$30,000**, use the appropriate bonus rate from the Bonus table.

   - For all others, the bonus rate is **0%**.

3. **Column G** should return the dollar amount of the bonus, rounded to the nearest **penny**.

Knowledge Check 16

Nesting Functions

File Needed

KnowledgeCheck_16.xlsx

Property Costs Analysis—Problem 1

Before purchasing a house, a potential homeowner must evaluate the total cost of ownership. Factors influencing this are the amount of money borrowed, the interest rate, the term of the mortgage, and the cost of homeowner's insurance, property taxes, and homeowner's association dues.

In the **KnowledgeCheck16.xlsx** workbook on the **Property Costs Analysis** worksheet, evaluate the total monthly cost of owning each of the properties being considered.

1. In cells **B6:D6**, solve for the amount of each home purchase to be financed. Assume that the sellers will get their asking prices and that the buyers will be able to make the planned down payment.

2. In cell **B7**, solve for the annual interest rate. The basic formula is

Standard Interest Rate - Interest Rate Discount

The standard rates and rate discounts are given in the tables on the **Rates** worksheet. Name these ranges, and when solving for the annual rate for Property1, make use of a function that can retrieve the appropriate value from each table.

3. Format the result as **Percentage** with **2** decimal places.

4. Copy cell **B7** to **C7** and **D7**.

5. Use an appropriate function in cell **B9** to determine the monthly payment.

6. Copy cell **B9** to **C9:D9**.

7. Use an appropriate function in cell **B13** to determine the total monthly payment for housing.

This amount is the sum of the loan payment amount, monthly property taxes, monthly insurance, and monthly association dues.

8. Copy cell **B13** to cells **C13:D13**.

Loan Payment Calculation—Problem 2

On the **Auto Loan Apps** worksheet, calculate the monthly payment for each loan. This is rather complicated, so be sure to examine the interest rates on the **Auto Loan Rates** worksheet before starting.

If the loan has not been approved by at least two loan officers, the monthly payment should be 0.

Round the final payment to two decimals, then format it as Accounting with two decimals. Note: There are two named ranges (auto_old and auto_new) on the last worksheet.

After completing these steps, go to the course website to answer Koin-earning questions.

Data Retrieval: INDEX and MATCH
Chapter 19

Outline

- Research & Exploration: Understand the Index Function
- In-Depth Case Application: Working with INDEX and MATCH Functions
- Review Problems: Practice Data Retrieval Functions, Knowledge Check 17

Objectives

- Return values using the INDEX function.
- Return position or rank using the MATCH function.
- Dynamically return values using a combination of functions.

RESEARCH & EXPLORATION

Research

Research the Excel function INDEX so you can answer the following questions. Be sure to take advantage of the tutorials available online at Microsoft's support site, http://office.microsoft.com.

How many forms does the INDEX function have? Have you seen any other functions thus far that have more than one form?

What is the array form of the INDEX function? What are the three arguments?

Exploration

Understanding the Different Retrieval Functions

In chapter 18, you learned how to retrieve data out of a data set using the VLOOKUP and HLOOKUP functions. You also learned how to use the MATCH function to count and find the col_index_num or the row_index_num.

You could do all the problems you learned in chapter 18 with an INDEX. However, in practice, most businesspeople have never heard of an INDEX function. In this course, you need to read the language of the problem carefully. If the problem says to **use a lookup**, then you must use either the VLOOKUP or HLOOKUP function. If the problem says to **use an index**, then you must use INDEX function. If the problem says to **use an appropriate retrieval function**, then you can use the VLOOKUP, HLOOKUP, or INDEX function. If the problem warrants, you may also be using a MATCH function nested inside the other functions.

It can be confusing deciding which function to use. In practice, you could always use INDEX and never use VLOOKUP or HLOOKUP. However, VLOOKUP and HLOOKUP are still widely used in business, so you still need to know how those functions work.

To understand how INDEX works, first review what VLOOKUP and HLOOKUP do and do not do.

Suppose the following table is filled with data. A VLOOKUP (vertical) looks **down** the **first** column to find a match with the lookup value. Then it looks to the **right** to the column indicated by the col_index_num; the following example assumes a col_index_num equal to 4. Importantly, the VLOOKUP must be looking in the **first** column in the array for the match, and it must look to a column to the **right** for the value needed.

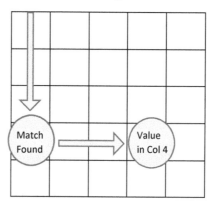

An HLOOKUP (horizontal) looks **across** the **first** row to find a match with the lookup value. Then it looks **down** to the row indicated by the row_index_num; the following example assumes a row_index_num equal to 4. Importantly, the HLOOKUP must be looking in the **first** row in the array for the match, and it must look **down** to a row for the value needed.

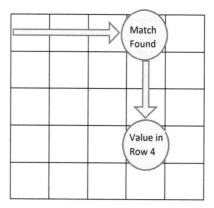

Thus VLOOKUP is limited, because it cannot look **down** a column and look to the **left**. Similarly, HLOOKUP is limited, because it cannot look **across** a row and then look **up**. What should you do if you need this?

For example, what if you have data that you need to match in the **third** column of the data and you need to retrieve data in the **second** column?

You cannot do this with a VLOOKUP. In this course, we call this a "backward" lookup. You can do one of the following:

1. Rearrange the data. This is not always feasible, and in this course, you should NOT do this.

2. Creatively use an HLOOKUP to solve a problem traditionally seen as a VLOOKUP. If you understand how to do this and get the correct answer, it will be graded correctly in this course. However, most people do not think this way. Logically, there is an easier way to solve the problem.

3. Use an INDEX function.

Using the INDEX Function

The INDEX function has two forms: Array form and Reference form. The Array form returns a value, and the Reference form returns a cell reference. In this course, you will use only the Array form.

The INDEX function works differently than the lookups. The INDEX function does not match values, either exactly or in a range. Instead, you must provide the INDEX function with both a row and column number. Then the INDEX simply finds the intersection of that row and column. In the following example, the row_num of 3 and column_num of 4 were used to retrieve the data at their intersection.

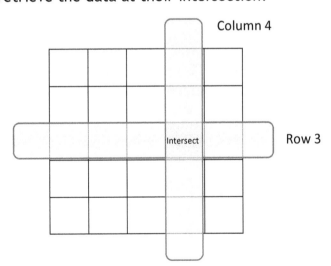

The arguments for the array form are listed first in the tag.

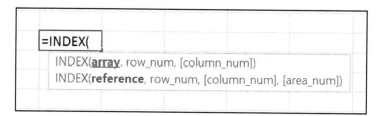

The arguments for the array form are as follow:

- **array**: "Array" means range of cells or table of data. Excel wants to know where the data are that you want to be able to retrieve.

- **row_num**: Starting in the upper left corner of your array, Excel wants to know the row number that contains the data you want to retrieve.

- **column_num**: Starting in the upper left corner of your array, Excel wants to know the column number that contains the data you want to retrieve.

If the array is only one row or one column, then the corresponding argument is optional. If the row_num is not given, then column_num must be given, and vice versa. If the array has multiple columns and multiple rows, then omitting the row or column number will return an array of that row or column. For the purposes of this course, you will treat the row_num and column_num as required.

In practice, you will rarely know the column and row number. Thus, you can use the MATCH function to do what it does best. First, you will practice using an index with no match functions, then one with only one match function, and finally one with two match functions.

1. Open **Chapter19-RetrievalFinctions-INDEX.xlsx**, then click on the **RE1** worksheet.

   Recently, Premiere ran a special on a holiday basket. Notice in cells I5:J14 a table exists with the quantity and then a shipping cost.

2. In cell **F5**, type **=INDEX($I$5:$J$14,E5,1)**

   a. $I$5:$J$14 are the cells where the data exist.

   b. Cell E5 refers to the number ordered and is also the row number in the data. Note this works **only** because the second column of the array contains consecutive numbers. In other words, the quantity ordered does not skip a number. If it did, then this formula would not work. For example, the first member, James Sanderson, ordered 7 baskets. Thus the index function counts down to the seventh row. Importantly, Excel is NOT matching the 7 with the 7 listed in J11.

    c. The value of 1 tells Excel you want the value in the first column. Shipping cost is always in the first column, so you can just enter a 1.

3. Autofill the formula down to cell **F51**.

Using the INDEX Function with One Match

As seen in the preceding exercise, rarely will a situation occur in which only the INDEX function is needed, for the INDEX function itself does not do any value matching. Quite frequently, in practice, you will nest either one or two MATCH functions for the row_num or the column_num or both.

In review, the match function counts what number an item is in a list and takes the following form:

=MATCH(lookup_value,lookup_array,[match_type])

MATCH arguments

- **lookup_value:** the value you are locating—F6 or the Employee's name

- **lookup_array:** the column or row where you are looking for the position rank of the Employee's name—B4:B25

- **match_type:** exact match, or 0

A utility company wants to be able to notify property owners in case of an emergency requiring the utility company to enter the property (tree down, gas leak, power line down, or the like).

Typically, a third party will report a problem at an address (represented by the parcel number). The utility company then must find the contact number of the owner associated with that address.

You want to lookup the owner's emergency contact number based on the parcel number for the land. In this instance, you will use the match function to count down a column to find the row number. This can be confusing at first, as it seems counterintuitive. The match function counts **down a column** to get the **row_number**. In this example, you always want to return the same column, so you will not need a match function for the column_number.

1. On the **RE2** worksheet in cell C3, type **=MATCH(C2,D8:D190,0)**

   The cell returns the value of 1. Excel took the value in cell C2 of 013-00470-00 and looked in the column D8:D190. Excel matched that value in the first cell, D8. Thus the match function returns a 1.

2. Click in cell **C2**, then select a **different parcel number** from the drop down list. Cell C3 changes to tell you the row number of parcel you selected.

3. In this case, you want the Emergency Contact Number, not just the row the parcel is in. Thus you will need to nest a MATCH function to accomplish your task.

4. In cell C4 type **=INDEX(B8:E190,MATCH(C2,D8:D190,0),2)**

   For the third argument, you entered a hardcoded 2, because you always want to return the value in column 2. Now cell C4 returns the Emergency Contact Number for the parcel selected in cell C2.

Using the INDEX Function with Two Matches

Premiere is creating a nutritional worksheet for an Employee Get Fit program. The user will select the Chip type and the Nutritional value wanted—Serving Size, Calories, Fat, Sodium, Carbs, or Protein. To solve this, an INDEX with two nested MATCH functions is needed.

The first MATCH function will count **down a column** to find the **row_number** like in the last problem. The second MATCH function will count **across a row** to find the **column_number**.

1. On the **RE3** worksheet, in cell **C5**, type **=MATCH(C2,I10:I31,0)**

   The position number returned by the MATCH function will also be the row number where Fritos information can be retrieved.

2. In cell **C6**, type **=MATCH(C3,B9:I9,0)**

   The position number returned by the MATCH function will also be the column number where Calorie information can be retrieved.

3. In cell **C7**, type **=INDEX(B10:I31,C5,C6)**

Note: *When defining the range of cells for multiple array arguments— e.g., lookup_arrays and arrays—all arrays must be either the same width or the same height as each other. Otherwise, the match function will count incorrectly and lead to incorrect results.*

4. Change cell **C7** to nest the match functions inside the formula. The final formula should be
   =INDEX(B10:I31,**MATCH(C2,I10:I31,0)**,**MATCH(C3,B9:I9,0)**)

5. Change the values in **C2** and **C3**; your MATCH functions should automatically update to a different row and/or column, and your INDEX function should now retrieve the updated value.

 # IN-DEPTH CASE APPLICATION

Use INDEX for a "Backward Lookup"

Some data retrieval problems are structured in such a way that they cannot be intuitively solved with VLOOKUP or HLOOKUP. A "backward lookup" problem can be solved by the use of INDEX and MATCH together. The MATCH function is used to determine the row number to use within the INDEX—or, in some cases, both the row and column numbers.

Consider the following table:

Company Name	Employees	Phone Number
Kirkwood Design Studio	8	812-331-0255
BG Hoadley Quarries Inc	44	812-332-1447
Bell Trace Health and Living Center	80	812-323-2858

You need to return the Company Name from column 1 based on a Phone Number; that is, you are looking up data in column 3 and returning data "backward," or from the **left** in column 1. To determine the row number for an INDEX function from which you want to return the data, you will have to use the MATCH function to match, say, 812-323-2858 with row number 3. The MATCH function will allow you to dynamically determine the row number given any Phone Number above.

Lollapalooza Band Acts

The Lollapalooza worksheet shows the schedule for the music festival of Lollapalooza. Premiere is a sponsor and wants to send people to check out certain acts and perhaps offer them products to promote.

For example, given the act in cell I3, we want to find when and where the show is. While the schedule looks like a VLOOKUP table, VLOOKUP cannot do what we'll call a "backward lookup": it can't scan down a column to see where your item fits and then read back a value from a column to the left of that. Accordingly, you must use an INDEX function.

The INDEX function needs a row and column number. While you do not have those, you can calculate them using the MATCH function. Be careful which ranges you use.

Note: *If a band played twice, this would return information for the first performance only. LOOKUP, MATCH, and INDEX functions locate only the first instance of the lookup_value and thus work best on unique values.* In I6, time will be returned as .75. In Excel, time is shown as a fraction of a day, so noon is 0.50 and 6:00 p.m. is 0.75. Format I6 as Time so it is shown as 6:00:00 PM.

1. On the Lollapalooza worksheet, enter a function in cell I5 that will return the Day on which the act in cell I3 performs. Write this function so it can be copied down to cell I7 and return the Time and Stage as well.

2. Format cell I6 as **Time**.

Product Analysis Worksheet

This worksheet contains some Premiere Foods product sales information for 2015.

1. In cell **H6**, use an appropriate function to retrieve the **Selling Price** for the Product ID in cell **H4**. Write the function so that it can be copied down to **H8** to automatically retrieve the **2015 Sales Volume** and **2015 Product Revenue** values. You can use either an INDEX or a LOOKUP function.

2. Appropriately format cells **H6** and **H8**.

3. In cell **K5**, use an INDEX function to retrieve the **Product ID** of the product that had the highest **2015 Product Revenue**. Write the

function so that it can be copied down to **K8** to automatically retrieve the **Product Category**, **Selling Price**, and **2015 Sales Volume**. What would happen if there was a tie? In other words, what if two different products had the exact same highest revenue? Format cell **K7** appropriately.

REVIEW PROBLEMS

Review Problem 1

1. On the Review1 worksheet, name the range of data on this sheet (starting in cell B5 or C5) **CategorySales**. Know what range you select for CategorySales. The formula you use in the next review problem will depend on how you set up the CategorySales named range.

2. Look over these data, then solve the problem on the Review2 worksheet.

Review Problem 2

1. On the Review2 worksheet, in **C7**, write a function that will return the sales value for the city in **B7** and whatever category is selected from the drop-down in **C2**.

2. Copy this function through **C12**. The chart should now display data for the selected category.

3. Change the category in cell **C2**, noticing the changes in both the values and the chart.

Review Problem 3

As a part of the Employee Get Fit program, Premiere wants to provide employees with a spreadsheet that displays calories burned while performing various activities.

1. On the Review3 worksheet, in cell **C4**, use an INDEX function (and other functions if needed) to return the calories for the Activity and Weight selected in cells C2 and C3.

2. On the Review3 worksheet, in cell **C5**, use a VLOOKUP function (and other functions if needed) to return the calories for the Activity and Weight selected in cells C2 and C3.

3. Which function did you prefer using, and why?

Knowledge Check 17

Retrieval Functions

File Needed

KnowledgeCheck_17.xlsx

For this Knowledge Check, you have the monthly sales revenue of each product category at Premiere in each of the three sales locations (OH store, IN store, Online). There is also a worksheet on which to consolidate this sales information, as well as a sheet to allow easy retrieval of sales figures for a particular category in a particular month.

1. In the KnowledgeCheck_17.xlsx workbook, on the All worksheet, in cell **B3**, enter a function that sums the values in cell B3 from the three location worksheets.

2. Copy your function through All!M8.

3. Assign the name all_locations to the range A2:N9 on the All worksheet.

4. Assign the names OH_store, IN_store, and Online to the same range on the OH Store, IN_store, and Online worksheets, respectively.

5. Cell **B8** on the **Retrieve figures** worksheet should return the appropriate revenue figure from the all_locations range, depending on what a user chooses from the drop-down lists in cells **B3** and **B4** for category and month.

Part of this knowledge check involves exploring and practicing various methods for retrieving data. For this one, use the VLOOKUP function.

6. Cells **B9**, **B10**, and **B11** should return the appropriate revenue figure for each sales location, again using VLOOKUP functions. **C9:C11** should calculate each location's percentage of the total.

7. Your results should at first reflect the sales revenue of perishable foods in all regions in November.

8. Format all sales revenue values as Currency. Format all percentages as Percent with 2 decimal places.

9. Test your functions by changing the values in cells B3 and B4 to answer the following questions:

   What was the sales revenue of perishable foods for all regions in January? In August?

   Which of the three sales locations brought in the most revenue from frozen foods sales?

10. For more practice (and to better understand the functions involved here), starting in cell **E8**, solve the problem using the INDEX function instead.

11. Last, starting in cell **H8**, solve the problem using the HLOOKUP function.

After completing these steps, go to the course website to answer Koin-earning questions.

Spreadsheet Models and Data Tables
Chapter 20

Outline

- Research & Exploration: Research Basic Components of a Spreadsheet Model, Create a One-Variable Data Table

- In-Depth Case Application: Design Characteristics of a Spreadsheet Model, Create One-Variable and Two-Variable Data Tables

- Review Problems: Creating a One- and Two-Variable Data Table, Knowledge Check 18

Objectives

- Understand the basic components and design principles of a spreadsheet model.

- Understand the difference between a descriptive and a prescriptive model.

- Create and use one- and two-variable data tables.

RESEARCH & EXPLORATION

Research

Research the following key terms to complete the Research section. Be sure to take advantage of the Excel tutorials online at http://ittraining.iu.edu and of online Microsoft Support at http://office.microsoft.com.

- One-variable data table
- Two-variable data table

You should be able to describe a situation in which a data table would be useful.

Exploration

Understanding the Basic Components of a Spreadsheet Model

A spreadsheet model is simply a spreadsheet that has been set up to resemble a real-world situation. The more realistic a model, the more useful it is. However, most models end up making some assumptions—either for simplicity or to compensate for lack of information. Different kinds of models exist, such as deterministic, probabilistic, and predictive, but some of these are beyond the scope of this course. This chapter will discuss descriptive and prescriptive models. All models contain these four basic components.

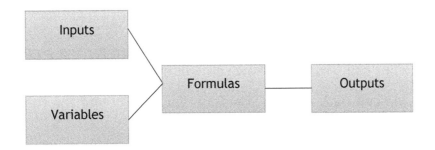

- **Inputs:** Known data that are required for calculations in the model—for example, cost of materials, selling price, and number of products sold.

- **Variables (Decision/Uncertain):** A variable over which a decision maker has control or a variable that is not yet known—for example, number of items to order, demand for a product, or rate of return on an investment.

- **Formulas:** Formulas and functions using the inputs and variables to arrive at the outputs.

- **Outputs:** Values of interest that are the result of calculations involving inputs and variables—for example, revenue, costs, or profit.

Creating a model, particularly from a blank spreadsheet, can be intimidating. Identifying the components of a model gives you a starting point and organization for the model.

Assume you want to create a model of your grades in this course. What component would your scores earned, current grade, and exam scores be in? Which would be inputs, variables, and outputs? Would grades be uncertain or decision variables—or somewhere in between as you decide how much time to study?

Creating a Grade Model

Navigate to your K201 files, open **Chapter20-Models-DataTables.xlsx**, and then complete the RE worksheet(s) using the following information.

A descriptive model describes the current state of a real-life situation. Use the following steps to complete the model of grades for the course:

1. In the file Chapter20-Model-DataTables.xlsx, on the RE1 worksheet, in cells **C4:C20**, enter the **points possible** for the graded items that you have completed and for which you have received a score. Leave this blank for the graded items that you have not yet finished or for which grades have not yet been posted. For now, leave cell C16 with a value of 200.

2. In cells **D4:D20**, enter the **points earned** for the graded items. For cell D16, guess how you will do on the second practical exam.

3. In cell **D22**, enter a SUM function to calculate the total points earned.

4. In cell **D23**, calculate the percentage of total points earned. Incorporate an IF statement so that the formula returns a blank if the value in D22 is **0**. Format as **Percentage** with **2** decimal places.

5. In cell **D24**, use an appropriate function that will return the letter grade from the named range **Scale** based on the percentage in cell D23. Incorporate an IF statement so that the function returns a blank if D23 is blank.

Creating a Prescriptive Model: One-Variable Data Table

Prescriptive models are adapted from descriptive models and can aid the decision making process by demonstrating how changing certain variables can impact the outcome. Prescriptive models perform a what-if analysis.

Now that you have completed the grade model, you have an accurate calculation of your current grade in the course. However, there are still several uncertain variables that will affect your final grade in the course, such as Lab Practical 2.

Use the following steps to create a one-variable data table that will allow you to estimate your final grade percentage and letter grade in the course based on several different Lab Practical 2 scores:

1. In cell **J7:J17**, type **100** through **200** in increments of **10** as possible Lab Practical 2 scores.

2. In cell **K6**, reference cell **D23** as an output cell of interest.

3. In cell **L6**, reference cell **D24** as the other output cell of interest.

4. Select the range **J6:L17**. To create a data table, the selection must include only the decision/uncertain variables and any references to output cells.

5. Click the **Data** tab; in the Data Tools group, click **What-If Analysis**, then **Data Table**.

6. In the Data Table dialog box, leave the **Row input cell** field blank, because the top row of this data table consists only of references to output cells.

7. Click the **Column input cell** box and reference cell **D16**, because in this data table, the left column consists of points possible for Lab Practical 2, and cell D16 is where that value is to be entered. If you click on cell D16 to select it, notice that Excel automatically puts in an absolute reference. If you type it by hand, you need the absolute reference $D$16.

8. Click **OK** to create the one-variable data table. Format the Percentage values as **Percentage** with **2** decimal places.

9. What is your estimated final letter grade if you earn 170 points on Lab Practical 2?

10. What other uncertain variables will affect your final grade, even though it was not accounted for in this model?

Creating a Usable Model

Spreadsheets are used in business to aid decision making. A perfectly accurate model that is misunderstood will mislead. A good spreadsheet model, accordingly, incorporates the following design principles. The lack of even one principle can render the model unusable.

- **Accuracy:** The values of your inputs are carefully verified, and your formulas are tested to ensure that your model's outputs are reliable.

- **Clarity:** Enables a spreadsheet model to effectively communicate its contents to other people or users.

- **Flexibility:** Using cell references instead of hardcoding values in formulas.

- **Efficiency:** Taking advantage of the many available functions available instead of creating complex formulas by hand.

- **Documentation:** Further explains how the model was created to other people.

  - *External:* General explanation of the model, information about the author, and information about the software version used to create the model

  - *Internal:* Labels, row and column headings, named ranges, text boxes, and the like

Using Custom Formats

While accuracy is the most important part of a model, the second design principle of clarity is equally important. If the user of the spreadsheet misunderstands the model, the model will lead to poor decision making. One tool you can use to help add clarity is custom formats.

For example, In Chapter20_SpreadsheetModelsAndDataTable.xlsx on the RE1 worksheet, look at cells K6 and L6. Those values must be there for the data table to work. If you did not know how a data table worked, what would you think these cells meant? A reasonable user of the model might think it means that on average, these grades will result in a B in the course. Is that accurate? In fact, if you average the potential outcomes in the table, on average these grades would result in a C+! This spreadsheet lacks clarity about these two cells.

You could add a note, or internal documentation, to clarify, but a better solution would be to use custom formats. During the In-Depth Application section, you will use custom formats to add clarity.

Excel has four levels of custom formatting: Positive, Negative, Zero, and Text. Each level is separated by a semicolon.

1. The first level specifies what the cell should look like if the underlying value is positive.

2. The second level specifies what the cell should look like if the underlying value is negative.

3. The third level specifies what the cell should look like if the underlying value is zero. If the third level is zero and the fourth level is not specified, it will give underlying values of zero the same format as an underlying value of positive.

4. The fourth level specifies what the cell should look like if the underlying value is text. If the underlying value will never be text in the model, you need not specify this level.

For this course, you need specify only the first two levels.

IN-DEPTH CASE APPLICATION

Creating a New Product Profit Model

Premiere Foods is considering a new product investment. This worksheet contains a partially created model to help determine whether it will be a profitable investment.

Premiere Foods will purchase the quantity in cell **B9**, and the estimated demand for the product is in cell **B11**. The cost per unit can be found in the table in cells **D5:E10**. The selling price is in cell **B6**; Premiere cannot sell more than the quantity purchased. If there are any leftover units due to demand's being lower than expected, they can be sold at the discounted price in cell **B7**.

1. In the file Chapter20-Models-DataTables.xlsx, on the Profit Model 1 worksheet, complete the model by entering appropriate formulas and functions in cells **B5** and **B15:B17**.

2. Once you have completed the model, create a **one-variable data table** to see how changes in **order quantity** affect the **Revenue**, **Costs**, and **Profit/Loss** for Premiere Foods.

3. **Order Quantity** should range from **1000** to **4000** in increments of **500**.

4. Delete cells **F13:H13**.

5. Right-click on cell **F14**, then select **Format Cells**.

6. On the Number tab under the Category, choose **Custom**.

7. In the **Type:** box, erase anything currently there, then type "Revenue";"Revenue"

8. Click **OK**. The cell now looks like it says Revenue. However, the value is still equal to B15. This custom formatting makes your model easier to understand.

   The first "Revenue" means that if the underlying value is positive, then make it look as if the cell says Revenue. The second "Revenue" (separated by a semi-colon) means that if the underlying value is negative, then make it look as if the cell says Revenue.

9. Repeat steps **5-8** for cell **G14** to display **Costs** and for cell **H14** to display **Profit/Loss.**

Creating a New Product Two-Variable Profit Model

The same profit model appears on this worksheet. It is important to note that there are two main factors that affect profit/loss in a business: supply and demand.

1. Create a **two-variable data table** to see how changes in **order quantity** and **estimated demand** affect **Profit/Loss,** a key output.

2. Again, **Order Quantity** should range from **1000** to **4000** in increments of **500.**

3. **Estimated Demand** should range from **500** to **5000** in increments of **500.**

4. Add a custom format to cell **E14** so that it appears blank. To do this, type **;;;** in the **Type:** box.

   Three semicolons in the custom format will always make the cell appear to display blank.

5. If the order quantity is 2,500, what is the approximate demand required to break even? Add conditional formatting to change the background color to **Dark Red** and a text color of **White** for those values less than **0.**

6. Explain which of the characteristics of good design are present in the model.

REVIEW PROBLEMS

Review Problem 1

Modeling Retirement

On the Review1 worksheet you have a partially created retirement model. You have $5,000 to deposit into the retirement account today and will make monthly deposits of $500 until you retire. The estimated interest rate on the account is 3.5%.

1. Examine the retirement investment model to determine which cells are the inputs, which cell the decision variable, which cell the uncertain variable, and which cells the outputs.

2. Apply a cell style of your choosing to each different type of variable.

3. In cell **B8**, enter your current age.

4. In cell **B9**, enter your desired retirement age.

5. In cell **B10**, enter a formula to calculate the number of monthly deposits you will make until you reach your desired retirement age.

6. In cell **B12**, use the FV function to calculate the amount of money that will be available in the account at your desired retirement age.

7. In cells **F3:L3**, enter possible interest rates for the retirement account, starting with **2.5%** and ending with **5.5%** in increments of 0.5%. Apply the same cell style to these cells as you did to B6.

8. In cells **E4:E14**, enter possible retirement ages, starting with **55** and ending with **75** in increments of 2. Apply the same cell style to these cells as you did B9.

9. In cell **E3**, reference the output cell that calculates the future value of the retirement account. Add a custom format to the cell so that the text **Retirement Savings** is displayed.

10. Complete the two-variable data table, then format the values inside the table as Currency.

11. If the actual interest rate earned on the account is 3.5%, what is the earliest age at which you can retire and have at least $1,000,000 in the account?

Knowledge Check 18

One- and Two-Variable Data Tables

File Needed

KnowledgeCheck_18.xlsx

Robin and Steve Witkemper own a bed-and-breakfast in Nashville, Indiana. Over the past 10 years since they opened, taxes have risen substantially, as have other costs. However, the Witkempers have resisted changing their nightly rate. As a result, their profits have steadily declined, dropping more than $15,000 per year. Faced with the reality of a nightly stay increase, they have requested your help in setting a base rate per night.

Understand the Business Model

The Profit Analysis worksheet already contains data about revenue and expenses, as well as formulas for calculating totals and net profit.

1. Click on cells **C10**, **C16**, **C23**, **C27**, and **C28** to examine those formulas.

2. Historically, the Witkempers average 800 stays per year (cell C3), with the lowest year having 700 and the highest year 1,000. Each stay consists of one guest room with a maximum of 2 guests for one night.

All calculations assume that each stay is at capacity.

Currently, the Witkempers charge a base rate of $139 per night (cell C7). That rate would apply to the value (off) season. During moderate-demand months, they would add a $30 upcharge; during high-demand seasons, they would add a $60 upcharge.

The Witkempers want to make at least $50,000 per year in profit. Remember: The Witkempers live at the bed and breakfast. They do not pay a mortgage as the company—the bed and breakfast—covers their residence. Thus, the profit is used only for other living expenses. With last year's rate and demand and the anticipated costs next year, the Witkempers would make only $34,800 in profit.

Identify and Format Model Components

3. Add a fill color for the various parts of your model according to the following guide:

   - Inputs: Any light blue color

   - Decision variable: Any light orange color

   - Uncertain variable: Any light red color

   - Outputs of interest: Any light gray color

Create a One-Variable Data Table

Create a one-variable data table that calculates the total revenue and net profit when rate per night ranges from **$139** to **$239** in increments of **$10**.

The one-variable data table has already been partially set up for you on the Analysis worksheet and needs to be completed in cells E3:G14.

4. To begin completing the one-variable data table, enter the desired values for nightly rates in cells **E4:E14**, then reference the relevant output cells in cells **F3** and **G3**.

5. Select the appropriate range, then complete the one-variable data table, referencing the correct input cell.

Can the Witkempers meet their goal of a $50,000 net profit given the current range of nightly rates considered?

If so, to what level would they need to increase it?

Create a Two-Variable Data Table

The Witkempers are concerned that a rate hike will decrease the demand (and thus the number of nightly stays). Complete the two-variable data table that has been started for you in cells E18:M29 on the Analysis worksheet. This table will illustrate how net profit changes as both rate per night and nightly stays per year change.

To save you time, the nightly stays per year variables have already been entered for you.

1. Enter the rate per night variables in cells E19:E29 (again, values vary from $139 to $239 in increments of $10).

2. Reference the appropriate output cell in **E18**.

3. Select the appropriate range, then complete the two-variable data table, referencing the appropriate variables.

Based on the rate required to meet the goal of $50,000 found in the one-variable data table, can the Witkempers meet their profit goal with the new rate if the demand is only 700?

After completing these steps, go to the course website to answer Koin-earning questions.

Data Validation

Chapter 21

Outline

- Research & Exploration: Research Formula Auditing and Data Validation, Create Simple Drop-Down Lists, Limit Dates That Can Be Entered into a Cell

- In-Depth Case Application: Improve an Existing Budget Application for Other Users

- Review Problems: Improve an Existing Price Quote Application for Other Users

Objectives

- Understand what an Excel application is.

- Troubleshoot designer- and user-introduced spreadsheet errors.

- Implement Data Validation rules to prevent data entry errors.

- Add internal documentation to an application.

- Implement features to prevent formula errors.

RESEARCH & EXPLORATION

Research

This chapter focuses on finding and fixing existing worksheet errors and preventing future errors from being introduced by users of Excel applications.

While errors like #NAME?, #VALUE!, and #DIV/0! typically stand out on a worksheet, how to correct them may not be immediately obvious, especially when they are associated with long formulas that reference many other cells. The utilities available in the Formula Auditing group on the Formulas tab can aid in such troubleshooting. You have already used the Evaluate Formula utility to examine nested AND and OR functions in chapter 17. To learn about other types of Formula Auditing techniques, open a browser, then use your preferred search engine to look up Formula Auditing in Excel.

After Formula Auditing helps fix problems that occur during worksheet design, Data Validation helps prevent data entry errors during worksheet use. To learn more about preventing user-introduced errors, read the introduction and the sections "What is data validation?" and "When is data validation useful?" in this Microsoft article.

Exploration

Circular References

Open the Chapter21_DataValidation.xlsx file. You will see a circular reference warning:

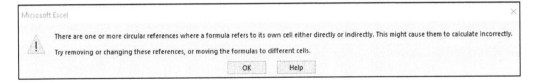

1. Click **OK** to continue. We will fix this problem in the In-Depth Case Application.

As the warning message explains, a circular reference occurs when a formula contains a reference to its own cell. This can be a direct reference or an indirect reference. In a direct reference, a formula refers immediately to the cell in which it itself resides. For example, the formula in cell B7 might contain a direct reference to cell B7:

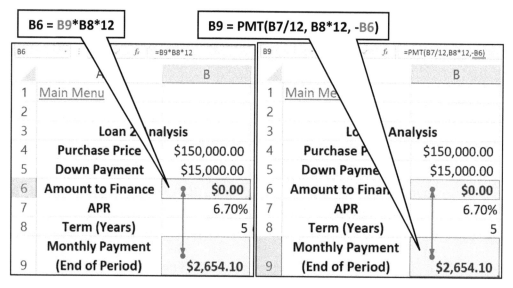

An indirect reference is more difficult to spot. It occurs when a formula in one cell contains a reference to another cell whose formula ultimately depends on a reference to the first cell. For example, in the following (incorrect!) calculation, cell B6 refers to cells B9 and B8. However, cell B9 refers to B6, leading Excel in a circle.

Excel will alert you when you type a circular reference; if it is an indirect circular reference, Excel will also draw a blue line linking the problematic formulas, as just illustrated.

Creating Drop-Down Lists and Restricting Dates

In the article linked in the Research section, you learned that you can use Data Validation to create a drop-down list of values from which a user can pick and that you can restrict user-entered dates to a certain time frame.

Navigate to the **RE1** worksheet. Premiere recently started offering an educational program focusing on healthy eating and cooking. The program is open to the public (not just Premiere Members), and participants can sign up for a 1-month, 3-month, or 6-month package of unlimited classes at one of several locations (Bloomington-Showers, Bloomington-Store, Chicago-Lincoln Park, Chicago-Pilsen, or Chicago-Store).

Premiere's data entry clerk needs to record the following for each student: class package, class site, whether the student is a Member of Premiere's loyalty club, and, if applicable, the student's loyalty club renewal date. Since there are limited and standardized input options for the Class Package, Class Site, and Club Member fields, it would be helpful to make drop-down lists of items from which the data entry clerk could select. This would save time and help prevent errors such as accidentally typing "5-month" instead of "6-month". Drop-down lists are a useful type of Data Validation in Excel.

Complete the following steps to create a drop-down list for the Class Package column:

1. On the **RE1** worksheet, select **D6:D26**.

2. On the **Data** tab, in the Data Tools group, click **Data Validation**.

3. In the Settings tab of the Data Validation utility, set the Allow field to **List**.

4. Click inside the **Source** box that appears.

5. The list items we want are contained on the Exploration Drop-Downs worksheet. Click on the **Exploration Drop-Downs** worksheet tab, then select cells **A4:A7**. Notice that cell A4 is blank; including a blank cell in the list allows the data entry clerk to select a blank value if necessary.

6. Click **OK**. Test the drop-down by selecting different membership types for a few of the listed students.

Rather than hand-selecting a range of cells to specify the Source of the list items, you can also refer to a named range. The class sites for the drop-down in Column E are contained in the ClassSite named range on the Exploration Drop-Downs worksheet. Use the Name Box to view this named range, then use the following alternate method to create the drop-down list of class sites:

7. On the **RE1** worksheet, select **E6:E26**.

8. On the **Data** tab, in the Data Tools group, click **Data Validation**.

9. In the Settings tab of the Data Validation utility, set the Allow field to **List**.

10. Click inside the **Source** box, then press **F3**. Select the **ClassSite** named range; click **OK**, then **OK** again. Test the drop-down with a few records.

11. Resize Column E if you wish.

In the previous two examples, the drop-down items we wanted to use were listed somewhere in the workbook. Be aware that this is not required; you can also simply type the list items you want directly into the Source box. For the Club Member column, the clerk should enter either Yes or No. Use the following steps to create this drop-down without referring to cells or named ranges for the Source:

12. Select **F6:F26**.

13. On the **Data** tab, in the Data Tools group, click **Data Validation**.

14. In the **Settings** tab of the Data Validation utility, set the Allow field to **List**.

15. In the **Source** box that appears, type **Yes, No**. This is a rare instance in which you should NOT put quotes around text in Excel.

16. Click **OK**. Test the drop-down.

The data entry clerk should not enter previous dates in Column G. To restrict the dates that can be entered, follow these steps:

17. Select **G6:G26**.

18. On the **Data** tab, in the Data Tools group, click **Data Validation**.

19. In the **Settings** tab of the Data Validation popup box, set the Allow field to **Date**.

20. In the **Data** box that appears, select **greater than or equal to**.

21. In the **Start date** box that appears, type **=TODAY()**. This will limit dates to only the current day's date and future dates.

22. Click **OK**. Test the validation rule by entering various dates (past, present, and future) for a few of the students.

Note that in each of these four examples, because you selected a multiple-cell range before clicking the Data Validation button, the Data Validation settings were applied to multiple cells, not to a single cell. If the same Data Validation rule should apply to multiple cells, then, to save time, you can set the rule for all those cells simultaneously rather than working cell by cell. Just make sure you select all the appropriate cells before you begin.

Protected Sheets

If someone were to change the values in the Exploration Drop-Downs worksheet, then the items in our drop-down lists in Column D and Column E of the RE1 worksheet would also change, since the Class Package and Class Site drop-down list items reference the values in the Exploration Drop-Downs worksheet. What if we accidentally ended up with the following list?

Name		Class Package C
Florence	EPLEY	
Thelma	MCCONNEL	
Jonathan	HEINZ	Bob 3-month
Cynthia	KEENAN	6-month

To prevent someone from changing the values on the Exploration Drop-Downs worksheet, it has been "protected." To see this protection in action, select the **Exploration Drop-Downs** worksheet and attempt to modify any cell's contents; permission will be denied. Protecting a worksheet is useful in preventing unauthorized changes and accidental errors from being made in cells that the user doesn't need to modify. Before any change can be made, the sheet must be unprotected; the spreadsheet designer can set a password for unprotecting the sheet to add greater security.

Although this entire worksheet has been locked against changes, it is possible to lock some portions of a worksheet but leave other portions available for editing. For instance, you could allow the user to change the contents of cells A1, A2, and A3 only. This process will be covered in the In-Depth Case Application.

Internal Documentation

Because you've added drop-down lists to the Class and Class Site fields on the RE1 worksheet, it should be fairly straightforward for the data entry clerk to fill in these details. However, the renewal date must still be typed by hand, and the clerk might not initially know that past dates are not allowed. To alert the user to this fact, a comment has been added. Navigate to cell **G5** on the **RE1** worksheet to examine this comment, the presence of which is indicated by a small red triangle in the upper right corner of the cell. Comments are only visible when you hover over or select cells that contain them. You will learn how to add comments and other types of internal documentation in the In-Depth Case Application.

In-Depth Case Application

Excel Applications

An Excel application, or "app," is a workbook or system of linked workbooks centered on a task with the aim of helping users complete that task simply while encountering as few errors as possible. Experienced Excel users often create apps for use by inexperienced users. Consequently, such apps must be easy to use, well documented, and error-free. They must also anticipate and include preventive measures against potential user errors.

Although Excel applications often help businesses solve problems and make decisions, their use is not limited to the corporate world. An Excel app could just as easily help a Little 500 team plan its training and its race-day tactics, help a group of friends track the successes of their NCAA tournament picks, or help a young professional manage his or her finances.

To build a robust Excel app, you must not only ensure that it is error-free and that it anticipates and prevents user-introduced problems but also understand the role that the application will play for the user and be well versed in any rules involved. For example, if you were building a Little 500 training and tactics app, you would need to know that the women's race is 100 laps long; if you were designing an NCAA tournament tracker, you would need to know that the winner of each game progresses to the next round. These types of parameters would need to be included in the finished application.

Budget Analysis Application Improvement

Navigate to the **Budget Analysis** worksheet. An intern created this application to help the Premiere team set budgets for the dairy department. The CFO is concerned because the app contains both intrinsic formula errors introduced by the designer and data entry errors introduced by a previous user. The CFO has asked you to revise the application with a focus on fixing these issues and preventing future problems. She wants the application to be well documented internally and easy to use, even for a novice Excel user.

1. Before starting to modify the app, navigate to the **Data** worksheet to examine its contents; it holds the flat data used for the budget analysis.

Troubleshooting Data Entry Errors

To begin the revision, we will find and fix data entry errors.

1. Return to the **Budget Analysis** worksheet.

2. This worksheet's table and chart—which are currently blank—are populated by the data corresponding to the Year and Location listed in cells B4 and B5. Change **B4** and **B5** as needed so that each of these matches a corresponding value on the Data worksheet.

Troubleshooting Formula Errors

Next we need to ensure that all of the built-in formulas are correct. When you opened the workbook, Excel alerted you to one problem—a circular reference error.

1. Rather than manually looking for the cell with the circular reference, let Excel find it. Click the **Formulas** tab, and then, in the Formula Auditing group, click the **Error Checking drop-down arrow.**

2. Hover over the **Circular References** item, then click the **cell reference** that appears next to it. Note that there are several cells containing circular references; the first cell that Excel identifies here may vary from computer to computer.

3. Notice that clicking on the cell reference activates the problematic cell. Examine the formula inside this cell; the formula references itself. Modify the formula to so that it references the correct cells.

4. **AutoFill** the change so that it applies to the entire range **N8:P8.**

5. Select cell **M13.** Notice that the formula in this cell results in a #NAME? error. Rather than searching for the error on your own, let Excel help you find it. On the **Formulas** tab, in the Formula Auditing group, click **Evaluate Formula.** In the Evaluate Formula utility, click **Evaluate** as many times as needed to determine where the error is.

6. Click **Close,** then correct the formula in cell **M13.**

7. You should now see an #N/A message in cell M13. Because cells O5:O7 are empty, Excel cannot calculate a maximum value for that range— the value is "not available." At this point, since you know you have fixed the formula error and you understand why you are seeing #N/A, it is safe to insert an IFERROR function to suppress this #N/A output, which otherwise might worry the user. In **M13,** place the **IFERROR** function around the existing IF function, using a **blank** as the value_if_error argument.

   Be careful to insert IFERROR functions *only* when necessary after you have verified your formulas without them. If the original app designer had hastily inserted an IFERROR function without troubleshooting the formula in cell M13, we would not have found the problem here, and the error would have persisted.

Preventing Errors with Data Validation

Now that we have corrected existing errors, we will apply Data Validation to prevent future errors from being made by users. A great place to start would be to create drop-down lists for Year and Location in B4 and B5, respectively. Then the user will not have to guess about appropriate entries, and potential spelling errors will be avoided.

1. Navigate to the **Drop-Downs** worksheet. In the Name Box, observe two existing named ranges: **Year** and **Location**. These can be used to populate drop-down lists on the Budget Analysis worksheet.

2. Return to the **Budget Analysis** worksheet, then select cells **B4:B5**. Selecting both cells simultaneously allows us to apply Data Validation settings to both cells at once for efficiency.

3. Click the **Data** tab, and in the Data Tools group, click **Data Validation**.

4. In the **Settings** tab of the Data Validation utility, set the Allow field to **List**.

   For the Source, we cannot use the Paste Name utility (the F3 key) to select a named range as we did in the Exploration. Since we are applying the rule to two cells at once, we need to specify two separate named ranges—but the Paste Name utility only allows selection of a single range. Instead, we will take advantage of the fact that the named ranges we need are identical to the labels in cells A4 and A5 by using the INDIRECT function to refer to these named ranges.

5. In the **Source** box, type **=INDIRECT(A4)**. The INDIRECT function interprets text in a cell as the name of a named range.

6. Click **OK**, then click on **B4** and then **B5** to examine the new drop-down lists.

7. Select cell **B5**. On the **Data** tab, in the Data Tools group, click **Data Validation**. The Source field should read =INDIRECT(A5). Recall that you typed =INDIRECT(A4) with no dollar signs when you specified the validation rule for both B4 and B5. Excel applied that formula to B4 and then shifted the cell reference inside it down one cell (to A5) when applying the formula to B5. Thus relative versus absolute cell

referencing makes a difference in Data Validation when you have multiple cells selected. Click **Cancel**.

8. To get a better idea of how the INDIRECT function works, select cell **A4**. Change its value to **Location**. Click on the drop-down in cell **B4**, noticing that it now lists locations. Change cell **A4** back to **Year**. Click on the drop-down in **B4**, noticing that it lists years again.

9. Try typing a non-existent datum value (e.g., **1985**) in cell **B4**. Notice that Excel gives you a generic alert message. It would be better to customize this alert to tell the user what the actual problem is and how to fix it. We can do this through the Data Validation utility. Click **Cancel**.

10. Select **B4** and **B5** again. Click the **Data** tab; in the Data Tools group, click **Data Validation**.

11. Click the **Error Alert** tab in the Data Validation utility. Enter text as shown in the following image:

12. Click **OK**.

13. Test one of the drop-downs again by attempting to enter a value not on the list. Observe the Error Alert. All validation rules should have an error alert set—always double-check the text of your Error Alerts. Click **Cancel**.

14. Select cell **N10**. We want to ensure that only positive whole numbers are entered for the available funds for the next budget year.

15. On the **Data** tab, click **Data Validation**. On the **Settings** tab of the Data Validation utility, set the Allow field to **Whole number**, the Data field to **greater than**, and the Minimum field to **0**. Click **OK**.

16. Test the rule by attempting to enter a **negative number** and then a **0** into **N10**. Always test your validation rules.

17. Select cells **N5:N7**. The value entered into each of these cells should not be less than the average of the past three years' costs for the corresponding store.

18. On the **Data** tab, click **Data Validation**. Set the Allow field to **Whole number**, the Data field to **greater than or equal to**, and the Minimum field to **=AVERAGE(H5:J5)**

    Note: *The H5:J5 reference in the Minimum formula must be relative so that the IL Store average costs and Online average costs—rather than the IN Store average costs—are used in turn when the Data Validation rule is extended from N5 to N6 and N7.*

19. On the **Input Message** tab, set everything to match the following image:

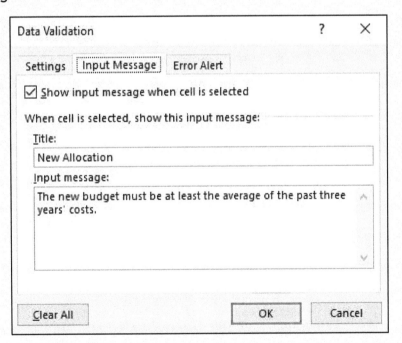

20. Click **OK**. Select one of the cells, then observe what the Input Message setting accomplished. Input Messages provide useful internal

documentation for the user. Always double-check the text of your Input Messages.

21. Select **H5:J5**, then view the average of these cells' values in the lower right corner of the Excel window. Notice that the current value in N5 is less than this average, but no error message has popped up. This is because Data Validation rules do not check existing data in the worksheet—they validate only new entries.

22. Type the existing value, **170000**, into cell **N5**, then press **Enter**. You should now see an error message. Click **Cancel**.

23. Select cell **N12**. It should not be allowed to display a negative number. However, notice that the user will never type directly into this cell; it contains a formula. Examine this formula, making note of the cell references therein that require user input.

24. Select cells **O5:O7**. These are the cells requiring user entry that affect the calculation in N12. Thus the values entered here by the user should not cause the output of N12 to be negative.

25. Click **Data Validation**. On the **Settings** tab of the Data Validation utility, set the Allow field to **Custom** and the Formula field to =$N$12>=0. We must use an absolute cell reference here, because we do not want the cell reference to change as the validation is applied to O5, O6, and O7. We are looking at the combined effect these three cells have on the single cell N12—not at their separate effects on cells N12, N13, and N14.

26. Click **OK**. Distribute bonus amounts in **O5:O7**, noticing how you cannot enter amounts that would allocate more Bonus funds than are available.

   Note: *Even though cell N11 is referenced in the formula in cell N12, we did not apply Data Validation to cell N11. This is because the user will never type anything into N11; N11 contains a formula. When applying Data Validation, select only cells in which the user will enter a value.*

Adding a Comment

You have learned how to add internal documentation in the form of an Input Message. Now let's learn how to add another type of documentation—a Comment.

1. Select cell **G8**. On the **Review** tab, in the Comments group, click **New Comment**.

2. In the Comment box that appears, delete the author's name and type the following:

   Sales/gross profit is the difference between revenue and the cost of making a product or providing a service, before deducting overhead, payroll, taxes, and interest payments.

3. Adjust the size of the Comment box to accommodate the text.

4. Click anywhere outside the Comment when you are finished editing it.

5. Hover your cursor over cell **G8**, noticing the difference between Comments and Input Messages.

Protecting the Budget Analysis Application

You have made excellent revisions to the budget application; now you need to protect the worksheet from unauthorized changes. When you protect a worksheet, by default, all cells become locked against editing. If you want to allow the user to make changes or enter data into certain cells after the sheet has been protected, then you must specify this before you apply protection to the worksheet.

1. Use the **Ctrl** key to select cells **B4:B5**, **N10**, and **N5:O7** simultaneously.

2. While hovering over one of the selected cells, **right-click** and select **Format Cells.**

3. On the **Protection** tab of the Format Cells utility, click the **Locked box** to uncheck it. Click **OK**. This tells Excel that the cells you just selected should not be locked against editing after the worksheet is protected (i.e., the user can change these cells).

4. You may deselect the currently selected cells if you wish, or you may leave them selected.

5. On the **Review** tab, in the Changes group, click **Protect Sheet**. Leave the password blank, then click **OK**. Sheet protection is very easy for an advanced user to undo, although adding a password can help with this. Protecting a sheet is most useful as a way of preventing a beginning user from modifying that worksheet.

6. Test the protection: try to change any cell that you did not unlock, then try to change a cell that you did unlock.

Hiding the Data and Drop-Downs Worksheets

Finally, we do not want the user to see the Data and Drop-Downs worksheets. Accordingly, we will hide these sheets from view.

1. Select the **Data** worksheet tab, then **right-click** on it. Select **Hide**.

2. Do the same for the **Drop-Downs** worksheet.

3. Observe that the corresponding worksheet tabs no longer appear at the bottom of the Excel window. If you need to make a sheet visible again after hiding it, then right-click on any of the visible worksheet tabs, choose **Unhide**, select the sheet to unhide, and click **OK**. Note that hiding sheets in this manner is most useful as a way of preventing a beginning user from viewing those sheets. Other methods (beyond the scope of this course) are more appropriate for hiding sheets from an advanced user.

The Next Step: Automation

The application is now in excellent form. To take it to the next level, we could think about using macros to automate tasks within the app. For example, using macros, we could automatically select the Budget Analysis worksheet, clear existing entries from cells N5:O7 and N10, and place the cursor in cell B4 whenever the app is opened so that each new user starts with a clean slate. With the click of a single button, we could copy a finalized Budget Analysis sheet to a new workbook with a meaningful filename and place it in a specific folder on the user's computer, or we could e-mail it to the dairy department manager with an automatically generated address or subject—even message text. Using macros, you can automate repetitive tasks, streamline the user's experience, and further customize an application.

Although macros are outside the scope of this course, an optional, brief introduction to recording and using macros is included in the appendix (chapter 25).

REVIEW PROBLEMS

Review Problem 1

Practice adding Data Validation to Premiere's catering service price quote application:

1. On the **Review1 Drop-Downs** worksheet, create two named ranges: **Service** (A4:A10) and **Item** (C4:C19).

2. Navigate to the **Review1** worksheet. Find and fix the one data entry error.

3. Set cell **B10** to allow only future dates.

4. Set cell **B11** to allow only events with 10 or more guests. Add a meaningful Input Message.

5. In cell **B12**, create a drop-down list of the service types listed on the **Review1 Drop-Downs** worksheet. *Challenge: Use the INDIRECT function to accomplish this.*

6. Set cells **A15:A26** to contain a drop-down list populated by the **Item** named range on the **Review1 Drop-Downs** worksheet.

7. Set an appropriate Data Validation rule so that the entries made in cells **C15:C26** do not allow cell B29 to become negative.

8. Set cell **B28** to allow only decimal values greater than 0. Add a meaningful Error Alert.

9. Add a comment to cell **C28** that says the following:

   The service fee includes table preparation, buffet setup, cake table setup, and servers.

10. Unlock all the cells that have a light green background, then protect the worksheet without a password.

11. Hide the **Review1 Drop-Downs** worksheet.

Working with Text Data

Chapter 22

Outline

- Research & Exploration: Research the LEN, FIND, LEFT, RIGHT, MID, CONCATENATE, TRIM, and CLEAN Text Functions; Explore Using Flash Fill

- In-Depth Case Application: Use Text Functions to Parse Names and Product Data

- Review Problems: Use Text Functions to Parse Product Data

Objectives

- Use Flash Fill, understanding its strengths and limitations.

- Solve problems using the LEN, FIND, SEARCH, LEFT, RIGHT, MID, and CONCATENATE functions.

- Understand how to use pattern matching with the FIND or SEARCH function in the context of nested text function problems.

RESEARCH & EXPLORATION

Research

Sometimes the data you need to work with will not be arranged in the most correct or most useful form. For example, you might receive a spreadsheet of employee details that uses a single column to hold each employee's combined name, address, city, state, and zip code rather than one that places each element in its own column. To perform sorting and analysis or to import these data into a table with separate name and address fields in Access, you would first need to parse the data into their basic components. Furthermore, you might find discrepancies in spelling, abbreviations, and capitalization that need to be standardized before analysis can begin, or you could encounter the leading zero problem and thus need to insert a variable number of zeroes at the beginning of each cell in a column of data. These are all examples of "dirty data." Fixing such issues is referred to as "data cleansing," and Excel is a powerful tool for doing this.

Data cleansing in Excel can of course be done by hand—one cell at a time. However, when you are dealing with more than a few records, this approach is untenable and error-prone. Fortunately, Excel includes many built-in text functions and other tools that can be used to efficiently parse and standardize large data sets.

Use your preferred search engine to research the following Excel text functions: LEN, FIND, LEFT, RIGHT, MID, CONCATENATE, TRIM, and CLEAN.

Exploration

Basic Text Function Examples

Now that you have researched several key text functions, navigate to the **Basic Text Functions** worksheet in the Chapter22_WorkingWithText.xlsx file and read through all of the provided examples. When you are finished, you should be able to describe what each listed text function does, and you should have a good idea of how each is used. You will practice using these functions to solve problems in the In-Depth Case Application.

Notice that these basic text functions can be used to return partial strings of text from the beginning (left side), middle, or end (right side) of a cell, and they can be used to separate or join strings of text. Text functions are most powerful for manipulating data when they are nested inside each other. However, formulas involving nested text functions can quickly become confusing, so before you attempt to nest any text functions, be sure to understand how each function behaves on its own.

FIND versus SEARCH

In your research, you looked up the FIND function. Notice that the Basic Text Functions worksheet also contains the SEARCH function. FIND and SEARCH are quite similar; the difference is that FIND is case-sensitive, whereas SEARCH is not. With the FIND function, Excel will return a value only if it finds *the exact combination of uppercase and lowercase characters you have specified*. With the SEARCH function, Excel disregards letters' case when looking for a match.

CONCATENATE versus CONCAT

In your research, you looked up the CONCATENATE function. Concatenation in Excel can also be accomplished by using the CONCAT function or by using ampersands. New in Excel 2016, the CONCAT function can be used in exactly the same way as the CONCATENATE function but does have some additional capabilities that we will not explore here. Be aware that CONCAT is not available in previous versions of Excel, and it may completely replace CONCATENATE in future versions.

More Text Function Examples

Now explore the **More Text Functions** worksheet, where you will find examples involving the TRIM and CLEAN functions. These two functions are often used together. TRIM removes all spaces other than single spaces between other characters; this includes all leading and trailing spaces at the beginning and end of a cell. It does not remove nonspace characters. CLEAN removes nonprintable and invisible control characters such as line breaks and escape characters that may be hiding in imported data.

Remember that you can refer to the Basic Text Functions and More Text Functions worksheets at any time to review how a particular text function works.

Exploring Flash Fill

In addition to text functions, Excel has a feature called Flash Fill that can sometimes parse large sets of data whose components are separated by a space or other predictable character. With Flash Fill, Excel attempts to detect a pattern that can be used to parse the data without the need of any formula or function. However, for Flash Fill to work, the dataset must be fairly simple and follow a predictable pattern. You should always double-check results obtained via Flash Fill, because even when handling data that seem simple to the human eye, Excel may not always parse each element in the exact manner you intend.

Navigate to the **RE1** worksheet to practice using Flash Fill:

1. In cell **B4**, type the last name **Daniels**, and then press **Enter**.

2. In cell **B5**, type just the first two letters of the next last name in the dataset (**De**), then pause there. As you start to enter the name Dewitt, Flash Fill recognizes a pattern in the dataset and guesses how you want to parse the data. It suggests the rest of the second last name, Dewitt, as the text to place in B5. Flash Fill also suggests entering all the remaining last names from Column A into Column B.

3. Press **Enter**. The entire Last Name column is finished.

4. Double-check the Last Name column to make sure the results are what you intended.

Flash Fill is a static rather than dynamic operation—the entries in Column B will not automatically update if you change any of the names in Column A.

5. In **A4**, type **SMITH, Larry** and press Enter. Notice that the last name "Daniels" remains in Column B.

6. Press **Ctrl+Z** to undo your typing. (You should again see "DANIELS, Larry" in A4.)

The keyboard shortcut for Flash Fill is **Ctrl+E**. Practice using this keyboard shortcut to fill in the First Name column:

7. In cell **C4**, type the first name **Larry**, then press **Enter**.

8. Press **Ctrl+E**. This applies Flash Fill to the column.

Troubleshooting

Flash Fill may not work in nonempty ranges. If there is already data in Column C when you try to use Flash Fill and Excel alerts you that it cannot find a pattern, then delete the contents of Column C and try again.

9. Double-check the First Name column to make sure that the results are what you intended.

Notice that the full name in A5 comprises three names. Flash Fill has parsed "Faye Ann" into the First Name column, but this name could be considered a separate first name and middle name. What if we want to ensure that all names in the First Name column contain only one word? Notice that there is a similar entry in A14. Must we correct each two-word entry by hand?

10. In **C5**, delete the name **Ann** and the **space** after the name "Faye." Press **Enter**.

11. Notice that Flash Fill learned from this correction and guessed that you wanted to similarly update the First Name entry in C14.

If after Flash Filling you need to make any corrections (e.g., "Faye Ann" to "Faye") and want Excel to automatically update similar entries throughout the range, then you must make the example correction immediately after performing the initial Flash Fill but before entering other data or formulas. Furthermore, always double-check the results of the entire range after making any corrections to Flash Fill—you must ensure that no previously correct entries were rendered incorrect.

Next, use Flash Fill to rearrange text in a cell.

12. In Column D, use the **Flash Fill** keyboard shortcut to create a column with a first name initial followed by a last name (e.g., **L. Daniels**).

13. Double-check the results to make sure they are correct. Make any changes if necessary.

Flash Fill can also be used to add symbols for dates, phone numbers, and the like.

14. In **G4**, type the formatted and rearranged date **07/31/2015**, then press **Enter**.

15. Press **Ctrl+E** to Flash Fill the date down the column.

16. Double-check the results to make sure they are correct. Notice that Flash Fill did not parse the dates correctly; it thought you wanted every month component to be July. Again, Flash Fill will attempt to learn from any corrections you make immediately after parsing the data. Type **10/26/2010** in **G5**, then press **Enter**. Notice that the other month components change.

Again, always check results obtained via Flash Fill to make sure they are what you intended. *For graded items in this course, you may use Flash Fill only if the instructions explicitly say to do so.* Keep in mind that for Flash Fill to work, the starting data must follow a simple pattern. There must also be no totally blank columns separating the starting data and the column you want to fill.

IN-DEPTH CASE APPLICATION

You have seen how Flash Fill can be used to statically parse very simple data sets. What if your data set is too complex for Flash Fill to parse properly? What if you need dynamic updates to occur? In these cases, you must use text functions.

Summary of Simple Excel Text Functions

- **LEN** returns the number of characters in a string of text.

- **FIND** or **SEARCH** returns the position number of the first character in a string of text you're looking for within some larger string of text. FIND is case-sensitive; SEARCH is not.

- **LEFT**, **RIGHT**, and **MID** return some number of characters from the beginning, end, or middle of a string of text.

- **CONCATENATE** combines text elements to create a single string of text. The **&** symbol also works, and so does the **CONCAT** function.

Parsing Employee Names

Navigate to the **Employee Name Parsing** worksheet.

Parsing Parts of a Name with Simple Text Functions

Working with a single text function is fairly straightforward. It's time to apply what you learned about basic text functions in the Research & Exploration section to parse parts of a name. Keep in mind that the LEFT, RIGHT, and MID functions output actual characters of text, whereas LEN and FIND output numbers.

1. Using the name in cell G3, enter the indicated function in each shaded cell in Column **T** to answer the corresponding question displayed in Column G.

Parsing Entire Names with Nested Text Functions

When working with text data, you will most often need to nest functions to return the appropriate results. Notice that the name on this sheet is written in *First space Last* configuration, so the first name occupies the left side of the cell and the last name occupies the right side of the cell. To have Excel output the first name, you would therefore use the LEFT function—but how many characters should you specify to output in LEFT's second argument? This is the tricky part, because you want this function to return the entire first name regardless of what *First space Last* combination is typed into cell G3. You cannot simply type a "4" here, because not all first names are four characters long; you need Excel to calculate how many characters are in the first name.

You know that the first name and last name are separated by a single space, so the length of the first name equals the position number of the space minus 1. As you know, the FIND function will output the position number of the space, so you need to use the FIND function, adjusted by 1 character, inside the LEFT function.

Remember this rule of thumb: Whenever you want to output a variable number of characters from the left side of a cell, use the LEFT function with a FIND in its second argument. You may need to subtract some number of characters from the FIND output depending on how the components of the cell are separated (e.g., by a space, by a word, by multiple pieces of punctuation, or so on).

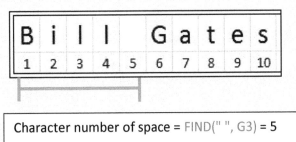

Character number of space = FIND(" ", G3) = 5

Length of first name = Location of space - 1 = 4

Returning the last name is slightly more complicated. The last name is on the right side of the cell in this example, so we need to use the RIGHT function to output it. To calculate the number of characters, however, we can no longer use the FIND function on its own. This is because the FIND function only counts characters from left to right; it cannot count characters from right to left, which is the behavior we would need in this case. To calculate the number of characters in the last name, we must therefore count how many characters are in the full name and subtract the number of characters up to and including the space. This operation is a LEN minus a FIND.

Remember this rule of thumb: Whenever you want to output a variable number of characters from the right side of a cell, use the RIGHT function with a LEN minus a FIND in its second argument. Again, you may need to subtract some number of characters from the LEN-minus-FIND result depending on how the components of the cell are separated.

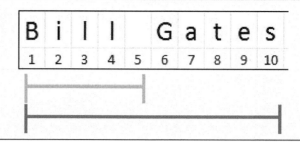

Length of whole name = LEN(G3) = 10

Character number of space = FIND(" ", G3) = 5

Length of last name = Length of whole name - character number of space = 10 - 5 = 5

Whether you are outputting text from the left or right side of a cell, it is always wise to check the number of characters in your result (use the LEN function to do this in some blank cell elsewhere on the worksheet). Compare the number of characters that Excel calculates with the number of characters that you count by eye; if there is any discrepancy, it means that you have extra spaces hiding in your answer that need to be removed. Adjust the second argument in your LEFT or RIGHT function by subtracting the appropriate number of characters. You may also use the TRIM function to remove extra spaces; however, TRIM will not remove any other extra characters such as punctuation or letters.

1. Using the name in cell G3, enter the appropriate nested functions in the shaded cells in Column **AL** to answer the corresponding questions displayed in Column **AA**.

2. Change the name in **G3** (use only *First space Last* format), observing how all the answers update dynamically.

Parsing a Middle Initial

1. Enter a function in **AD35** to return the middle initial from the name in S32. Think through the situation: You want to return 1 character from the middle of a cell, starting one character after the space. Thus you will need to use a FIND function to determine the position of the space and increase that number by 1; this will be the start_num argument inside the MID function.

2. Change the name in **S32** (use *First space Middle space Last* format), observing how the answer changes.

Combining Names

1. Enter a **first name** in cell **G41** and a **last name** in cell **G42**.

2. In cell **AD44**, concatenate the first name, a space, and the last name using the **ampersand** symbol as you learned in Access.

3. In cell **AD46**, join the first name, a space, and the last name using the CONCATENATE or CONCAT function. Each text element to be joined should be a separate argument within the function.

Parsing Products

Navigate to the **Product Parsing** worksheet. The dataset on this sheet is a list of Premiere Foods products with brand names and item codes combined in one cell (e.g., "Country Life product 009017"). Having the products listed this way would be problematic if you wanted to, say, import brand and item code as separate fields into an Access database. Because there is consistency in the way the data are represented, you might try to use the Flash Fill feature in Excel to parse the data into separate columns:

1. In cell **C6**, type the brand name **Country Life**, then press **Enter**.

2. Press **Ctrl+E** to Flash Fill the result down the column.

Notice that for some brand name values—particularly "Healthy 365" and "Alvita 2"—the Flash Fill feature does not appropriately parse the data. While Flash Fill can be very helpful and is easy to use, in some cases the data structure may be too complex for Excel to decipher the appropriate pattern to parse. You could try to correct the results, but that would be inefficient. For this particular problem, you should use text functions to appropriately separate the data.

3. **Delete** the contents of **C6:C68**.

4. In cell **C6**, enter the appropriate nested text functions to return only the brand name (Country Life) from cell **B6**.

5. In **C4** or some other blank cell, use the **LEN** function to check the length of your solution. Remove any blank spaces from your solution in **C6** if necessary, either by subtraction or using the TRIM function. You may delete the contents of **C4** when you are finished.

6. **AutoFill** the solution down to **C68**. (Remember: AutoFill and Flash Fill are different processes!)

7. In cell **D6**, enter the appropriate nested text functions to return only the item code (009017) from cell **B6**. Although all the item codes here are six characters long, do not assume that this will always be the case. Write a formula that can handle a flexible item code length.

8. In **D4** or some other blank cell, use the **LEN** function to check the length of your solution. Remove any blank spaces from your solution in **D6** if necessary. You may delete the contents of **D4** when you are finished.

9. **AutoFill** the solution down to **D68**.

REVIEW PROBLEMS

Review Problem 1

You have been given a list of items in Premiere's International product category and need to make tags to label the shelves that will hold these items. You have a list of Products with their Wholesale Codes (for ordering from the supplier) and their Prices. You will need to separate and rearrange the various elements in these data to create the shelf labels.

Parse the Brand and Description

The Product field in Column A is a combination of the brand name, a space, the word "brand", a space, and the product's description.

1. In cell **D5**, enter a solution that will return the Brand (Generic House) from the text in cell A5. Before you begin, carefully examine how the word "brand" is variously written in the first few records.

2. **AutoFill** your solution down the column. If you see errors, investigate the difference between FIND and SEARCH.

3. In cell **E5**, enter a solution that will return the Description ("Sushi Mat w/Bamboo Paddle") from the text in cell A5.

4. **AutoFill** your solution down the column.

Parse the Item Code

Each Wholesale Code in Column B adheres to this pattern: the letters "INTL" to indicate the International category, followed by the product's six-character Item Code, followed by the first three characters of the product's brand name.

5. In cell **F5**, enter a solution that will return the Item Code from the middle of the Wholesale Code. Here you may assume that all Item Codes will be exactly six characters long.

6. **AutoFill** your solution down the column.

Concatenate Fields to Make Shelf Labels

7. For the shelf labels, cell **G5** should use the contents of cells **D5**, **E5**, and **F5** to return the following (be sure to include all punctuation, *single* spaces between elements, the word *item*, and

a dollar sign as shown):

Generic House Sushi Mat w/Bamboo Paddle; item 213924; $2.19

8. **AutoFill** your solution down the column.

Tables and Charts

Chapter 23

Outline

- Research & Exploration: The Purpose of Excel Tables, Creating Basic Charts

- In-Depth Case Application: Create and Modify a Chart with Data in a Table

- Review Problems: Practice Creating Charts, Knowledge Check 19

Objectives

- Format data as an Excel table.

- Use table filters.

- Add totals to a table.

- Identify the type of chart suitable for the analysis intended.

- Create basic charts (column, pie, line).

- Modify chart settings.

RESEARCH & EXPLORATION

Research

It should be very obvious by now how valuable Excel skills are in any industry. What may not be obvious is that you don't need to be an expert in Excel to realize Excel's value. One of the most basic tools that Excel offers, for example, is the table. Tables make it easier to manage and analyze data by providing options to help you easily view, sort, filter, and calculate totals in your data. Read Create a table in a worksheet in Excel, a blog post from the Microsoft Office support site, to learn more about Excel tables and how to create them.

Excel also provides easy-to-use tools to visualize data with a variety of charts. Charts are commonly used in presentations and reports to summarize data in a way that is easy to interpret at a glance. Browse Available chart types in Office 2016 for Windows, a blog post from the Office support site, to get an idea of the variety of charts available and how to create them.

Before you begin creating charts in Excel, it is crucial that you understand how to discern which type of chart is appropriate—for different chart types convey different meanings. For example, a line chart is best used when you are trying to represent a trend over a specific period of time, whereas a column chart is best used when you want to compare data side by side. Additionally, pie charts are best used when you want to illustrate the relationship of parts to a whole.

Exploration

Navigate to your files, download and open the **Chapter23_TablesAndCharts.xlsx** workbook, then complete the following exercises.

Creating a Line Chart

In this exercise, you will create a line chart to easily see any trends in revenue for each department from 2012 to 2015.

1. Click the **RE1** worksheet tab. This worksheet contains revenue data from Premiere Foods' top-performing departments from 2012 to 2015.

2. Select the range **B4:F7**. Click the **Quick Analysis** button located in the bottom right corner of the selection.

   This button appears whenever a contiguous range of cells are selected and provides a variety of tools to enhance the data.

3. Click the **Charts** tab in the Quick Analysis options to see which chart types Excel recommends based on the data in the selection.

4. Click **Line** to insert a line chart showing the revenue trend for each of the three departments across the 4-year period.

5. Move the **chart** so that it is positioned below the data.

6. Click the **Chart Title** placeholder once, type **Top Department Revenue, 2012-2015** (look to the formula bar to see the text as you type), and then press **Enter**.

7. Click any **cell** in the worksheet to deselect the chart.

Creating a Column Chart

In this exercise, you will create a column chart to easily compare total departmental revenue earned from 2012 to 2015.

1. Click the **RE2** worksheet tab.

Since the cells containing the department names and the total revenue are noncontiguous, the process of selecting the cells is a little different:

2. Select the range **B5:B7**. Press and hold **Ctrl**, select the range **G5:G7**, and then release the **Ctrl** key. Since this range is noncontiguous, the Quick Analysis button does not appear.

3. Click the **Insert** tab on the Ribbon. In the Charts group, click the **Insert Column or Bar Chart** button , and then, under 2-D Column, select **Clustered Column**.

4. Move the **chart** so that it is positioned below the data.

5. Click the **Chart Title** placeholder, type **Top Department Revenue, 2012-2015**, and then press **Enter**.

6. Click any **cell** in the worksheet to deselect the chart.

Creating a Pie Chart

In this exercise, you will create a pie chart to illustrate the percentage of total revenue derived from the Personal Hygiene department from 2012 to 2015.

1. Click the **RE3** worksheet tab.

2. Select the range **B5:B7**. Press and hold **Ctrl**, select the range **G5:G7**, and then release the **Ctrl** key. Since this range is noncontiguous, the Quick Analysis button does not appear.

3. Click the **Insert** tab on the Ribbon. In the Charts group, click the **Insert Pie or Doughnut chart** button, and then, under 2-D Pie, select **Pie**.

4. Move the **chart** so that it is positioned below the data.

5. Click the **Chart Title** placeholder, type **Top Department Revenue, 2012-2015**, and then press **Enter**.

6. Click the **pie** to select all three pieces.

7. Click the **piece** representing the Personal Hygiene department.

8. Click and drag the **piece** slightly to the left to explode the pie, creating emphasis on the Personal Hygiene department.

9. Click any **cell** in the worksheet to deselect the chart.

Notice that all three charts use the same data and have the same chart title, but each chart illustrates a different aspect of the data.

IN-DEPTH CASE APPLICATION

Enhancing Data with an Excel Table

You can format a range of data as an Excel table to more easily manage and analyze the data. There are many benefits to using Excel tables:

- Data become easier to read through the use of banded rows or columns with alternating colors.
- Data in any column can be easily sorted in ascending or descending order.
- Data in any column can be easily filtered so that you only see the data you want to see.
- Totals such as sums, averages, counts, and more can easily be added to each column.
- Column names remain visible no matter how far down you scroll in the spreadsheet.

1. Click the **Sales Volume Data** worksheet tab.

The data on this worksheet represent the quantity of items sold for the Premiere Foods "Generic House" brand for each product category and quarter in 2015. Also included in the data is the 2015 average sales volume for each product category.

2. Click any **cell** inside the data range, then press **Ctrl + A** to select the range A5:F49.

3. Press **Ctrl + T** to begin the process of converting the range to a table.

4. In the Create Table dialog box, make sure the **My table has headers** check box is checked, and then click **OK**.

The range of cells is now formatted as a table, and the Table Tools Design contextual tab appears on the Ribbon with a variety of options for modifying the design and function of the table. Note that the Table Tools Design tab appears only if a cell inside the table is selected.

5. Click the **Design** tab.

6. In the Table Style Options group, click the **Total Row** check box. A Total row appears at the bottom of the table (A50:F50).

7. In cells **B50**, **C50**, **D50**, and **E50**, select Sum from the drop-down menu as the summary function to apply in the total row. Although SUM is selected as the function, Excel inserts the SUBTOTAL function in

each of the cells. Since tables are designed to easily filter out any undesirable data, the SUBTOTAL function is used, because it will only conduct the chosen mathematical operation on data that are visible in the table, ignoring any records that have been filtered out.

8. Click the **filter** drop-down arrow next to the Category header in cell A5. Click the **(Select All)** check box to deselect all categories.

9. Scroll through the list of categories, click the **Hair Care** and **Health and Beauty** check boxes to select those categories, and then click **OK**.

The table has now been filtered to only show sales volume for the Hair Care and Health and Beauty categories. Notice how the Total row only calculates the total sales volume for the visible categories.

Creating a Combination Chart to Analyze Sales Volume

Visualizing data with charts can often provide a better understanding of your data. When a chart is created using data formatted as a table, the filters can be used to easily modify the chart as needed.

1. Select the range **A5:C23**, press and hold **Ctrl**, select **F5:F23**, and then release **Ctrl**.

2. Click the **Insert** tab; in the Charts group, click the **Insert Combo Chart** button , and then select **Clustered Column—Line**.

The combo chart combines a clustered column chart and a line chart in a single chart object. This combination chart makes it easy to compare quarterly sales volume by category, as well as to compare these values with the average sales volume for 2015.

Moving the Chart to a Different Worksheet

3. With the chart selected, on the Design tab in the Location group, click **Move Chart**.

4. In the Move Chart dialog box, click the **Object in** radio button and select **Qtr 1 and 2 Sales Volume**, then click **OK**.

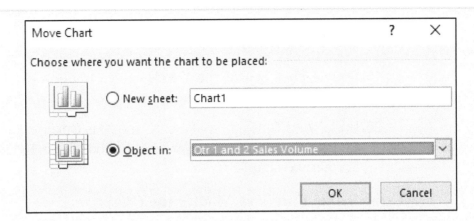

5. The Qtr 1 and 2 Sales Volume worksheet becomes active with the chart inside it. Position the chart inside the shaded area (cells B7:H22), resizing the chart if necessary so that it fits inside the shaded area.

Improving the Design of the Chart

6. With the chart still selected, to the right of the chart, click the **Chart Styles** button to view a list of predefined chart styles.

7. Click **Style 3** to apply the style to the chart.

10. Click the **Chart Title** placeholder, type **Quarter 1 and Quarter 2, 2015**, and then press **Enter**.

11. Use the Font group tools on the Home tab to set the chart title in 12-point bold Century Gothic type.

12. To the right of the chart, click the **Chart Elements** button to view a list of commonly used chart elements.

13. Point to **Axis Titles**, click the **arrow** to the right, and then click the **Primary Vertical** check box.

14. Notice that a vertical axis title has been added to the chart and is currently selected. Type **Sales Volume**, then press **Enter** to rename the axis.

15. Format the axis title in 10-point bold Century Gothic type.

16. Click the **Chart Elements** button, point to **Legend**, click the **arrow** to the right, and then select **Top** to move the legend to the top of the chart.

17. Double-click one of the **columns** in the chart to open the Format Data Series pane on the right.

18. Adjust the value in the Series Overlap box to **-25%** so that there is space in between the columns.

19. Double-click one of the **Y-axis** values to open the Format Axis pane on the right.

20. Under Axis Options, make sure the Axis Options icon is selected. Change the value in the Major Units box from 10.0 to **5**, then close the Format Axis pane.

Using Table Filters to Modify the Chart

Since the chart was created from a range of cells in an Excel table, you can modify the filters to see different data in the chart.

21. Click the **Sales Volume Data worksheet** tab.

22. Click the **Category filter**, click the **Bath** check box to include that category of data in the chart, and then click **OK**.

23. Click the **Qtr 1 and 2 Sales Volume** worksheet tab, noticing that the sales volumes for the Bath category are now included in the chart.

REVIEW PROBLEMS

Review Problem 1

On the Review1 worksheet, edit the existing pie chart:

1. Change the data source of the chart to be QTR2 sales revenue instead of QTR3.

2. Change the chart type to a **3-D Pie** chart.

3. Adjust the **3-D Rotation** of the pie so that the **X rotation** is set to **50** degrees and the **Y rotation** is set to **30** degrees.

4. Change the Chart Style to **Style 7** and the Color theme to **Color 3**.

5. Add **Data Labels** as Data Callouts, with the Value and Percentage showing.

6. Emphasize the Perishable piece (the largest) by pulling that piece of the pie away from the others to "explode" that piece.

7. Edit the **Chart Title** so that it reads **QTR 2 Sales**.

8. Make the **Legend** formatting **Bold** with a type size of **11pt**.

9. Compare your chart to the graphic next to it.

Review Problem 2

On the Review2 worksheet, create a line chart to illustrate the revenue trend for each Premiere Foods location across all four quarters of 2015:

1. Use the range **B7:F10** to create the chart.

2. Change the Chart Title to read **Revenue by Location and Quarter, 2015**

3. Add a title to the vertical axis. It should read **Sales Revenue**.

4. Modify the vertical axis values so that the minimum bound is set to **1500.0**, the maximum bound to **3000.0**, the major unit to **500.0**, and minor unit to **100.0**.

5. Apply **Chart Style 9**, then add a **Data Table** chart element to the chart.

6. Remove the Legend, which is no longer needed.

7. For each data series (IN Store, IL Store, and Online), in the Format Data Series pane, Line options, change the Width of the lines to **1pt.**

8. Change the **Line Color** for the line representing the IL Store to **orange**.

9. Compare your chart to the graphic next to it.

Knowledge Check 19

Visualizing Data with Charts

File Needed

KnowledgeCheck_19.xlsx

Create an "Exploding" Pie Chart—Problem 1

On the **Q3 Sales by Region** worksheet, create a pie chart that illustrates the percentage of revenue earned by each US region for the third quarter. Refer to the following image and specifications for guidance.

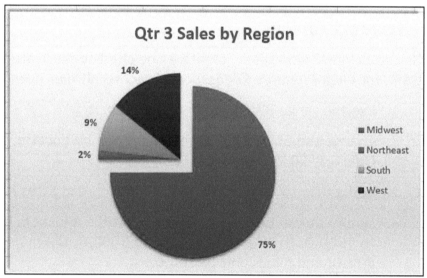

Specifications

- Apply Style 5 and Color 3.

- Set the chart area fill to gradient.

- Set the legend position to right.

- Set the data labels as Percentage in the outside end position in bold type

- Set the chart area shadow to offset diagonally to the top left.

- Explode the Midwest piece.

- Resize and move the chart appropriately.

Create a 2D Clustered Column Chart—Problem 2

On the **Sales-Discount Ratio** worksheet, begin in column E and create a formula that will calculate the ratio of discounts to sales for each of the employees listed. Calculate this by dividing the discount amount by the sales amount. (The higher the percentage returned, the more we are giving up in discounts to generate each dollar of sales.)

Then create a 2D clustered column chart displaying the ratio of discounts to sales for employees at the Indiana store only.

Hint: You will need to sort the data in a particular way to be able to select the correct range of cells for the chart.

Refer to the following image and specifications for guidance.

Specifications

- Apply Style 9 and Monochromatic Color 6.

- Set the legend to none.

- Set the text direction to horizontal, with a custom angle of -70 degrees.

- Set the axis titles in 10-point type.

- Set the chart title border to use a 1.75-point gradient line border, and apply the preset gradient Bottom Spotlight—Accent 2.

- Change the vertical axis scale from 1% to 8%, with a major unit of 0.5%.

- Resize and move the chart appropriately.

After completing these steps, go to the course website to answer Koin-earning questions.

PivotTable and Power View Reports

Chapter 24

Outline

- Research & Exploration: PivotTables, Power View Reports, Data Models, Create a Basic PivotTable

- In-Depth Case Application: Analyze Revenue Data with a PivotTable, Build a Relational Data Source with Power Pivot, Create a Simple Dashboard and Power View Report

- Review Problems: Creating PivotTables, Knowledge Check 20

Objectives

- Create PivotTables to analyze and organize data.

- Create a relational data source with Power Pivot.

- Create a simple dashboard and Power View report.

RESEARCH & EXPLORATION

Research

A PivotTable is a powerful data analysis tool that allows you to easily organize, explore, and summarize large amounts of data. The data being analyzed are typically organized into columns and rows where the top row consists of headings for each of the columns. When organizing data in this way, there cannot be any blank rows in the data set, although blank cells do not pose a problem.

Using your preferred search engine, search for *examples of PivotTables in Excel*.

PivotTables in Excel 2016 can also be developed from multiple data sources that can exist inside and outside of Excel. For example, you might want to analyze sales data for each employee, and the sales data might be one data source and the employee data another. In such a scenario, you can create a data model using Excel's Power Pivot, bringing the data in these sources together into a relational data source within Excel. Read the Office Support blog post Create a data model in Excel to learn more.

Power View reports, another tool available in Excel 2016, are designed to help you explore, visualize, and present large amounts of data. Power View reports were introduced in Excel 2013 and can be created using data from one or multiple sources. Read the Office Support blog post Power View: Explore, visualize, and present your data to learn more.

Exploration

Navigate to your files, download and open the **Chapter24_PivotTables.xlsx** workbook, and then complete the following exercises.

Using the Recommended PivotTables Feature

Excel can recommend various PivotTables based on the type of data in your data set. In this exercise, you will use the recommended PivotTable feature to summarize transactional data so that you can see total sales revenue by product category.

1. Click the **Transaction Data** worksheet tab. This worksheet contains transactional data from 2015.

2. Click the **Insert** tab. In the Table group on the left, click **Recommended PivotTables**.

3. In the Recommend PivotTables dialog box, scroll through the recommendations to see the variety of ways that PivotTables can organize data.

4. Select the fourth option, **Sum of Sales by Category**, and then click **OK**.

   A new sheet (Sheet1) is inserted to the left of Transaction Data containing the recommended PivotTable.

5. Right-click the **Sheet1** worksheet tab, select **Rename**, type **Sales by Category** as the new sheet name, and then press **Enter**.

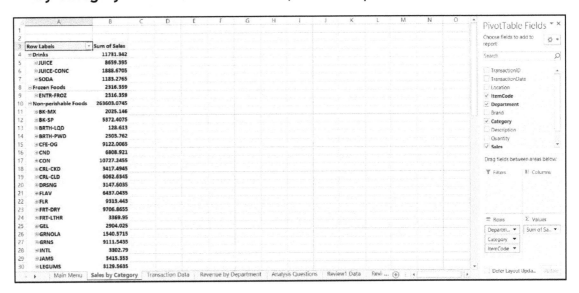

Notice the **PivotTable Fields** pane on the right. This pane serves as the Design view of a PivotTable. The field names are derived from the column labels in the data set, and their placement inside the four areas in the bottom half of the pane determines the structure of the PivotTable.

Improving the Design of a PivotTable

The Recommended PivotTable feature does an excellent job of creating a basic PivotTable to explore various aspects of your data, but the default design could use some improvements.

1. In cell A3, delete the text **Row Labels** and insert **Departments/Categories**, which is a more appropriate label.

2. Resize column **A** so that the entire label is visible.

The values in the Sum of Sales column are not formatted appropriately. It is important to note that PivotTables are designed to be modified in order to easily explore the data. For example, the cells that currently have revenue values in them may be replaced with quantity values when analyzing sales volume. Therefore, to format cells in a PivotTable, you will apply the formatting to the field, not the cells.

3. In the PivotTable Fields pane, click the **Sum of Sales** field, located in the Σ Values area, and then select **Value Field Settings** from the menu.

4. In the Value Field Settings dialog box, in the Custom Name box, type **Revenue** to replace the Sum of Sales text.

5. Click the **Number Format** button at the bottom of the dialog box.

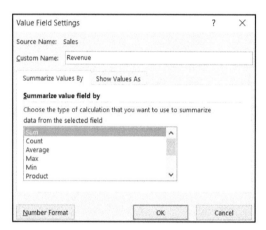

6. In the Format Cells dialog box, select the **Accounting** category, click **OK**, and then click **OK** again.

One of the benefits of PivotTable is the ability to drill down into the data. Notice the + and – signs to the left of each department and category in column A. These provide the user with the ability to expand (drill down) and collapse (roll up) the data.

The Drinks department is currently expanded to show the three categories of items within the department and the revenue generated from 2015 sales.

7. Click the **+** sign next to the Juice category to drill down, viewing the individual item codes that belong to the Juice category. Now

you can easily see how much revenue came from the sale of a specific item within a product category for a department.

8. Click the – sign next to the Juice category to roll up the data.

 # In-Depth Case Application

Analyzing Revenue with a PivotTable

Once you become more familiar with creating and working with PivotTables, you will most likely want to create them yourself rather than using the recommended PivotTable feature in Excel. In this exercise, you will create a PivotTable report that will allow management to view sales revenue broken down by each department and product category summarized monthly and quarterly.

Note: This section has two separate workbooks: Chapter24_PivotTables.xlsx and Chapter 24_DataModelAndPowerView.xlsx.

1. Download and open the **Chapter24_PivotTables.xlsx** workbook, then click the **Transaction Data** worksheet tab.

2. Click the **Insert** tab. In the Tables group, click **PivotTable**.

3. In the Create PivotTable dialog box, verify that inside the Table/Range box **'Transaction Data'!$A$1:$J$48744** is the range that will be used for the PivotTable.

4. Under **Choose where you want the PivotTable report to be placed**, click **Existing Worksheet**. Click inside the **Location** box, click the **Revenue by Department** worksheet tab, and then click cell **A3**.

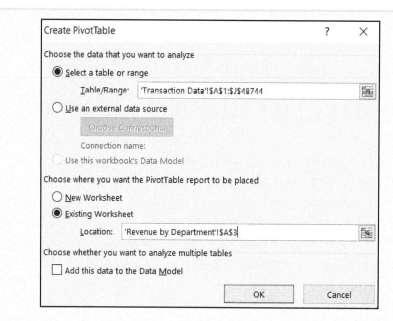

5. Click **OK**. The PivotTable is now ready to be designed on the Revenue by Department worksheet, starting in cell A3.

Structuring the PivotTable Using the PivotTable Fields Pane

Creating a PivotTable report consists mostly of dragging fields from the top of the PivotTable Fields pane into areas below the field list. Each of the four area has a different purpose.

1. In the PivotTable Fields pane, drag the **Location** field into the **Filters** area. This creates a filter in the top left corner that can later be used to see data from only specific locations.

2. In the PivotTable Fields pane, drag the **Brand** field into the **Filters** area, below the Location field. This creates a second filter just below the Location filter. Once the PivotTable report is completed, the user can decide to see data from only specific locations or brands.

3. In the PivotTable Fields pane, drag the **TransactionDate** field into the **Rows** area. This creates row headings where Excel automatically groups the transaction dates into months with the ability to drill down to view each transaction date within each month. You will modify this grouping later, as that level of granularity is not necessary for the members of management who will be using this report.

4. In the PivotTable Fields pane, drag the **Department** and **Category** fields into the **Columns** area. Make sure that Department is above Category, because a department may have multiple product categories. This

creates column headings for each of the departments for which a user could drill down to see details from each category within a department.

5. In the PivotTable Fields pane, drag the **Sales** field into the **Σ Values** area. Any field placed into the Σ Values area will be summarized with an aggregate function. By default, Excel will make an assumption about which aggregate function is to be applied based on the type of data in the field. In this case, Excel applies the SUM aggregate function to the Sales field and renames the field Sum of Sales.

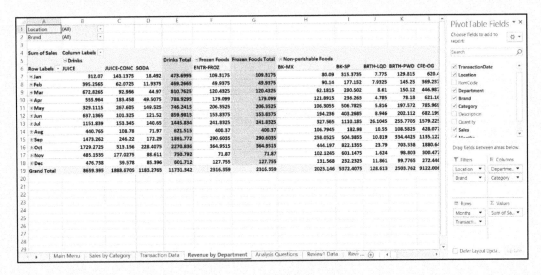

Grouping Dates into Months and Quarters

When the TransactionDate field was added to the Rows area, Excel automatically grouped the dates into Months. Businesses often report on their earnings every quarter. You can easily modify how dates are grouped in PivotTables.

1. Right-click cell **A7** or any cell that contains a month, then select **Group**.

2. In the Grouping dialog box, click **Days** to deselect the grouping by days.

3. Click **Quarters** to group the dates by quarters in addition to months, then click **OK**.

Adding Quarterly Subtotals

In addition to grouping dates by quarters, subtotals can be added to calculate the totals for each quarter.

1. Right-click cell **A7** or any cell that contains a Qtr label, then select **Subtotal "Quarters"** to add subtotals for each of the four quarters.

Formatting a PivotTable

Before a PivotTable is considered finished, you should ensure that columns and rows are clearly labeled, that values are formatted appropriately, that the PivotTable is appropriately named, and that the PivotTable is easy to read.

1. In the PivotTable Fields pane, click the **Sum of Sales** field in the Σ Value area, then select **Value Field Settings**.

2. Type **Revenue** in the Custom Name box.

3. Click **Number Format**, then format the field as **Accounting**.

4. Click cell **A6**, then replace the text Row Labels with **Time Period**.

5. Click cell **B4**, then replace the text Column Labels with **Departments**.

6. Adjust the column widths as necessary to accommodate the new labels.

PivotTable styles are a way to change the look and feel of a PivotTable. Excel provides several different built-in styles that change based on the workbook theme. You can even create custom styles to match an organization's branding.

7. Click the **PivotTable Tools Design** tab; in the PivotTable Styles group, select **Pivot Style Medium 7**.

By default, Excel names PivotTables with names like PivotTable1, PivotTable2, and so forth. These default names are not very descriptive. Since a workbook may contain many different PivotTables, it is best practice to provide them with a descriptive name.

8. Click the **PivotTable Tools Analyze** tab; in the PivotTable group, click inside the PivotTable Name box, then type **RevByDep**.

Adding Slicers to Filter a PivotTable

Slicers allow you to filter PivotTable data in a way that makes it much easier to see the current filtering options being applied than when using the Report Filter. Slicers also provide buttons for the filtering options.

First, to make the PivotTable smaller and more manageable, you will "roll up" the data to view the revenue at the department level.

1. Click cell **B5**, and on the PivotTable Tools Analyze tab, in the Active Field group, click the **Collapse Field** button.

2. On the PivotTable Tools Analyze tab, in the Filter group, click **Insert Slicer**.

3. Select the check boxes for the **Location** and **Brand** fields, then click **OK**.

4. You can move the slicers anywhere on the worksheet and resize them; move them to the right of the PivotTable.

5. Use the **Ctrl** key to select both the Location and Brand slicers. On the Slicer Tools Options tab, choose **Slicer Style Light 6** so that the slicer buttons match the style color of the PivotTable.

You can have both the Report Filter and slicers in a PivotTable together, or you may choose to use one or the other. Slicers do provide the added benefits of a visual display and an easy-to-use interface for anyone using the PivotTable.

When finished, the PivotTable should resemble the following figure:

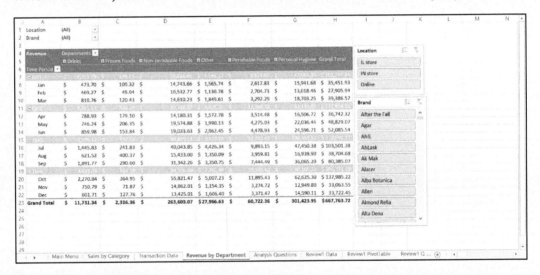

Using the PivotTable to Answer Questions about Premiere

PivotTables are not designed to be static views of your data. They are designed to "pivot" so that you can see your data from a variety of perspectives.

1. Click the **Analysis Questions** worksheet tab.

2. Use the PivotTable filters, drill down, and roll up to answer the questions. If correct, your answers will appear in blue type.

3. Once you are finished, save and close **Chapter24_PivotTables.xlsx**.

Building a Data Model Using Power Pivot

As you learned in the Research & Exploration section of this chapter, Excel's Data Model can be used to bring data from multiple sources, external and internal, creating a relational data source within Excel.

1. Download and open the **Chapter24_DataModelAndPowerView.xlsx** workbook.

All the data sources for this exercise are in different Excel tables, located o different worksheets in this workbook. Each worksheet, in essence, is like a Access table, although the data might not be normalized like in a relational database.

2. Examine the table on the **Calendar** worksheet.

As done previously when you created the RevByDep PivotTable, date fields can be grouped by months, quarters, and so forth. However, this is limited in that the quarterly groupings can only be aligned with the calendar year— Quarter 1 must be January, February, and March. Many organizations operate on a fiscal year that differs from the calendar year. The table on the Calendar worksheet can be used to define the dates that fall within the fiscal year quarters.

3. Click the **Data** tab, in the Data Tools group, click **Manage Data Model**. If prompted to "Enable the Data Analysis add-ins to use this feature," click **Enable**. A Power Pivot window opens in front of the Excel workbook.

4. Minimize the Power Pivot window, noticing that the Ribbon in the Excel workbook now has a Power Pivot tab.

5. With a cell inside the Calendar table selected, click the **Power Pivot** tab then, in the Table group, click **Add to Data Model**. The Power Pivot window is now active, and the Calendar table is displayed in the data model.

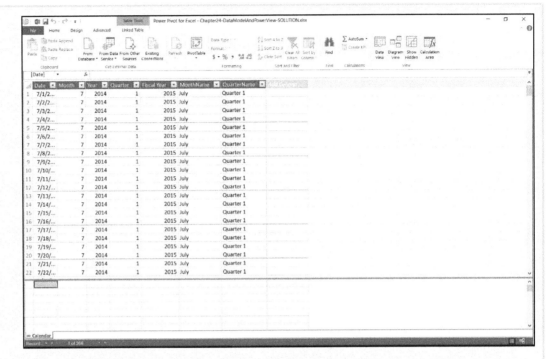

6. Minimize the Power Pivot window, then return to the Excel workbook. You may see a yellow banner at the top notifying you that the Data Model changed—this is to be expected.

7. Repeat steps 5 and 6 to add the tables on the **Transactions**, **TransactionDetails**, and **Products** worksheets to the data model. Save the workbook after each table is added. Power Pivot has a greater likelihood of crashing because of the intense memory usage. Best practice dictates that you save often.

Connecting Data Sources with Relationships

The Power Pivot window provides more advanced functionality. For example, you can add calculated fields, establish key performance indicators (KPIs), and establish relationships. You can even link into Microsoft's Azure cloud database and access millions of data records—some of them for free.

Creating relationships between tables with common fields will allow you to analyze the data more effectively and efficiently.

1. In the Power Pivot Window, click the **Design** tab; in the Relationships group, click **Manage Relationships.**

2. In the Manage Relationships dialog box, click the **Create** button.

3. In the Create Relationship dialog box, in the first drop-down, select **TransactionDetails.**

4. In the preview of the TransactionDetails table, click the **ItemCode** column to select it.

5. In the second drop-down, select **Products**.

6. Confirm that the ItemCode field is highlighted in the preview of the Products table.

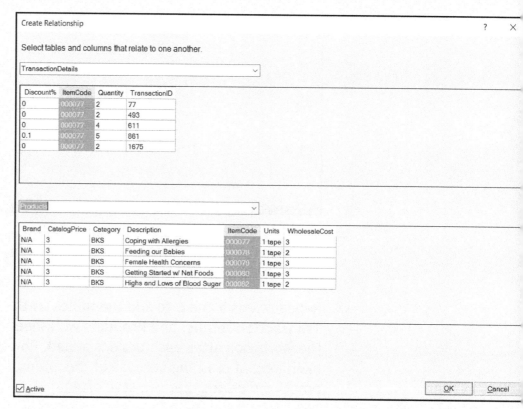

7. Click **OK** to create a relationship between the TransactionDetails and Products tables using the shared field ItemCode.

8. Continue creating relationships between the **Transactions** and **TransactionDetails** tables using the **TransactionID** field and between the **Transactions** and **Calendar** tables using the **TransactionDate** and **Date** fields.

9. Close the Manage Relationships dialog box, then save the workbook.

10. To view the relationships, in the Power Pivot window, click the **Home** tab; in the View group, click **Diagram View**.

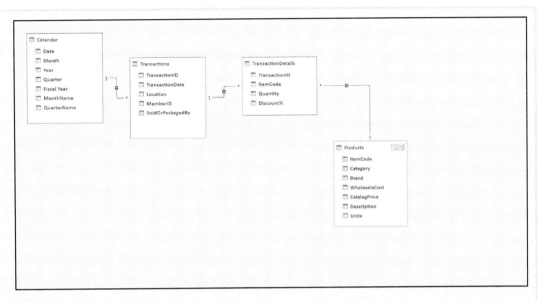

If you are familiar with Microsoft Access, you will notice the similarity between this and the Relationships window in Access.

11. On the Home tab, in the View group, click **Data View** to return to the default view in the Power Pivot window.

Creating Formulas That Use Fields in Related Tables

Power Pivot uses a type of function known as DAX functions (Data Analysis eXpressions). DAX functions are a cross between Access database calculations and Excel formulas. The **RELATED** DAX function will allow you to look up data in another table in the data model, much like with a VLOOKUP.

1. In the Power Pivot window, click the **TransactionDetails** sheet tab.

Notice that no calculation for revenue exists. Premiere calculates its revenue using the fields Quantity, CatalogPrice, and Discount%. In an Excel workbook, you would normally reference cells and use a VLOOKUP to retrieve CatalogPrice from the other Excel table. In the Excel data model, using DAX functions like RELATED, you can ask Excel to use the connection between TransactionDetails and Products via the common field ItemCode to find the appropriate CatalogPrice for each item.

2. Select the column titled **Add Column**.

3. Click into the Formula Bar.

4. Type the following formula:
   =[Quantity]*RELATED(Products[CatalogPrice])*(1-[Discount%])

5. Press **Enter**.

Notice how the calculation is automatically applied to the whole column.

6. With the column selected, right-click, and then select **Rename Column.**

7. Type **Revenue** for the column title, then press **Enter.**

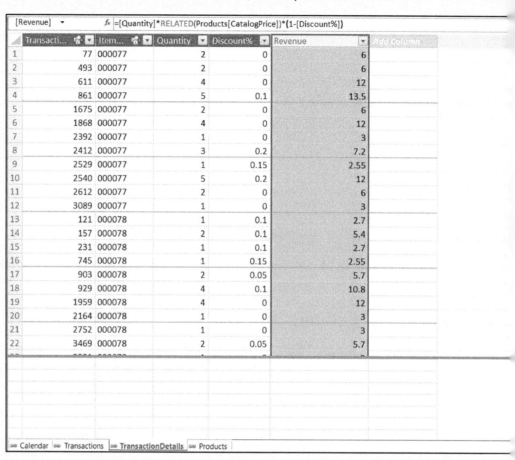

Creating a Simple Dashboard with Power Pivot

Dashboards are very common in business. A dashboard consists of interactive data and charts that track metrics that the organization's decision makers consider are important for success. The Power Pivot window provides tools to quickly create PivotTables and PivotCharts, using any of the fields in the Data Model, that can serve as a simple dashboard:

1. In the Power Pivot window, on the Home tab, click the **PivotTable arrow**, and then select **Chart and Table (Horizontal).**

2. In the Create PivotChart and PivotTable (Horizontal) dialog box, click **Existing Worksheet**, and then click inside the **Location** box.

3. Click the Collapse dialog button. Click the **Premiere PowerPivot** worksheet tab, then click cell **A4.**

4. Click **OK**, then **OK** again.

5. A PivotChart and PivotTable object are embedded into the worksheet:

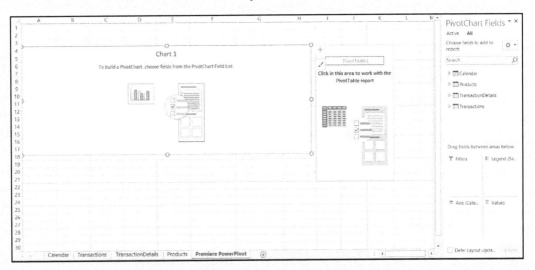

6. Click the **PivotTable1** object, noticing that the PivotTable Fields pane looks the same as it did when creating the RevByDep PivotTable except that you can now select fields from multiple tables.

7. In the PivotTable Fields pane, click **Transactions** to expand and view the fields in the table. Drag the **Location** field to the **Columns** area.

8. In the PivotTable Fields pane, click **Calendar** to expand and view the fields in the table. Drag the **QuarterName** field to the **Rows** area.

9. In the PivotTable Fields pane, click **TransactionDetails** to expand and view the fields in the table. Drag the **Revenue** field to the **Σ Values** area. Format the Revenue field with a custom name of **Quarterly Revenue** and as **Accounting** with **0** decimals.

10. Click the **Chart 1** object and in the PivotChart Fields pane, drag the **QuarterName** field from the **Calendar** table to the **Axis (Categories)** area.

11. In the PivotChart Fields pane, drag the **Location** field from the **Transactions** table to the **Legend (Series)** area.

12. In the PivotChart Fields pane, drag the **Revenue** field from the **TransactionDetails** table to the **Σ Values** area.

13. Click the **PivotChart Tools Design** tab; in the Type group, click **Change Chart Type**.

14. Select **Line** from the All Charts tab, select **Line with Markers**, and then click **OK**.

15. Apply the **Style 9** Chart Style to the chart.

Creating a Simple Power View Report

Power View adds sophisticated data visualization to Excel. Here you will create a simple Power View report using the fields in the Data Model.

Adding the Power View Button to the Ribbon

In Excel 2016, the Power View button is not enabled by default, so you must customize the Ribbon to add it.

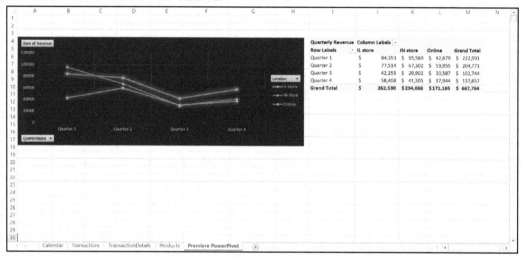

1. Click the **File** tab; in the left pane, click **Options**.

2. In the Excel Options dialog box, click **Customize Ribbon** on the left.

3. On the right, under Main Tabs, click on the + to expand the **Insert** groups list. The Insert tab will be the tab on the Ribbon where you will add the Power View button.

4. At the bottom of the Main Tabs section, click **New Group**.

5. On the left, under **Choose commands from:**, click the drop-down arrow, and then select **Commands Not in the Ribbon**; from the list, select **Insert a Power View Report**.

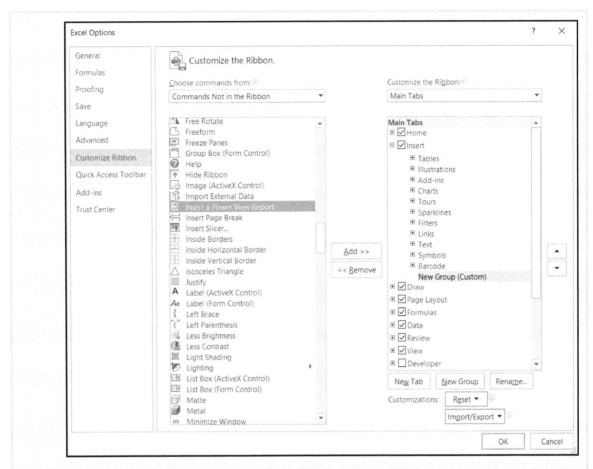

6. With both Insert a Power View Report and New Group (custom) selected, click **Add**, then **OK**. The Insert a Power View Report button is now available to the far right of the Insert tab.

7. On the Premiere PowerPivot worksheet, click inside the PivotTable.

8. Click the **Insert** tab; in the far right, click **Power View**. Once it loads, it should look like the following:

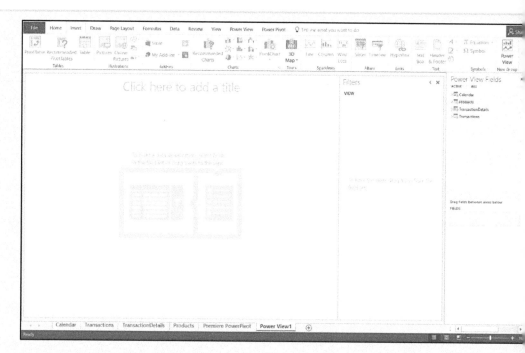

9. In the Power View Fields pane, click the arrow to the left of **TransactionDetails** to expand the table and view the fields. Click the **Σ Revenue** check box.

10. In the Power View Fields pane, expand **Transactions** to view the fields. Click the **Location** check box.

11. On the DESIGN tab, in the Switch Visualization group, click **Column Chart**, and then select **Stacked Column Chart**.

12. In the Power View Fields pane, expand **Calendar** to view the fields. Drag the **QuarterName** field into the TILE BY on the bottom half of the Power View Fields pane.

13. Resize the chart so that all data are visible.

14. Click a blank area to the right of the column chart.

15. In the Power View Fields pane, click the **QuarterName** check box in the Calendar table, and then click the **Σ Revenue** check box in the TransactionDetails table.

16. In the Switch Visualization group, click **Other Chart**, and then select **Line Chart**.

17. Reposition the line chart below the column chart, resizing appropriately.

18. Click on the **Title**; name it **2015 Sales Report**.

19. Click the **Power View** tab. In the Themes group, click **Themes**, and then select **Theme6**.

20. Close the **Filters** pane, located in between the Power View Fields pane and the Power View report.

21. Click the **Online column** in the column chart to view only online sales in both visualizations. When completed, your Power View report should resemble the following:

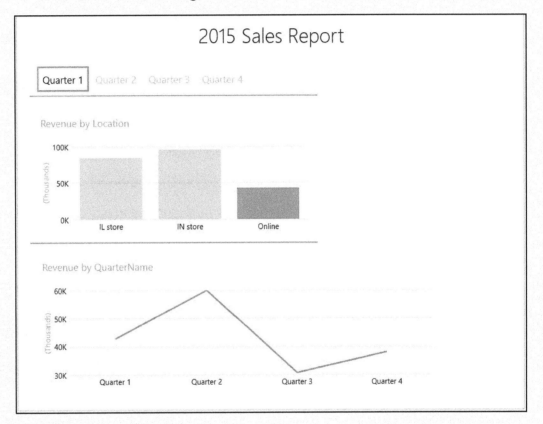

22. Save and close the file.

REVIEW PROBLEMS

Review Problem 1

GP Golf is a manufacturer of golf apparel that specializes in golf gloves. They sell three types of gloves: Regular, Pro, and SoftGrip. GP Golf creates separate versions of its gloves for women and men as well as for right-handers and left-handers.

You are interested in yearly, quarterly, and monthly sales volumes for each type of glove. You want to be able to view sales volumes by gender.

In the Chapter24_PivotTables.xlsx file, complete the following steps:

1. Navigate to the **Review1 Data** worksheet.

2. Use the data on this worksheet to create a PivotTable.

3. Locate the PivotTable on the **Review1 PivotTable**, in cell **B4**.

4. Place the Date field in the Rows area, the Type field in the Columns area, the Gender field in the Filters area, and Sales Volume in the Σ Values area.

5. Group by months, quarters, and years. Create subtotals for quarters and years.

6. Format your PivotTable with any of the predefined styles.

7. When finished, use your PivotTable to answer the questions on the **Review1 Questions** worksheet. If correct, your answers will appear in blue type.

Knowledge Check 20

PivotTables

File Needed

KnowledgeCheck_20.xlsx

Create and use a PivotTable to analyze rep sales by item type and customer state for the Electronic Products Corporation.

Create the PivotTable

Using the data on the Rep Sales Summary worksheet, build a PivotTable, locating it in cell A4 of the PivotTable worksheet. Configure it to initially look like the following figure:

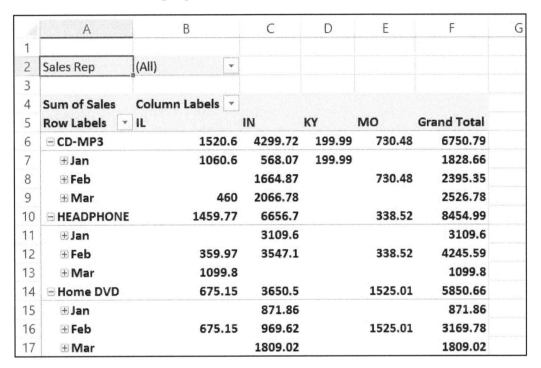

Format the PivotTable

Make the following changes to the pivot table. When finished, your PivotTable should match the following figure.

1. Group the Order Date field by months only.

2. Format the PivotTable using Pivot Style Medium 2.

3. Format all sales figures as Accounting with 2 decimal places.

4. Change the Column Labels header to read Customer State.

5. Widen columns A through F to make the data easier to read.

	A	B	C	D	E	F	G
1							
2	Sales Rep	(All) ▾					
3							
4	**Sum of Sales**	Customer State ▾					
5	Row Labels ▾	IL	IN	KY	MO	Grand Total	
6	⊟ CD-MP3	$ 1,520.60	$ 4,299.72	$ 199.99	$ 730.48	$ 6,750.79	
7	Jan	$ 1,060.60	$ 568.07	$ 199.99		$ 1,828.66	
8	Feb		$ 1,664.87		$ 730.48	$ 2,395.35	
9	Mar	$ 460.00	$ 2,066.78			$ 2,526.78	
10	⊟ HEADPHONE	$ 1,459.77	$ 6,656.70		$ 338.52	$ 8,454.99	
11	Jan		$ 3,109.60			$ 3,109.60	
12	Feb	$ 359.97	$ 3,547.10		$ 338.52	$ 4,245.59	
13	Mar	$ 1,099.80				$ 1,099.80	
14	⊟ Home DVD	$ 675.15	$ 3,650.50		$ 1,525.01	$ 5,850.66	
15	Jan		$ 871.86			$ 871.86	
16	Feb	$ 675.15	$ 969.62		$ 1,525.01	$ 3,169.78	
17	Mar		$ 1,809.02			$ 1,809.02	

After completing these steps, go to the course website to answer Koin-earning questions.

Appendix: Box at IU, Query Guide, Reports in Access, Automating Tasks with Macros

Chapter 25

Outline

Objectives

- Learn and practice how to use your IU Box account.

- Learn and understand the basic process for creating queries.

- Learn and practice how to create reports in Access.

- Learn and practice how macros are used to automate tasks.

BOX AT IU

Research

When you have a question about information technology at Indiana University, the Knowledge Base, found at http://kb.iu.edu, often has the answer.

Read the following Knowledge Base articles about your Box account:

- About Box at IU
- Best Practices for Box at IU

Exploration

Box at IU provides IU students and faculty and staff members with unlimited secure cloud storage allowing them to store music, homework, pictures, videos, and the like and to access their stored files from virtually anywhere using any device. If you are new to cloud storage in general or to Box at IU specifically, the following may shed some light on some of the options you have for using this service.

IU Box on the Web

You can upload, download, and share any file by using any web browser, such as Internet Explorer, FireFox, Chrome, or Safari. Log onto https://box.iu.edu with your IU username and passphrase to get started.

Box Sync and Other Apps

If you have a personal computer or smartphone that you would like to use to access, store, share, and edit your files, Box has apps for PCs, Macs, iPhones, iPads, the Windows Phone 8, Android phones, and other devices. Installing Box Sync on your personal computer will allow you to sync folders to your computer. This allows you to access those synced files from your file explorer or "finder." Any changes made to the documents stored in these synced folders will be automatically backed up to Box. To learn more, and to install Box Sync, read this Knowledge Base article, then follow the steps in the article.

You may find other apps, such as Box Edit and Box for Office, useful as well. To learn more about using Box apps, read this Knowledge Base article.

IU Box Mapped Drive

The ability to set up your Box account as a mapped drive is available only in the STC computer labs on the campus of IU Bloomington. You can easily create a mapped drive to your Box folder in order to access all your files stored on Box from the "This PC" shortcut on each STC computer's Desktop. To configure your Box account as a mapped drive, go to http://cloudstorage.iu.edu, log in with your IU username and passphrase, and then authorize Box or other cloud services of your choosing. Once After doing so, you can go to any STC computer lab on campus and view your files from all authorized services by clicking on **This PC**. You can read more about Cloudstorage at IU by reading this Knowledge Base article.

The "This PC" shortcut looks like this on the STC computers:

After you map your Box account as a drive, when you double-click on the This PC shortcut on any STC computer, the window will look as follows:

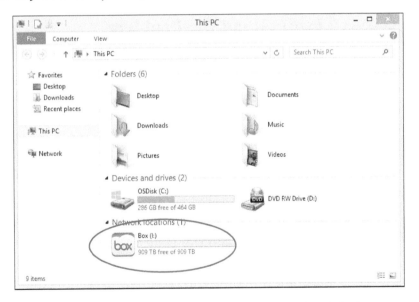

Note: *These mapped drives are not recommended for use with Access databases or very large files. You should instead download these files and work on them from the Desktop, then upload them back to Box after completing your work.*

GUIDE TO CREATING QUERIES

Research

Microsoft Office's support site contains helpful articles and step-by-step instructions for performing tasks in Microsoft applications. For example, the following article explains how to create various types of queries:

- <u>Introduction to queries</u>

Exploration

Although queries can sometimes be created in different ways, it is important that you be able to efficiently identify what is needed to create the query, build it, check your work as you go, and return the results in a way that makes sense. Use the following guidelines when creating and using queries to retrieve data in Access.

Understand the Problem

Read the problem for general structure. The first time you read the problem, focus on determining just three things:

1. Fields that you need to display
2. Fields that you need to specify criteria
3. Fields that you need to use in calculations

Use the Relationships window. Sometimes you will be able to view the Relationships on paper, but other times you will need to open the Relationships window and take the time to look at the tables and their fields and how the tables are joined to one another. Referring to the relationships helps you become familiar with the database quickly and should also help you keep in mind how the database is structured. It will also likely save you time: instead of randomly opening tables to see what fields are in them, you can view all tables and fields at once in the relationships window.

Select Necessary Tables

Next, focus on the top half of the query design window. Add the table(s) that contain the fields that you have identified as ones that you need in the query. Keep the following in mind:

- When a field that you need exists in more than one table, use the table in which that field is the primary key.

- Do not just add all tables. Adding unnecessary tables can lead to incorrect results.

- Check to make sure that the tables you need are all joined by relationships. If any are not, you must also add the table(s) that will complete the join(s). Omitting those joining tables can cause Access to become unresponsive.

Select Necessary Fields

Add the appropriate fields to the bottom half of the query design window in the order requested. Run the query to check your work so far and to help you think ahead.

When you run the query, look for just two things:

1. Does the number of records listed make sense? If the largest table included in your query has, say, 4,000 records and your query returns 80,000 records (or seems to hang), check to make sure you haven't left out a joining table.

2. What do the data look like? As you look over the data, think of how you will need to specify criteria. The language in the problem description might not match the data values exactly. Pay attention to spelling in general, as well as abbreviations and multiple spellings (for example, singular and plural forms).

Specify Criteria

Reread the problem to determine criteria. What limiting factors are there? What's to keep you from selecting all of the records in the database? This might be a good time to highlight words in the problem description that point out how you want to limit the data.

Add criteria <u>one by one</u>, running the query after each criterion is added to the design. This will save you time in the long run; if your query suddenly breaks, you will know that it broke as a result of the criterion that you last added. In general, follow these steps:

- Add one criterion, then run the query. Do your results make sense so far? If not, fix the criterion.

- Add the second criterion, then run the query again. Do the results make sense so far? If not, fix the second criterion.

- Add the third criterion, then run the query again—and so on.

Create Calculated Fields

Create calculated fields as needed, putting field names in brackets [ ]. It might help to first think in concrete terms.

- You might have a hard time figuring out how to calculate sales revenue by just looking at the database field names. Instead, open up the tables, thinking about how to calculate revenue for the sale of a single product by hand. If a customer bought 3 items priced at $110.00 and received a 15% discount, the math problem to calculate the total revenue for the transaction would be 3 * 110 * (1 – .15). (It may help to write this down.) Once you have a concrete example worked out, substitute field names in the appropriate places in the formula. In this example, 3 might be replaced by the field name [Quantity], 110 may be [CatalogPrice], and .15 may be [Discount%], so the calculation becomes

  [Quantity]*[CatalogPrice]*(1-[Discount%])

  Notice the placement of the parentheses to enforce the desired order of operations.

- To rename a calculated field, type the new field name before the calculation, separating the field name and the calculation with a colon:

  Total:[Quantity]*[Price]

  Note: Do not change the Caption property. Doing so will not change the actual field name.

- You can rename a field in a query even if it is not part of a calculation. Last:[LastName] will cause the "LastName" field to be called "Last" in the query.

Aggregate Data

If you need to summarize the records in any way, turn on the **Total row**. By default, **Group By** is used for every field in your query. Group By will group together any duplicate records that the query has found if those records are indeed identical in every field that is showing.

- Consider the difference between **Count** and **Sum**. **Count** tells you how many records were selected; **Sum** adds data values. One way to remember the difference is that you can use **Count** on a text field, but **Sum** can be used only with numeric data.

- Consider the difference between **Group By** and **Where**. Using **Group By** on a field tells Access to organize the query results according to the values in that field. Using **Where** on a field allows Access to ignore that field when organizing the query results. For example, with **Group By** on the TransactionDate field, results will be listed according to the date of the transaction. With **Where** on the TransactionDate field, results will not be listed according to date; the fact that the results might contain different dates will be ignored.

In general, if you are already using the Total row for something, you can use Where for fields that have specified criteria but that do not need to be displayed in the results.

Sort Results

Sort as needed. You must sort in Design View so that your sort sequence is saved as part of the query design. Otherwise, the query results would need sorted each time the query is opened.

Show/Hide Fields

Display only the fields that you are asked to list. Return to Design View; in the Show row, uncheck the appropriate boxes.

Save the Query

Save your query using the name indicated in the directions or, if the database is for business or personal use, a name that makes sense to the user. If you misspell a query name (including by using a space where you should have used an underscore or where you should use neither), this can greatly affect the integrity of your database and can cause confusion when you try to use the query in other objects in the database.

CREATING REPORTS IN ACCESS

Research

Reports are created to view and summarize data from multiple sources in one place. Reports are often printed out and used for recordkeeping, discussions, and presentations. For this reason, when designing a report, do not make the report too wide. Otherwise, extra pages of paper that are almost blank will be used. Also, since a report is likely going to be shared with other stakeholders, pay close attention to the alignment, formatting, and sizing of the controls within the report so that it looks as professional as possible.

Read the following articles to familiarize yourself with reports in Access:

- Introduction to reports in Access
- Create a grouped or summary report
    - Be sure to specifically read about using the Report Wizard and about adding or modifying grouping and sorting in an existing report.

If needed, you may find additional support articles using the online Microsoft Support, available at http://support.office.com.

Exploration 1

Go to your storage device or cloud storage, download your most recent **Premiere** database to the desktop, and then open it.

Create a Report of the Class Rosters for Each Training Class

Reports are often based on queries that have been created to pull data from tables, possibly using criteria to narrow the results and using aggregate functions to summarize the data. In this problem, you will ultimately create a report that generates a roster for each training class that the employees are attending. First, you must create a query that will generate a list of the employees enrolled in each class. The results of this query will depend on a specific ClassID that the end user types when prompted after the query is run; accordingly, the query will be a parameter query.

Create a Parameter Query

1. Create a parameter query that will generate a list of employees enrolled for any desired course.

2. The query should list **ClassID**, **ClassName**, **Date**, **StartTime**, **EndTime**, **Location**, **MaxEnrollment**, **EmployeeID**, **First**, **Last**, **JobTitle**, **Department**, and **Phone**.

3. Each time this query is run, it should prompt the user to enter a ClassID. To accomplish this, in the query design, type **[Enter a ClassID:]** on the criteria line below the **ClassID** field, as shown:

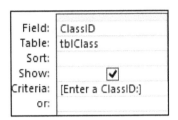

4. Run the query to test your results. When prompted, type in any ClassID (e.g., **PM0101** or **PP0102**).

5. Save the query as **qryTrainingRosters**, then close it.

Use the Report Wizard to Create Printouts of Class Rosters

1. On the **Create** tab, in the **Reports** group, click **Report Wizard**.

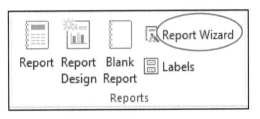

2. On the first screen of the wizard, select **qryTrainingRosters**, then move all fields from the query to the Selected Fields list. Click **Next**.

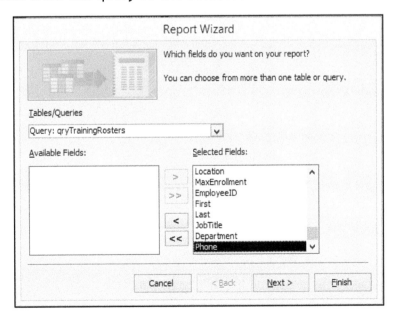

3. On the next screen, select to view your data **by tblClass**. Click **Next**.

4. On the next screen, do not add any additional levels of grouping; just click **Next**.

5. Sort by **Last**, then **First** in **ascending** order. Click **Next**.

6. Verify that the **Stepped** Layout and **Portrait** Orientation options are selected. The check box next to **Adjust the field width so all fields fit on a page** should be selected, too. Click **Next**.

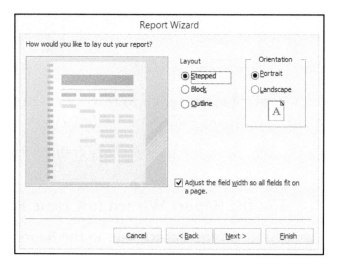

7. Name the report **rptClassRosters**. Click **Finish**.

8. You should be prompted to enter a ClassID. Type **PM0101** into the parameter value box to view your report. All the data are there, but the layout makes it difficult to read.

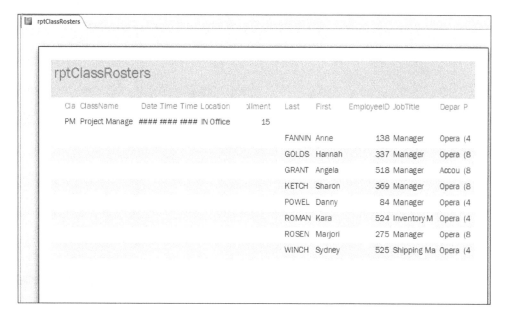

9. Close **Print Preview** to see the report in **Design View**, then make changes to the design of the report as indicated in the directions that follow.

   There are four ways to view a report: Report View, Print Preview, Layout View, and Design View. The most useful of these views are Print Preview, Design View, and Layout View. Use Print Preview when you want to see what the Report View would look like if it was printed on paper, which is usually a goal of creating reports. Use Design View to move, size, and align controls, and change the width of the report. Switch between Design View and Layout View to immediately see the results of your changes, then fine-tune your report as needed to make it look more professional.

   ### Troubleshooting

   If you are in Design View and you are trying to move just one control but find that all the controls are moving with it, you may need to remove the layout control. Press **Ctrl+A** on your keyboard to select all controls, then click the **Arrange** tab. Then click the **Remove Layout** button, which is in the Table group. This will allow you to work independently with the controls.

   If you select all your controls, then click on the Arrange tab and find that the Remove Layout button is gray, then your controls are already independent of one another.

Modify the Report in Design View

1. Delete the **rptClassRosters** label from the Report Header section.

2. Drag the **ClassID** text box from the ClassID Header section to the Report Header section.

3. Make the type in the ClassID text box **16-point** and **bold**. Adjust the size of the text box as needed. Click the top of the Page Header bar, then pull it up to adjust the height of the Report Header section to about half an inch to avoid wasting space.

4. Delete the **ClassID** label from the Page Header section.

5. Click the top of the **Detail** bar, then pull it down to create more space in the **ClassID Header** section.

6. In the Page Header section, select the labels for **Last**, **First**, **EmployeeID**, **JobTitle**, **Department**, and **Phone**. Drag them to the ClassID Header section, placing and sizing these labels as shown:

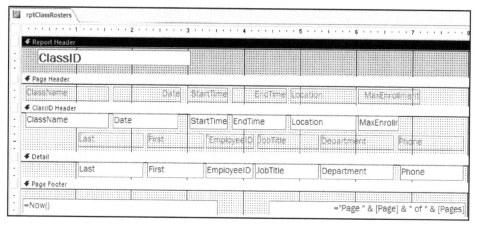

7. In the Detail section, select the **text boxes**, then drag them below their corresponding labels as just shown.

8. Arrange and resize the labels and text boxes in all the sections to match the following screenshot. Do not widen the report by dragging it past 8 inches on the horizontal ruler. This will cause blank pages in the report, which wastes paper and is unprofessional.

9. Switch to **Print Preview**. Enter a ClassID when prompted, such as PM0101. Your report should look similar to the following image. The navigation buttons at the bottom of the screen should be grayed out, because your report for one class should be just one page.

Summarize Employee Course Enrollment Using a Calculated Field

1. In **Design View**, on the Design tab, in the Grouping & Totals group, click the **Group & Sort** button.

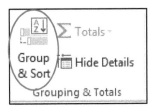

The Group, Sort, and Total pane will open at the bottom of your screen.

2. In the ClassID group, click **More**.

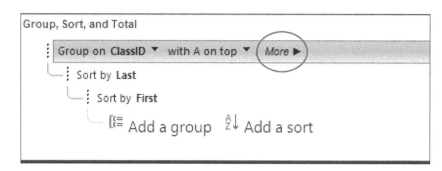

3. Click the arrow to the right of **with no totals** so that you can add a calculation.

4. You want the number of employees enrolled in the course to appear below the class roster. This means that you need to Total On the **EmployeeID** and to tell Access to **Count** those **Values**, since each EmployeeID is unique. Select the check box for **Show subtotal in group footer** so that the number of employees enrolled appears below the class roster.

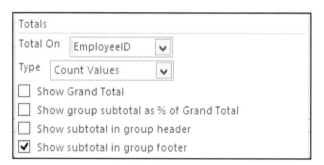

5. You should now see a ClassID Footer section in the report design grid, along with a function that counts the EmployeeID values. You may have to increase the width of the text box to see the entire function.

6. Add a **label** next to the count of EmployeeID values; in it, type **Total Enrolled:**

7. When you select this new label, you will see a warning appear. Click the warning, then choose **Associate Label with a Control**. Access should offer you the following option. Click **OK**.

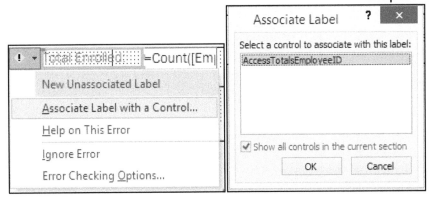

8. Switch to Print Preview to test your work. When prompted, type **PM0101** as the ClassID.

   Your results should be similar to the following screenshot. Again, the navigation buttons at the bottom of the screen should be grayed out, because the report for this class is only one page.

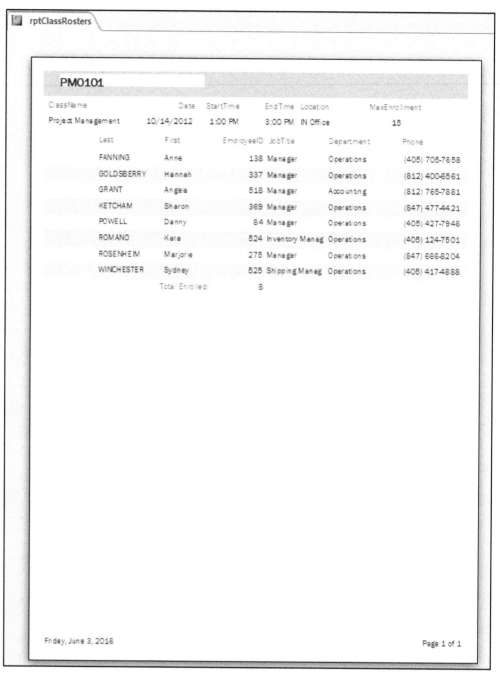

| rptClassRosters | | | | | | |

PM0101

ClassName		Date	StartTime	EndTime	Location	MaxEnrollment
Project Management		10/14/2012	1:00 PM	3:00 PM	IN Office	15

Last	First	EmployeeID	JobTitle	Department	Phone
FANNING	Anne	138	Manager	Operations	(405) 705-7658
GOLDSBERRY	Hannah	337	Manager	Operations	(812) 400-6561
GRANT	Angela	518	Manager	Accounting	(812) 765-7881
KETCHAM	Sharon	369	Manager	Operations	(847) 477-4421
POWELL	Danny	84	Manager	Operations	(405) 427-7948
ROMANO	Kara	524	Inventory Manag	Operations	(405) 124-7501
ROSENHEIM	Marjorie	275	Manager	Operations	(847) 666-8204
WINCHESTER	Sydney	525	Shipping Manag	Operations	(405) 417-4888
	Total Enrolled:	8			

Friday, June 3, 2016   Page 1 of 1

9. Save and close the report.

Exploration 2

Create an Annual Physical Inventory Report

Every year, Premiere Foods conducts a physical inventory audit in which an employee counts exactly how many items of each product are on the shelf. These data are then cross-referenced with the actual inventory system for accuracy. This yearly physical inventory helps determine theft levels, other inventory loss, and the accuracy of the electronic system.

For this report, each employee needs a listing of products per Department per Category per Aisle. The first number in the item code represents the aisle in the store where the item is located. Premiere's database already includes the needed query, named qryProductInventory.

1. On the **Create** tab, in the Reports group, click **Report Wizard.**

2. Select **qryProductInventory**, then click the **double-right-arrows** to add all the fields to the report. Click **Next.**

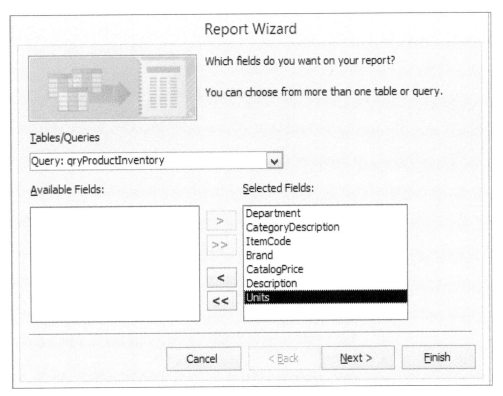

3. View the data by **tblProductCategory.** Click **Next.**

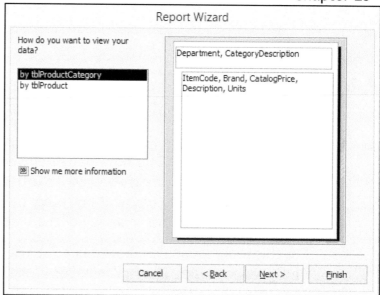

4. We know that each item is placed in an aisle based on its ItemCode. Add **ItemCode** as an additional level of grouping. Then click the **Grouping Options button** to modify the grouping intervals.

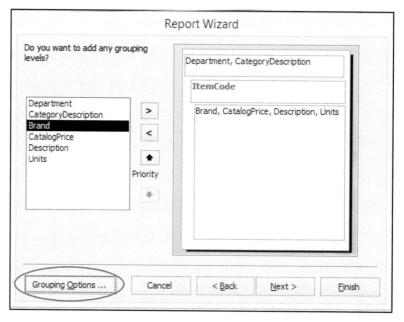

5. The first character of the ItemCode indicates the aisle in which the product is placed. Click the **Grouping intervals** drop-down, then select **1st Letter**. Remember, even though item codes are numeric, the ItemCode field has a ShortText data type, since we do not perform calculations with it. This is why the drop-down says 1st Letter instead of 1st Number.

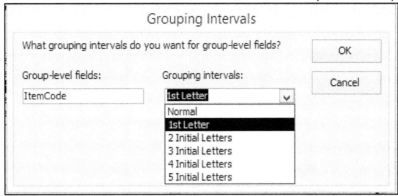

6. Click **OK**, then click **Next**.

7. Set the records to sort by **Description** in **ascending** order, then click **Next**.

8. Choose **Stepped**, **Portrait**, **Adjust the field width so all fields fit on a page**, and then click **Next**.

9. Name the report **rptPhysicalInventoryAudit**, then click **Finish**.

The report will open in Print Preview. The top of your report should look like the following image:

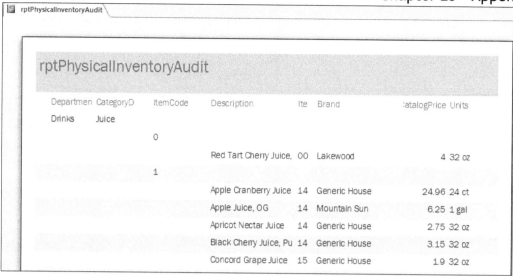

Modify the Physical Inventory Audit Report

Wizards in Access rarely give you a finalized version of the object created, including reports. Complete the following steps to clean up the report. Refer to the two figures at the end of this exploration as you work through the directions.

1. Close **Print Preview**.

2. Delete the **Department, CategoryDescription**, and **ItemCode by 1st Letter** labels in the Page Header section. Make sure that you delete the labels and NOT the text boxes.

3. Move the **Department** and **CategoryDescription** text boxes to the Page Header section. Set both to **13 pt** type size, resizing as needed.

4. Add a label to say **Aisle** next to the text box in the ItemCode Header section, then set both the label and text box to **13 pt** type size. Resize as appropriate. Notice the formula in the text box, which retrieves just the first character of the ItemCode.

5. Rearrange and resize the labels and text boxes to resemble the following figure:

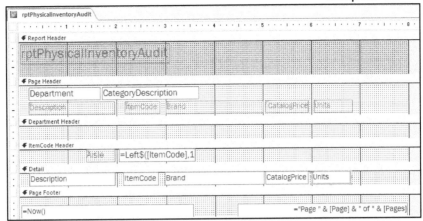

6. Change the report title to **Premiere's Annual Physical Inventory Audit**.

7. On the Design tab, find and select the **Line Control**.

8. Draw a **line segment** at the end of the text boxes in the Detail section.

This will be a place for employees to write in the actual inventory count when they go through the aisles and count the items. You can hold down the **Shift** key while dragging to ensure that the line is straight.

Troubleshooting
If your line doesn't appear in Print Preview, make sure the Border Style Property is set to solid.

9. Add a **label** to the end of the labels in the Page Header section that reads **Physical Count**.

10. Increase the height of the Detail area slightly to allow space for the inventory count to be written on the line.

11. Switch to **Print Preview** to check the progress of your report.

Add Totals to the Report

At the beginning of each department in the report, you want the number of products in the that department to be counted and documented. This can be done by counting the ItemCodes in each department and putting that answer in the Department Header.

1. Click the **Group & Sort** button on the Design tab.

2. On the Group on Department row, click **More**, then click the arrow to the right of **with no totals**. Set everything to match the following image:

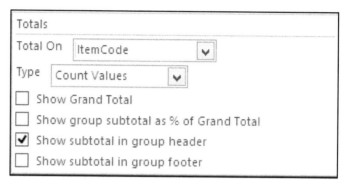

3. Move the new text box that appears in the Department Header to the left side of that section, between the 1-inch and 2-inch marks. Set the type size of the text box to **14 pt**.

4. Add a **label** to the right of the new text box that reads **Unique Products in this Department** in bold type.

5. Format the **CatalogPrice** text box as currency.

6. Set the **Can Grow** property for the **Description** text box to **Yes**. This will allow the Description text to wrap for descriptions that are longer than the current size of the text box allows.

7. Adjust all fields so that the data can be read and so that your report resembles the following figures.

8. When you are finished, save and close the report.

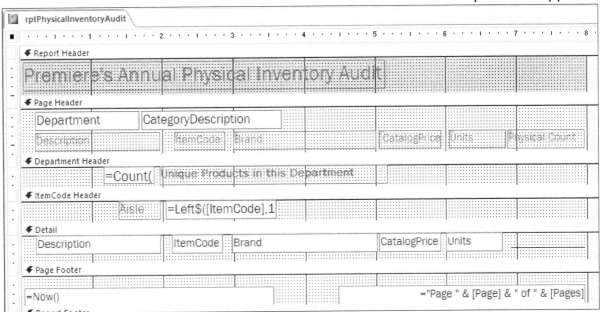

Design view of Premiere's Annual Physical Inventory Audit

Print Preview of Premiere's Annual Physical Inventory Audit

Knowledge Check 10

Summary Reports

For this Knowledge Check, you will create a report that will serve as a catalog of products sold by the Artful Yard.

Report Guidelines

Refer to these guidelines and the images on the pages after the guidelines to create the report. Placement need not be exact.

- The report is based off the PRODUCTS Table.

- Do not include Product Line, Wholesale Price, Units in Stock, Max Units, or Warehouse from the PRODUCTS table.

- Include a Grouping of Product Categories, sort in ascending order by Product ID, and then choose a Stepped Layout.

- In the Report Header, create label(s) to display the following information. Use any type style of your choosing.

- Edit the appropriate property of the Product Category field so that all values appear as UPPERCASE.

- Change the label for Our Selling Price and Competitor's Selling Price to be **Our Price** and **Their Price**, respectively.

- The last item in the Detail section is a text box control that contains the image of the product, if there is one. In Design View, decrease the height of this control to about an inch so that your report can fit more products on a page.

- Add a rectangle control object around the details of each product. It should have a transparent back style and a 2-point sparse dot border.

- Create a calculated field with the label **You Saved:** that calculates the difference between their price and our price. Format as Currency. Change the Border Style of this calculated field to Transparent.

- In the Product Category footer and Report footer, calculate the total number of products and the average savings on products in terms of our price versus their price. Refer to the images for labels and placement. Change the Border Style of these text boxes to Transparent.

- At the end of the report, draw a line with a weight of 2 points between the last category calculations and the calculations for the entire catalog. Refer to the End of Report image for the placement of this line.

After completing these steps, go to the course website to answer Koin-earning questions.

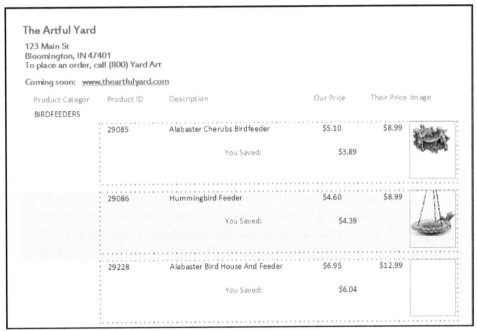

Page 1 of Report

| 33875 | Alabaster Sun/Moon Hanging Feeder | $6.00 | $10.99 | |
| | You Saved: | | $4.99 | |

Total products in this category: 25
Average savings on products in this category: $6.88

BIRDHOUSES

| 27101 | Wood Bed & Breakfast Birdhouse | $6.00 | $10.99 | |
| | You Saved: | | $4.99 | |

End of BIRDFEEDERS Category

| 33913 | Frog Lovers On Moon Windchimes | $5.00 | $8.99 | |
| | You Saved: | | $3.99 | |

Total products in this category: 33
Average savings on products in this category: $5.83

Total products in this catalog: 165
Average savings on products in this catalog: $6.23

End of Report

AUTOMATING TASKS WITH MACROS

Research

What Are Macros?

Macros are a powerful tool that allow you to customize and automate Excel. Macros are technically computer programming code written in Visual Basic for Applications (VBA). Luckily, macros can be recorded without writing a single line of code in Excel. VBA and macros can be used in all of the Microsoft Office Programs, but only Excel and Word have recorders. Access, however, does have a robust macro designer. If you are interested in learning how to write VBA code rather than record the code, talk with your instructor about upper-level courses.

Macros can be used to automate both simple and complicated tasks. Any common repetitive task, such as printing worksheets, can be made easier with macros. Another example of the use of macros is when a user is prompted to enter identifying information when a file is first opened. All Excel files with macros have an extension of .xlsm rather than .xlsx.

You can read more about macros in the following Microsoft Office support article:

- Create or delete a macro

Exploration

Show the Developer Tab

Before you record macros, you need to show the developer ribbon to access some advanced features. Although you can record a macro without the developer ribbon, you cannot attach the macro to a button without using the developer ribbon.

1. Open Excel to a new blank workbook.

2. Click the **File** tab, and then, on the left-hand side, click **Options**.

3. In the dialog box that appears, click on **Customize Ribbon** on the left-hand side, as shown in the following figure.

4. Under the list of tabs on the right, check the box next to the **Developer** tab, then click **OK**.

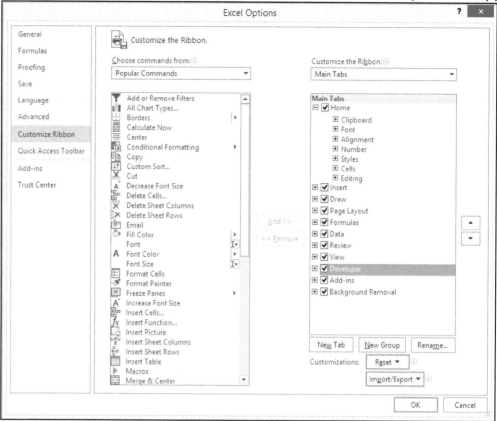

Create a Simple Macro

You will create a very simple macro on this new worksheet. Before you record a macro, you should know exactly what your macro will do. You will create a worksheet, add a new worksheet, and record a macro that, when run, takes the user to the new worksheet and selects cell A1.

1. You should still have Excel open to your new, blank worksheet. Save the file to the desktop of your computer as **macros.xlsm**. Notice that the extension is a macro-enabled spreadsheet or .xlsm. Make sure to save it with the correct extension.

2. Add a second worksheet. By default, Excel will name the second sheet Sheet2.

3. Select Sheet1.

4. On the **Developer** tab in the Code group, click on **Record Macro**.

5. In the Record Macro dialog box, name the macro **SelectSheet2**. In the **Description**, type **This macro will take the user to Sheet2 and make cell A1 the active cell**. Although you are not setting a keyboard shortcut, you can do that in this dialog box as well. Click **OK**.

6. You are now recording. Everywhere you click, everywhere you scroll, Excel is creating code that does the same thing you do. Click on **Sheet2**. Then, click in cell **A1**. When you are at the end of a macro, always think about what cell should be active at the end. Accordingly, even if cell A1 is already active, click on the cell anyway to make sure it is in the recording.

7. The most important thing to remember when recording macros is to stop the recording when you are done. If you do not, you will create an endless loop that could crash your computer. On the Developer tab in the Code group, click **Stop Recording.**

8. After you stop recording, click on any cell other than A1, then click back to **Sheet1.**

9. On the Developer tab in the Code group, click on **Macros**. With the SelectSheet2 macro selected, click on **Run** to test the macro. If it worked properly, it will take you to Sheet2, and cell A1 will be selected.

10. On the Developer tab in the Code group, click on **Macros**. With the SelectSheet2 macro selected, click on **Edit** to see the code that Excel wrote for you. Excel opens a new window: Visual Basic for Applications Editor.

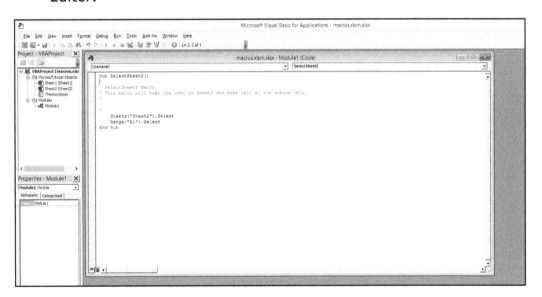

11. Close the **Visual Basic for Applications Editor**, then return to Excel.

12. Select **Sheet1.**

13. On the Developer tab in the Controls group, click on **Insert**, then select the first tool, named **Button (Form Control).**

14. Click and drag on Sheet1 to draw a **rectangle** of any size. When you release the mouse button, the Assign Macro dialog box will appear. Select the macro **SelectSheet2**, then click **OK.**

15. Select and delete the text Button 1, then type **Go to Sheet2**. If you have any trouble, right-click on the button, then select Edit Text.

16. Click anywhere outside of the button.

17. Then click on the button to test the button/macro. The macro should take you to Sheet 2, cell A1.